S0-BBF-313

perspectives on DEATH

perspectives on DEATH

Liston O. Mills, editor

abingdon press - nashville and new york

PERSPECTIVES ON DEATH

Copyright © 1969 by Abingdon Press

All rights in this book are reserved.
No part of the book may be reproduced in any manner whatsoever without written permission of the publishers except brief quotations embodied in critical articles or reviews. For information address Abingdon Press, Nashville, Tennessee.

Standard Book Number: 687-30824-0

Library of Congress Catalog Card Number: 69-19742

"The Sacral Power of Death in Contemporary Experience," by William May, is based on his article "Death: The Conspiracy and Silence," which appeared in *Christianity and Crisis,* April 16, 1962.

Scripture quotations noted RSV are from the Revised Standard Version of the Bible, copyrighted 1946 and 1952 by the Division of Christian Education, National Council of Churches, and are used by permission.

SET UP, PRINTED, AND BOUND BY THE PARTHENON PRESS, AT NASHVILLE, TENNESSEE, UNITED STATES OF AMERICA

contents

introduction

Until recently death has been largely the domain of the Christian church in the Western world. Man's birth was interpreted as a creation in the image of God. His death was understood as a going to be with God. In between, he passed the days of his years as a pilgrim in preparation for that meeting.

Over the past decade numerous books and essays have appeared describing a transition in the Western—and particularly the American—view of death. A break with the tradition is said to be in process. Medical science continues to push back the boundaries of life expectancy; some optimistic doctors even speak of an indefinite life span. The rituals and practices surrounding death reflect, not faith, but profound change and society's disenchantment with the church's ceremonies. Religiously, modern man no longer speaks with the assurance he once did of meeting God and of eternal life.

There was a certain security and steadfastness about life and death in the earlier view of man and his place in the world. One writer says it enabled man to take a death-defying stance. Death could be faced; it could be talked about with friends and neighbors; it could be treated as normal and as a natural end. For the conviction that all was in the hands and will of God made it possible to gaze at the end of life with hope. Meaning and fulfillment in life and in death were possible within the bounds of a personal relationship to God. This is not to say that ideas of judgment and torment were not often abused. The Middle Ages and some of the revival preachers belie this. And it is also not to say that this world and its woes were not often neglected in a preoccupation with the next world and its bliss. But at its best the conviction that man and the issues of life were in God's hands enabled one to live his threescore and ten with some sense of who he was and what he was to be about.

The transition described by recent literature is a movement away from this defiance. "Death-denying" is the phrase used to characterize the new stance. Beginning with the Enlightenment, and perhaps before, man was glorified, and the issues of life and death were separated. Modern man, it is said, opts for life, and he refuses to face the fact of his inevitable demise. Sociological and psychological studies are replete with examples of the ways death is avoided.[1] It is treated, says one writer, as "a communicable disease." Theological understandings are not sought; death is the result of an accident or of negligence or of disease. The dying are isolated in hospitals and the elderly are removed to "Sunset Villages." Ministers are requested to speak briefly at funerals and not to mention the deceased. And the American funeral director has come in for scathing attacks because of his euphemistic and romantic (and profitable) dealings with death.

The results of the present stance have been to rob life of much of its depth and meaning. The neglect of death has led to an antiseptic and superficial view of health and well-being—the absence of pain, the absence of conflict, living

[1] An excellent volume to which the editor is indebted which deals with the denial of death from both a sociological and psychological perspective is Robert Fulton, ed., *Death and Identity* (New York: John Wiley & Sons, 1965).

life as a blonde. Carl Jung spoke of man's need to come to terms with his own death. And Viktor Frankl says that to ignore the "tragic triad" of pain, death, and guilt is to lay aside the sources from which man has discovered his deepest meanings. It was partially out of a sense of outrage over oppression and the death of the martyrs that the Israelites began to see death as a theological and moral issue. They asked how a good Creator could permit his apparent defeat and the thwarting of his own purposes—a question which led eventually to faith in a resurrection.

Death does not seem to plumb such depths in us. The tragic murders of John and Robert Kennedy, of Medgar Evers and Martin Luther King, shock us, but they do not goad us into a hard look at the "tragic triad" and they do not alter our confidence in science and technology as our salvation. Thus death for us is neither a theological nor a moral issue. It is merely "the inevitable conclusion of a natural process. . . . It is a fact in a world of facts, and [thus], our lives lose their essence and we must search in vain for our lost selves." [2]

Since these are the ideas and currents among which practicing clergy, laymen, and seminary students and professors must make their way, several members of the Vanderbilt Divinity School Faculty, together with guests from other institutions, offered a course called "perspectives on death" during the spring semester, 1967. This volume contains the revised and edited versions of the lectures. A fourfold purpose guided our decisions to offer the course and to publish the results. First, we wanted to make available the biblical teachings on death and their subsequent development and interpretation by the church. Second, we wanted to investigate current concepts of death as these are reflected in contemporary literature and contemporary theology. Third, we sought to include material which would help the students and the reader to appreciate the mean-

[2] *Ibid.*, *pp.* 337-38.

ings of death as a psychological and a social event. Finally, we wanted to present some of the pressing ethical and pastoral problems associated with the care of the dying and the bereaved.

Obviously the book is incomplete. A case could be made for another group of essays written from different points of view than the ones included here. Our reasons for selecting these particular perspectives had to do with our audience, with what is already in print, and with the implementation of our purposes. Thus, although there is a great deal of material on the psychological and sociological aspects of death, a fair amount on the theological, and more still on the pastoral care of the dying and the bereaved, it is difficult to find material depicting the *development* of the Hebrew-Christian view,[3] and more difficult still to find the socio-psychological, the theological, the biblical, and the pastoral placed in any kind of relation. Again, we wanted our selection to demonstrate, at least in part, the contexts and epochs in which various aspects of the church's teaching emerged. It seemed important to point out that the concepts of death and afterlife did not spring "full blown from the head of Zeus"; they were the products of intense struggles with real issues. Also, we desired our selection of perspectives to provide some insight into the relation of thought and behavior—i.e. that a society's or institution's practice reflects its attitudes and convictions. Finally, we hoped for the development of some sensitivity, perhaps even compassion, for the persons who must face death or who are bereaved.

At no time have we considered these statements to constitute the Christian view of death. We have simply desired to raise issues arising out of Christian faith which appear pertinent to our current situation.

I wish to express my gratitude as editor to the con-

[3] Jacques Choron, *Death and Western Thought* (New York: Collier Books, 1963), is an exception to this generalization.

tributors to this volume. At every point they have been concerned for the problems involved in publication and considerate of the editor.

A special word of thanks is due to my colleague, Professor Leander E. Keck. He was both an early consultant on the course and a helpful friend as the plans for the volume took shape. The late Professor Walter Sikes of Christian Theological Seminary and Vanderbilt Divinity School also is remembered with gratitude and affection for his counsel and encouragement as this work was developing.

I would like to thank Dr. John Wilson, staff psychiatrist at Vanderbilt Student Heath Center, and the Rev. Wayne Bell of the Vine Street Christian Church for their friendly interest and helpful suggestions.

The Vanderbilt University Research Council provided a research grant which provided leisure to do many of the editorial duties, and for this I am grateful.

My wife, Jennie, has been a model of helpfulness and patience. My gratitude to her for her confidence and trust is deep indeed.

Liston O. Mills

Vanderbilt Divinity School
November, 1968

Lou H. Silberman, Hillel Professor of Jewish Literature and Thought at Vanderbilt University, suggests that the Hebrew view of death was undergirded by confidence in Yahweh as the creator and sustainer of life and in his purpose for Israel. Their ideas on death and the afterlife developed out of their experiences of oppression and suffering. Their Scriptures and apocalyptic literature reflect their moral conflict over the question of how a good Creator could permit his people to suffer and his purpose to be thwarted. The beginnings of the concepts of resurrection—not immortalty—and judgment are evident as their response.

I

Death in the Hebrew Bible and Apocalyptic Literature

Lou H. Silberman

H. Wheeler Robinson began his essay "Hebrew Psychology" with the assertion that "the modern study of anthropology has done as much for the elucidation of the Old Testament as that of archeology." He continued: "Just as we re-date the fall of Nineveh from 606 B.C. to 612 B.C., on the evidence of a Babylonian tablet, so we interpret the Hebrew idea of 'soul' from parallel ideas about the breath-soul amongst primitive peoples." [1]

It is to the insights of such scholars as Robinson that we must turn in order to approach our topic, the idea or ideas of death in the Old Testament and apocalyptic writings. Yet two words of warning are due at the outset. Granted that anthropological studies have had an important role in helping scholars break through the barriers of conventions that read and understood this literature in the light of

[1] In Arthur S. Peake, ed., *The People and the Book* (London: Oxford University Press, 1925), pp. 353-82.

later theological affirmations, it is a risky undertaking to generalize about "primitive" man and to apply such generalizations to our study of Israelite man. The authors of the Hebrew Bible, whatever else one may say of them, do not fit the anthropological category of "primitive peoples" if this phrase means a relatively simple culture composed of largely illiterate people.[2] Hence, though we may be indebted to the study of primitive man for insights that may help us fashion conceptual tools with which to examine the ideas about man found in the Hebrew Bible and in apocalyptic literature, we must be on our guard lest we primitivize where our fathers theologized.[3]

A second word of warning concerns our temptation to think of the theme at hand in isolation. While methodologically this may be a necessity, nonetheless ideas of death did not exist by themselves but rather within a constellation of other ideas and attitudes with which they cohered. Whatever ideas about and attitudes toward death the Israelites held, such ideas and attitudes stood in some crucial relationship to what they believed about life; and that in turn was related to other spheres of interests until, as D. R. G. Owen has suggested,[4] these were ultimately connected to a way of understanding God. Again, we must be careful of unexpected traps. It is not being suggested that the Israelite ideas about death are logically deducible from a concept of God. All that may be claimed, but that quite firmly, is the coherence of the ideas and attitudes in the Israelite thought-constellation, a coherence that may be something quite other than a linkage of logical necessities.

[2] R. H. Lowie, *Primitive Religion* (New York: Boni and Liveright, 1924), p. ix.

[3] In fairness to the authors utilized in this study—Robinson, Johnson, Owen, *et al.*—it should be said that they were, and particularly Johnson, aware of the pitfalls of too great a reliance on parallels.

[4] D. R. G. Owen, *Body and Soul* (Philadelphia: Westminster Press, 1956), p. 164.

Having thus set out our caveats, we turn now to the substance of our problem.

Hebrew Understanding of Life

To grasp what the Hebrew Bible says about death requires, as has been indicated, that we first comprehend what it understood life to be. For biblical thought—and it is, as Aubrey Johnson meticulously notes, "predominantly synthetic"—life is understood not in abstract terms, but as it was met in "a unit of vital power," most particularly, though not exclusively, in man. Johnson, in his concern to use parallel materials from anthropology to illuminate the discussion, described that totality, man, as he has been presumed to be understood by the primitive mind, by the term "soul-stuff" or "soul-substance." Later, however, he in effect withdrew approval of the term in a critical footnote in which he pointed out that the use of such terms "serves to encourage what appears to be a question-begging use of the term 'soul' " in just such an undertaking in which he and we are involved. For man (and on a few occasions animals) as that "unit of vital power" is referred to by the Hebrew term, *nefesh,* which if understood as "soul" in common usage gets us exactly nowhere in our understanding of biblical anthropology.[5]

Robinson, examining the 734 instances of the word *nefesh,* pointed to "three more or less distinct meanings." The first "relates to the principle of life, without any emphasis on what *we* should call its psychical side." The second is "the only one which can be called psychical in the proper sense." The third "denotes 'self,' or the personal pronoun." [6] Johnson agrees that "each of these meanings may be distinguished in certain passages," but found "the

[5] Aubrey R. Johnson, *The Vitality of the Individual in the Thought of Ancient Israel* (2nd ed.; Cardiff: University of Wales Press, 1964), p. 2, note 3. See also p. 3, note 4.

[6] *The People and the Book,* p. 355.

meaning of the term as a whole far too fluid to be able to accept so definite a classification." It denotes at one extreme, as he pointed out, "that common vital principle in man or beast which reveals itself in the form of conscious life." [7] It is that life of the flesh, *basar b'nafsho,* equated in Gen. 9:4 with *dammo,* blood. In this context, when the blood gushes forth, it is the life of the flesh that flows away. Thus it is possible to distinguish between the flesh and its life without suggesting any sort of body/soul dualism.

The equation of life and blood in the passage at hand discloses how far that term has moved from its original meaning, "breath," or perhaps at its earliest stage "neck" or "throat," to a meaning in which the physical function primarily evidencing livingness, i.e., breathing, has entirely vanished. The word has here come to mean that state, aliveness, of which the physical function breathing or its manifestation breath are the evidence. Johnson's examination of the word as it functions in Hebrew disclosed that the original meaning did on occasion remain—as for example in Isa. 5:14, *lakhen hirḥibhah she'ol nafshah,* "Therefore *She'ol* has widened its throat," and Jon. 2:5, *'afafuni mayim ad nefesh,* which should be rendered "water encompassed me up to the neck," rather than "the waters compassed me about, even to the soul," being followed as it is by the continuation of the picture of the prophet sinking down into the sea. However, such usage represents but a small fraction of the occurrences.[8]

It is not our task to repeat the careful examination of this word begun by Wheeler Robinson and carried forward with great insight by Johnson. What we are concerned with are the results of such an inquiry which make it unmistakably clear that to understand and to translate *nefesh* as soul, in the ordinary sense of that word, i.e.,

[7] *Vitality of the Individual,* p. 8, note 2.
[8] *Ibid.,* pp. 4-7; see also pp. 90 ff.

as one side, the psychical, of a physical/psychical pairing, is to impose upon the Hebrew Bible a point of view its authors did not share. For these writers man did not *have* a *nefesh,* he *was* a *nefesh,* an animated being, a total person. The *nefesh* is very often the living person in his entirety as Genesis 2:7 says; *wayyitzer YHWH 'elohim 'et ha'adam 'afar min-ha'adamah wayippah be'appaw nishmat hayyim wayehi ha'adam l'nefesh hayyah* "And the Lord God formed man of dust from the ground and breathed into his nostrils the breath of life and the man became a living being (Johnson, living person)." In this verse, too, we see the way in which the word's earlier meaning, "breath," has been replaced, for here "breath" is referred to by the word *neshamah* which in large measure is the general term in biblical Hebrew to indicate the manifestation of the physiological activity. Indeed, there is no agreement as to whether *nefesh* retains this meaning in any passage, and since its usage as throat is quite limited, we are left with a term pointing to aliveness in a variety of situations, whose exact nuance of meaning is determined not by its etymology or even by available terms borrowed from the so-called parallels of primitive peoples, but by its function in the particular context in which it occurs.[9]

Before pursuing our examination of this aliveness, in order to determine what is meant in the Hebrew Bible by death, we need to make a brief excursion in order to understand yet a third word belonging to this meaning cluster, "breath," the term *ruaḥ.* It, Johnson wrote, "points to an initial awareness of air in motion, particularly 'wind.'" The variability of its intensity and the changeability of its ways gave rise to a secondary use, to quote Johnson "broadly corresponding to the term 'spirit,'

[9] See Johnson, *The Vitality of the Individual,* p. 6, note 2. In this entire discussion it is important to keep in mind James Barr's insights regarding the functional use of a term; see his *Semantics of Biblical Language* (London: Oxford University Press, 1961).

in order to denote the equally varied behavior of human beings." Here again we must tread carefully. *Ruah* in this meaning is not *a* spirit, but *spirit* as it functions in such English phrases as "a man of spirit," "a spirited response," "in high spirits," that is, full of life; or contrariwise, "in low spirits," "dispirited," "spiritless," that is, lacking liveliness. There is, however, an added aspect to this term, for it is not only used to describe the ebb and flow of a man's powers, both in their physical and psychical manifestations, but it is also used to describe an external power that touches and affects man, as for example *ruaḥ YHWH,* "The Spirit of the Lord." [10]

This term, unlike *nefesh,* held its ground on its several levels of meaning. It means wind; it is a synonym for *neshamah,* breath, in its physical connotation, albeit a gift of God; it functions in descriptions of the intensity of emotional response, or, with the proper qualification, as an external power affecting man, the scale running from *ruaḥ YHWH,* "the Spirit of the Lord" that transforms a person, i.e., charisma bestowed, to *ruaḥ zenumim,* "a spirit of whoredom" (Hos. 4:12). The reason we must attend to this term is simply that when *nefesh* is understood as "soul" in a dualistic body/soul pairing, i.e., in a psycho-physical dichotomy, then *ruaḥ* is either equated with it, i.e., soul = spirit, or it is added as an extra layer to man, providing a trichotomy, body, soul, spirit. But, as Wheeler Robinson has written: "There is no trichotomy in Hebrew psychology, no triple division of human personality into 'body, soul, and spirit.' . . . There is not even a dichotomy in any strict sense. . . . The Hebrew idea of personality is an animated body, and not an incarnated soul." To continue: "For the Hebrew man is a unity, and . . . that unity is the body as a complex of parts, drawing life and activity from a breath-soul, which

[10] Johnson, *The Vitality of the Individual,* pp. 23-27.

has no existence apart from the body." [11] Thus an accurate understanding of the meaning of *ruaḥ* prevents its equation with *nefesh* and avoids the error against which Wheeler Robinson warned.

Hebrew Understanding of Death

It is this "animated body," this "unit of vital power," this "psycho-physical organism," this livened dust that is man. Death is to be understood as the dissolution of this unit. Its aliveness has drained away. Man is, in the phrase from II Sam. 14:14 to which Johnson referred, "like water spilt upon the ground that cannot be gathered up." Yet this dissolution is not utter extinction. Some of the power that functioned in the unit may continue, Johnson speculates, to inhere ever more faintly in some of the parts of the person, the bones, the blood, the name.[12] Johnson writes: "Death is to be explained in terms of life. It is a weak and indeed, insofar as it marks the final disintegration of one's *nefesh,* the weakest form of life; for it involves a complete scattering of one's vital power." [13] I find this statement lacking in Johnson's usual clarity. The source of the difficulty is, I suspect, primarily linguistic.

[11] *Ibid.,* pp. 362-66.

[12] *Ibid.,* p.88, notes 2, 3, and 4. A fuller examination of this "survival" is called for. Johnson also notes in passing "possible survival within the social unit," referring to his own work *The One and the Many in the Israelite Conception of God* (2nd ed.; Mystic, Conn.: Verry, Lawrence, 1961), especially pp. 4-13. The potency inhering in the name is part of the attitude of the Israelite toward language and its direct and immediate relation to its referent. See Johannes Pedersen's *Israel: Its Life and Culture,* Vols. I-IV (London: Oxford University Press, 1926–40).

[13] Johnson, *The Vitality of the Individual,* p. 88. In another place (pp. 94-95) he writes: "At death a man's vital power is found to be broken up in disorder, its unity shattered; and the result is that as an individual he drags on in a relatively weak existence, which is as opposed to life in its fullness as darkness is to light." He follows this immediately with a statement that again speaks of death as the weakest form of life. It seems clear that Johnson takes life and existence as synonyms.

Johnson has used "life" with a double meaning. It is on occasion synonymous with vitality, and on others, with existence. But he has not been careful with this distinction, nor perhaps aware of it. It cannot be said at one and the same time that death is "the weakest form of life" and that "it involves a complete scattering of one's vital power." But, preserving the distinction, one can say that death is the weakest form of existence, that form of existence involving a complete scattering of vital power. Indeed, when we turn to the biblical concept of death it is quite clear that the dead exist; they do not live.

The existence of the dead has its locus in *She'ol,* a name whose etymology is in dispute. It is the lower world, *'eretz tahtiyot,* lying below the cosmic ocean, the waters beneath the earth, on which the very bases of the mountains rest.[14] The Bible has a variety of descriptive names for it: *'abhaddon,* perdition, destruction; *bor,* the pit; *shaḥat,* either the pit or corruption; *qebher,* the grave *par excellence; bet 'olam,* eternal home. Like the Babylonian *Arallu,* it is the land of no return.[15] David, confronted by the child born of his illicit union with Bathsheba, abruptly ceases his self-abasement and addresses God: "Now he is dead, wherefore should I fast? can I bring him back again? I shall go to him, but he will not return to me." (II Sam. 12:23) It is the land of forgetfulness (Ps. 88:12), silence, quiet, inaction. "For then should I have lain down and been quiet; I should have slept; then I should have been at rest," declares Job (3:13).

> There the wicked cease from troubling,
> and there the weary are at rest.
> There the prisoners are at ease together;

[14] *Ibid.,* p. 91.

[15] Robert Martin-Achard, *From Death to Life,* trans. J. P. Smith, (Edinburgh: Oliver and Boyd, 1960), pp. 38, 40.

they hear not the voice of the taskmaster.
The small and great are there,
and the slave is free from his master. (Job 3:17-19)

For Job in his despair, *She'ol* seems almost inviting, but for a man in the vigor of life, it promises despair, for it represents the emptying out of life, the ultimate weakness whose partial experience, sickness, turns man's days into sorrow.[16] Yet after his outburst, reflecting on *She'ol,* that earlier seemed so inviting, Job would rather have a few days of comfort in life:

before I go whence I shall not return,
to the land of gloom and the deep darkness,
the land of gloom and chaos,
where light is as darkness. (10:21-22)

The dead themselves are shadows, shades, ghosts in this far land. At most, as in the case of Samuel to whose shade some of the *mana* of his life still adhered, they are called *'elohim,* "divine beings" who come out of the ground at the bidding of the necromancer. (I Sam. 28:13) The more common term for such summoned visitors is *'obot,* ghosts, whose behavior is obliquely described by Isaiah in his threat to Jerusalem:

Thou shalt speak out of the ground
and from the dust thy speech shall squeak.
Thy voice will come forth from the earth like a ghost's
from the dust thy word will chirp. (29:4)

For the dead are but echoes of the living; perhaps they are even fading echoes.

[16] See Johnson, *The Vitality of the Individual,* p. 44, and later in this chapter, the discussion of death as the analogue of all human weakness.

The most common term for the dead is *refa'im,* again a word whose etymology is in dispute. There is some evidence that it may be a loanword referring to chthonic deities or to agents of the underworld. If this is so, then, as is not infrequent in such cases of borrowing, it may not have been clearly understood and taken to refer to all dwellers in the underworld, i.e., the dead. Further, as is often the case, an indigenous etymology may have been invented so that an original Ugaritic *rp'um* was understood as being derived from the Hebrew root *rph* "to be weak." Thus in the warning to the "king of Babylon" in Isaiah we read:

> *She'ol* beneath is stirred up
> to meet you when you come,
> it rouses the *refa'im* to greet you,
> all who were leaders of the earth;
> it raises from their thrones all
> who were kings of the nations.
> All of them will speak and say to you:
> You have become as weak as we!
> You have become like us! (14:9-10)

Here the *refa'im* who are specified as "the earth's leaders," "kings of the nations," terms reflecting another possible meaning of the root, "nobles," address the newcomer to *She'ol* with words that interpret their own present state and thus suggest another meaning for the name by which they are called: "You have become weak as we!" "You are like us!" [17]

[17] See *Ibid.,* pp. 89-90, note 3. As to the way in which such substitutions and meanings may have come about, see Lowie, *Primitive Religion,* p. 300. He points out that the Oglala Sioux claimed their Badger Dance Society was modeled on a society with the same name among the Crow. No such dance, however, was noted among this tribe. The solution was found when it was recognized that the Oglala word for badger was practically identical in sound with the Crow word for kit-fox. "Comparison of the regalia and mode of ceremonial organi-

As has been indicated, Johnson sees death as the weakest form of life, a position he supports by pointing to the way in which "any weakness in life is a form of death." Without arguing the details, it seems to me that the confusion between existence and life again obscures the issue. The weakness which is death is used, rather, as an analogue for a whole series of human situations in which the individual and the community experience varying degrees and kinds of weakness, e.g., the failure of bodily power or vigor; the disruption of what we call interpersonal relations; the disorder of society. All of these are seen and described in terms of movement toward death, as a falling out of life rather than the actuality of death. This in no way invalidates Johnson's entire discussion with its careful consideration of the meaning of the root *ḤYH* "to live," but only argues that at the lower end of the scale there comes the point where cumulative quantitative weakness arrives at a qualitative difference.[18]

The danger involved in the failure to recognize the way in which *She'ol* and death are used as analogues to human situations is most clearly evident in Martin-Achard's *From Death to Life*. Here *She'ol* is seen not as a "mere remote region passively waiting for mankind to die one by one; it is a power endlessly threatening the living, an insatiable monster opening its paws to devour Israel. The kingdom of shades is found not only in the depths of the Abyss, at the opposite extreme of Heaven [Isaiah 7:11], it is everywhere and surrounds God's creation on every side." Again: "*She'ol,* the Abyss, and the Wilderness are revealed as powers inimical to life, places where darkness and disorder reign, they are the manifestations of Chaos." Finally, "*She'ol* is seen as a reality, in some

zation indicated that the Oglala borrowed the kit-fox dance of the Hidatsa or Crow and naïvely interpreted the alien name as though it were a vocable of their own tongue."

[18] See page 19, note 13.

sense autonomous, which is not the work of Yahweh and which, by its dynamic, disputes the authority of the God of Israel over the creation and seeks to bring it back into primal chaos again." [19]

What has happened here is clearly the failure of the author to recognize and understand the demythologizing program and process of the Old Testament. It is an example of that continually compounded genetic fallacy that insists that words and phrases continue to function at their most primitive level. Now I do not deny that archaic meanings often lurk within the more sophisticated developments. But one cannot therefore begin with the assumption that the mythic is always the effective meaning. Martin-Achard, having committed himself, beats a hasty retreat at this point. "Nevertheless the Old Testament rejects dualism: the destiny of the world is not to be explained as an interminable struggle between two divinities of co-equal power." But then he marches back into battle: "He is the God who has made the heavens and the earth, but not *She'ol,* the God of the living, and not of the dead [Mark 12:27], calling His creations to life, the God of Abraham and of Isaac and of Jacob, leading history on towards the manifestation of His kingship, the God who rejects the *Nihil* before annihilating it." [20] That is, indeed, vigorous theological homiletics, but it is also a kind of theological shell game in which the pea moves faster than the eye, and, to change the metaphor, you can have your cake and eat it too.

Whatever mythological origins *She'ol* and *Mot*=Death may have had, and however they may reassert themselves on occasion, they function, for the most part, in the Old Testament otherwise. When they are used as analogues to human experiences, they indeed seem to be independent forces, for the situations they are used to illustrate

[19] Martin-Achard, *From Death to Life,* p. 42.
[20] *Ibid.,* p. 45.

are the processes of growth and decay, of health and sickness, of civic well-being and disorder. When they are disengaged from their function as analogies and from their mythological origins, they have a kind of grey matter-of-factness. Death is the spilling out of life. The dead are the echo of life; they are not part of creation but its shadow. When the psalmist declares "In death there is no remembrance of Thee; in *She'ol* who can give Thee praise?" (Ps. 6:5), he is not making a claim about the inability of YHWH to be present in *She'ol,* he is pointing to the unreality of the dead. *She'ol* is the underside of creation. Again, when the psalmist still asks: "Dost Thou work wonders for the dead?" (Ps. 88:10) it is not to point to a weakness in God, but it is rather a recognition that the *pele',* "wonder," is something done within the context of man and his history. God is *'oseh fele',* "the doer of wonder," for Israel at the Sea (Exod. 15:11); but there are not events hence no wonders for the dead. Psalm 139 affirms the pervasive presence of YHWH, he is *ba-shamayim,* in the heavens, i.e., the skyey region above, in *She' ol,* the netherworld beneath the cosmic sea, *be'aḥarit hayyam,* the far west where the sun falls beneath the sea. He is there, says the psalmist, for and to the living, the "unit of vital power" who may seek to hide from him; for the dead, that presence is unexperienced. The dead have no experience either of God or of anything else. They are shadows gone from the scene where God and man are related in event. As Wheeler Robinson put it, "The life of Sheol affords formal and not real continuity of life." [21]

It is difficult for modern man to understand this Israelite stance since it is so different from his own. Robinson suggests that the real clue to this view of death lies in the idea of corporate personality. He says that "the Israelites seem to have been content with this shadowy 'life

[21] Wheeler Robinson, "Hebrew Psychology," pp. 378-79; 375-78. See also Johnson, *The Vitality of the Individual.*

after death' that was no life, so long as the idea of corporate personality enabled them to think of themselves as living on in their children or their nation." Corporate personality, as Wheeler Robinson defined it, means "the treatment of the family, the clan, or the nation, as the unit in place of the individual. It does not mean that no individual life is recognized, but simply that in a number of realms in which we have come to think individualistically, and to treat the single man as the unit, e.g., for punishment or reward, ancient thought envisaged the whole group of which he was a part." [22] Viewed in this way, death, though no less the dissolution of individual, lost its ultimacy, for the corporate person, family or clan or all Israel, endured. Perhaps it was that enduring that gave the shades in *She'ol* their existence. So long as family, clan, Israel lived, the shadow life cast, though it was not life, existed.

The Appearance of the Resurrection Idea

When this strong sense of corporate personality began to fade and the singular individual with his own self-consciousness began to move toward the center of thought, the old answer no longer sufficed and new answers had to be sought.[23] But what sort of new answers? and whence were they sought? Harris Birkeland, in his essay "The Belief in the Resurrection of the Dead in the Old Testament," is concerned to trace the emergence of that idea, for it seems something quite other than the position we have been examining, with the evidence pointing to an external source. Yet he is not satisfied to see it as a borrowing pure and simple. Such a mutation, he concludes, "cannot become an integral part of a religious complex when this complex is not prepared for that idea." Hence,

[22] Robinson, *Ibid.*
[23] *Ibid.*, p. 379.

whether there were outside influences or not is secondary to the internal disposition that made the acceptance and integration of such ideas possible.

Birkeland's essay is concerned to examine the various factors that may in one way or another have been involved in such an emergence: (1) the idea of the resurrection of the deity in Canaanite religion, a possibility Birkeland rejects as having no positive, although he allows for a negative, effect; (2) the occasional miraculous revivals which, although exceptional and not intended to say anything about a common occurrence, nonetheless indicate the possibility, albeit yet limited to a special "I" (I Kings 17:17 ff; II Kings 4:35, 13:21). As Birkeland notes at this point: "The Psalmists do not show us more than the belief in the possibility of a divine miracle endowing a man with new life after death." (3) Again, the concept of the historical restoration of Israel, a figurative resurrection, Birkeland suggests, may have played an important role, particularly as it is so vividly described in Ezekiel 37. If then at some point there is thrown into this complex of ideas an external factor that catalyzes the situation, the belief may emerge—but only if there have already existed within the totality of Israelite religion some such tentative receptivities as those described above. It is from Iran that many scholars see this impulse deriving, for in the dualistic struggle that makes up Iranian religion, life is understood as finally conquering death through the resurrection of the dead body. The eschatological conquest is not, writes Birkeland, "fully historical-ethical. It is partly physical." It is contact with Iranian religion, argues Birkeland, that added to the belief in the eschatological restoration of the people, among several traits, that of physical resurrection.[24]

Now while schematically I find Birkeland's essay at-

[24] *Studia Theologica* (Lund, 1950), III, 1, 60-78.

tractive I would not insist upon the details of his analysis, although there is no doubt in my mind that for an idea such as the resurrection to cohere to the totality of Israelite belief there must have been dispositions within the totality, i.e., attitudes, ideas, that could receive the new impulse and not, by the sheer obstinacy of the belief-structure, reject them out of hand. Thus in Isaiah 26:19, in the apocalypse that includes chs. 24 through 27 (coming, according to many scholars, from around 300 B.C.), the prophet, viewing the coming age in which the destitute land shall be restored when the world power that now subjects Israel has been destroyed, adds to the promise of restoration spoken by his predecessors a new note:

> Thy dead shall live, their bodies
> shall rise.
> O dwellers in the dust, awake
> and sing for joy!
> For thy dew is a dew of light,
> and on the land of the shades
> thou wilt let it fall.

This passage and Daniel 12:2 (dating from c. 165 B.C.) are the only two, writes Wheeler Robinson that "explicitly declare a life after death."[25] Birkeland views the Isaiah passage as the disclosure of the crucial influence Iranian thought had on Israel although he argues "nothing essentially new has been added to the Jewish faith. The resurrection of the dead is only another more physical way of conceiving the eschatological restoration contained in the Jewish belief itself."

The further working out of this impact is, writes Birkeland, to be found in the addition of the cosmic dualism

[25] Robinson, "Hebrew Psychology," p. 379. "Life after death" here does not mean immortality, i.e., separate survival of the soul *post mortem*, but a life that has come to an end and shall be restored. It does not deny the reality of death.

of Zoroastrian religion to the ethical dualism of Judaism. "The physical and cosmic aspect was transferred from the former to the latter and the dualism as a whole was more strongly stressed even on the ethical line. Hell as opposed to Heaven comes into existence and God gets Satan as his counterpart." [26] Yet at the point where the influence appears in Isaiah 26, these later developments are not apparent. Resurrection seems to be a divine gift bestowed upon the martyrs. It is, writes Wheeler Robinson, "a resurrection of the good alone." The Daniel passage: "And many of them that sleep in the dust of the earth shall awake, some to everlasting life and some to shame and everlasting contempt," more clearly represents the working out of ethical dualism, cosmically-physically projected. What is important to recognize is that this life after death is conceived of as a resurrection, a resurrection of the body, which is, as Wheeler Robinson writes, "the only real life which the Hebrews could conceive." [27]

What happened is that under the influence of a highly sharpened sense of the importance of the singular individual, various moves were made that culminated in the emergence of the idea of resurrection of the dead. The structure of foreign ideas that assisted in the birth of this new stance within Jewish thought was effective because its own historical perspective was able to relate to the eschatological hopes of Israel that were by no means displaced by the individualistic interest that made the doctrine of resurrection attractive and important. The result was not a diminution of what might be called the horizontal or historical axis but an enlargement of possibilities by the addition of this new vertical or individual axis. More could now be said; the future hope could be enlarged; the corporate personality, Israel, that

[26] See page 27, note 24.
[27] "Hebrew Psychology," pp. 379-80.

was to enjoy the fulfillment, would now do so not merely as it would be at the end of days, but as it had been, all of it, from the very beginning of its trek through history.

Apocalyptic Thought

It is this restatement of Israelite thought in which possibilities and potentialities are transformed into actualities; in which ethical dualism is stamped with a cosmic-physical impress, that lays the groundwork for the seed-bed of apocalyptic thought which has its flowering and fruit in Judaism and in Christianity. D. S. Russell, writing in *The Method and Message of Jewish Apocalyptic,* reports: "An examination of the relevant terminology of the apocalyptic writers shows quite clearly that their 'psychology,' though influenced in part by foreign ideas, is nevertheless fundamentally Hebrew in character and represents a continuation, and in some respects an interesting and significant continuation, of the prophetic consciousness." However, he notes in discussing the term *nefesh* in apocalyptic writings that "there is one use of the word that is not found at all in the Old Testament. This distinguishes the soul from the body and conceives of it as existing separately, or as capable of doing so, in a disembodied state after death. Such a conception is a radical departure from the outlook of the Old Testament." He adds: "though the apocalyptists believe in the separate survival of the soul after death, it cannot ultimately express the survival of the soul after death, it cannot ultimately express the surviving personality in terms of soul alone, but must add more to the conception of a bodily resurrection." [28] But once this distinction is made and accepted, the whole development now moves in another direction. The shades in *She'ol* are now souls or

[28] (Philadelphia: Westminster Press, 1964), p. 147.

spirits. Personal survival, continuity between life on earth and in *She'ol* is now posited. And a body/soul dualism has begun to function.

It is at this point that the impact of still other ideas, this time of Greek origin, introduced ever greater complexity into the formulations. The previous syntheses, while including individualistic concerns, did so primarily from an eschatological perspective, seeking to provide a place for the individual in the final historical consummation. The new elements had little or no interest in such final events but were primarily directed toward the fate of the individual understood not within history but as soul released from the bondage of matter. The afterlife of the resurrection was thus challenged by the afterlife of immortality.

While some apparently held on to the classical biblical position, denying both resurrection and immortality, others, affirming both, found themselves involved in intricate formulations that sought to relate the horizontal-historical axis of thought to the vertical-individual and vice versa. Each position was colored by the other. Judgment, characteristic of the historical consummation, was now seen in individual terms as well. The shadowy realm of *She'ol* now became the abiding place of disembodied souls. In some writings it was merely a temporary residence for the souls awaiting the resurrection and final judgment, although even here a distinction was made between the righteous and the wicked. As is evident, the emphasis was still upon the eschatological event.

In other writings the distinction between the righteous and wicked had immediate results in the situation of the souls. *She'ol* provided a foretaste of the final judgment based upon the moral behavior of the soul before death. The good enjoyed in some measure the eventual happiness that would be theirs in the resurrection; the wicked suffered the torments their actions deserved. In this setting the individualistic factor had moved toward the fore. Again, *She'ol* was looked upon by others as the final destination of the wicked, with punishment during the intermediate period and obliteration at the final judgment, while the righteous were destined, after the foretaste of the future, to enjoy the life of the resurrection in the final consummation. A still more radical bifurcation or division of *She'ol* into at least two separate regions, *Gehinom* (Gehenna, Hell), the place of punishment, and *Pardes* (Paradise, Heaven) is found in other apocalyptic writings.

At all events, the somber classical position of the Hebrew Bible had given way as the Jews responded to their historical situation and to the infiltration of ideas from abroad. The former challenged the ancient ideas as insufficient; the latter, insofar as they were not inimical to the crucial structures of Jewish thought and were able to find foothold in the ideas of the past now subjected to reinterpretation, provided the means by which other perspectives on death were made available to the Jewish Community. These were, in the course of the years, developed in yet new ways by Rabbinic Judaism and the Christian Church.[29]

[29] *Ibid.*, pp. 357-90. For the development in Rabbinic Judaism see George Foot Moore, *Judaism in the First Centuries of the Christian Era, the Age of the Tannaim* (Cambridge, Mass.: Harvard University Press, 1932), II, 279-395.

Leander E. Keck is Professor of New Testament at Vanderbilt Divinity School. He states that Jesus worked within the apocalyptic tradition with its emphasis on judgment, the defeat of Satan, and resurrection. But death was not the focal point of his message; he called instead for repentance and trust in God. Later writers saw in Jesus the beginnings of the new age. Paul, in I Corinthians 15, reflects the apocalyptic understanding of death as he confronts the Greek world and rejects immortality for resurrection. For him also, death is a moral question; that is, will God vindicate himself by redeeming his creation? John presents another alternative in describing eternal life as already present.

II

New Testament Views of Death

Leander E. Keck

There is no such thing as "the New Testament doctrine of death." For one thing, the New Testament is a selection of twenty-seven writings which reflect theological work done in two cultures and languages, Semitic (Hebrew and Aramaic) and Hellenistic. When Christianity moved from Palestinian soil to the Hellenistic world, questions arose and answers were forged which simply had not been developed in Palestine. Second, the New Testament does not discuss death as a theme; rather, it treats the theme of death in a great variety of settings that control what specifically is said (and not said). For example, a certain view of death is built into Jesus' words to the penitent thief, "Today you shall be with me in paradise," but the saying itself concerns forgiveness. Shall we use such sayings to talk about what Jesus taught about death? Because each setting for statements about death and life brings to the surface those aspects of the matter which are pertinent to the general theme while leaving other aspects untouched, one cannot simply compile New Testament phrases about death, drawn from a concordance, into a systematic statement of the theme. Rather, one should penetrate the various formulations to discern whether they have a common underlying center.

To do this, we must deal with the New Testament piecemeal rather than as a block. Only so can we do approximate justice to the diversity and the development which it represents. We will begin in Palestine, with Jesus and the earliest church. Then we will note how Paul engaged his Palestine-based tradition with the Greek mind and its view of death. After that we shall see how John displaced the old Jewish theology of death and resurrection by a new emphasis, whose roots also go back to earliest days. Finally, we will draw some conclusions concerning the historical and theological significance of New Testament views of death.

It is clear, of course, that resurrection is the dominant idea in the New Testament, not immortality.[1] Equally evident is the fact that the early Christian understanding of resurrection was inherited from that strand of the Old Testament and of Judaism which we call apocalyptic.[2]

[1] Oscar Cullmann has laid out the issue cogently and convincingly, though he has not paid sufficient attention to the encounter between resurrection and immortality theologies. Hence this discussion is a tacit conversation with Cullmann's analysis, "Immortality or Resurrection of the Dead?" recently republished in *Immortality and Resurrection,* ed. Krister Stendahl (New York: The Macmillan Co., 1965). In this edition Cullmann comments on criticisms levelled at his analysis. Because C. Ryder Smith's *The Bible Doctrine of the Hereafter* (Naperville, Ill: Alec R. Allenson, 1958) coordinates statements about life beyond death into a logically coherent system (whose historical orientation is to the Old Testament and Intertestamental ideas only), the whole treatment of the New Testament hangs in midair.

[2] There is reason to believe that first-century Pharisaism was much more open to apocalyptic than later rabbinic materials suggest. Apocalyptic theology, as will be argued and assumed here, is not to be

Inevitably, the entire discussion takes on the character of a conversation with the apocalyptic understanding of man and his dying.

Jesus

Because the Synoptic data are so diverse, it is useful to classify the sayings and deeds of Jesus.[3] To begin with, several kinds of materials will *not* be discussed. (a) Some passages are wrongly thought to refer to life after death because they speak of heaven. For example, "Lay up for yourselves treasures in heaven" (Matt. 6:20) does not speak of life after death at all because here "heaven" is simply a traditional Jewish circumlocution for God (as the parallel in Luke 12:21 sees). (b) Nor will we deal with those passages where Jesus speaks of his own death, because they do not properly belong in a discussion concerning every man's dying. (c) The Gospels also contain stories of Jesus' restoring the dead to life, such as Jairus' daughter (Mark 5:21-43) and the man from Nain (Luke 7:11-17). These stories were told to exalt Jesus' power and do not really belong in our discussion either. We will deal with two basic kinds of materials: those in which Jesus refers to death in connection with a major point that does not concern death, and those in which death and life after death are the explicit focus of concern.

1. When Jesus speaks of death in connection with his major concern, repentance and discipleship, we see what he *assumes* about death. Sometimes he merely mentions

---

identified simply with apocalyptic imagery about cataclysmic events at the end of the world, nor with theologically based chauvinism. The most recent monograph on apocalyptic is that by D. S. Russell, *The Method and Message of Jewish Apocalyptic* (Philadelphia: Westminster Press, 1964); Chap. XIV surveys the apocalyptic understanding of future life and compares it with previous Hebrew views.

[3] William Strawson's *Jesus and the Future Life* (Philadelphia: Westminster Press, 1959) does not distinguish clearly enough between assumptions and assertions, thereby making Jesus "teach" more than the material actually warrants.

death without disclosing any particular idea about it. For example, Matt. 16:25-26 reads, "For whoever would save his life will lose it, and whoever loses his life for my sake will find it. For what will it profit a man if he gains the whole world and forfeits his life?" Or we recall that Jesus did not shrink from making a would-be follower choose between burying his father, the most elemental family duty, and following him promptly: 'Let the dead bury their dead" (Matt. 8:22).[4]

At other times Jesus revealed what he assumed about death and what follows it. Thus Matt. 5:29-30[5] says that if one part of the body causes sin, it is better to amputate the part than to send the whole body to hell (Gehenna).[6] Luke 14:7-14 ends by saying those who invite outcasts to the wedding feast will be "repaid at the resurrection of the just," implying a view of limited resurrection as reward rather than a general resurrection which makes it possible for all men to be judged. Luke 16:9 mentions being received into "eternal habitations" after death. Matt. 10:28, part of a collection of sayings concerning discipleship, says: Do not fear those who can merely kill you; fear him who can send you to hell (Gehenna).[7]

Such sayings reveal three important things about Jesus' understanding of death. (a) Death is interpreted with categories drawn from apocalyptic (whence they entered

[4] Some scholars have seen this as an unfortunate translation (into Greek) of an Aramaic phrase which means, "Leave the dead to their burier of the dead [undertakers]." See I. Abrahams, *Studies in Pharisaism and the Gospels* (2nd Series; London: Cambridge University Press, 1924), pp. 183-84.

[5] Matt. 18:9 uses a different form of the saying and expressly mentions the hell of fire (see note 28 on page 51).

[6] It is important here not to let English usage confuse us. In common English, "hell" sometimes refers to the place of punishment ("hellfire and damnation"), sometimes to the abode of the dead ("He [Christ] descended into hell"); the latter translates the word Hades (the equivalent of Hebrew Sheol), the former Gehenna (as in Mark 9:43).

[7] The same point is made, in effect, by Acts 5:29: "We ought to obey God rather than men."

the stream of rabbinic thought also), such as judgment, resurrection, reward, punishment. There is no evidence that Jesus had any quarrel with such ideas; to the contrary, he found it possible to work within this perspective. (b) There is no interest in disclosing mysteries of death and what lies beyond. Rather, the references to death function as sanctions. They suggest the serious consequences of today's decision; they mark out the horizon against which Jesus expects his hearers to act. Because Jesus and his hearers shared views of death he could use them to undergird the urgency of his appeal. (c) In themselves, these views of death are not the source of Jesus' appeal for repentance and discipleship; his summons is grounded in his perception of the God whose kingship is actualizing itself in a decisively new way, and his preaching is not motivated by fear of death but by a sense of his own destiny. Death was not the central problem to be resolved. Jesus did not see it as his task to explain the problem of death or to overcome its power.[8] As we shall see, this distinguishes Jesus from many elements in the Greek world.

2. This is confirmed by that material in which Jesus expressly discusses death and its meaning. Luke 13:1-5 is especially suggestive, for two kinds of death are linked by the catastrophic circumstances: the death of the Galileans whom Pilate killed at the temple and the tragic victims of an accident. Neither group was killed because God decided to punish them for exceptional wickedness. Thereby Jesus shut the door to that kind of speculation that always tries to find a moral reason in the will of God for tragic death, as if it were God's retribution. This view is really the other side of the coin of Jesus' view that God's

[8] This judgment is not altered even if one were to regard the predictions of his resurrection to be authentic. The Jesus of the Fourth Gospel, on the other hand, makes overcoming death and mortality central to his task.

sunshine and rain fall indiscriminately on the just and unjust (Matt. 5:45). Positively, Jesus adds a summons to repentance: "Unless you repent you will all likewise perish." This does not mean that God threatens with catastrophe only the unrepentant, or that repentance brings immortality. Rather, the crowd should use such occurrences to reflect on the tenuousness of their own lives and to use the opportunity to repent lest death overtake them.[9] This note sounds like the stern preaching of John the Baptist (Matt. 3:7-12; Luke 3:7-9, 15-17).

The story of Jesus' conflict with the Sadducees (Mark 12:18-27) makes death and resurrection central. This story now stands as one of several controversies in Jerusalem. This gives the story a stylized character which must not be overlooked. The Sadducees, who regarded only the Pentateuch as Scripture, denied the resurrection and appealed to the absence of this doctrine from the Pentateuch (among other arguments) for support. Their opponents, the Pharisees, not only developed the synagogue in which the Scriptures were expanded to include Prophets and Writings (in which resurrection appears), but took pains to show that resurrection was taught in the Pentateuch as well. In our story, the Sadducees come at Jesus with an argument designed to expose the absurdity of the belief in resurrection by appealing to what both he and they regarded as Scripture.

They appeal to Deut. 25, according to which the brother

[9] Strawson reviews the various meanings of "perish" and concludes that probably Jesus was, like the Old Testament prophets, warning that national disaster could be avoided only by national repentance, a common change of course (probably with respect to insurrection against Rome); *Jesus and the Future Life*, pp. 76-78. The recent book by S. G. R. Brandon sees the anti-political character of the Lukan context in which this story is found, but refuses to infer from this that the materials originally had the same anti-Zealot thrust. *Jesus and the Zealots* (New York: Charles Scribner's Sons, 1968), p. 316, note 6. Rudolf Bultmann's hesitation about the historicity of the tradition is not persuasive. *History of the Synoptic Tradition*, trans. John Marsh (New York: Harper & Row, 1963), pp. 54-55.

of the deceased must marry the widow, and if possible, add to the family. Whether this law, called "Levirite marriage," was enforced, or became custom, is unimportant for the argument. The Sadducees' question is designed to show that resurrection is impossible because God would not contradict his own will. The argument assumes that life after resurrection continues this life and its relationships;[10] hence the question, "Whose wife will she be?"

Jesus' reply is a double one: Vss. 24-25 answer the immediate question concerning the *manner* of the resurrected, vss. 26-27 argue for the *fact* of resurrection by appealing to precisely that part of Scripture which Sadducees accepted. The first answer itself is twofold: First,

[10] In Jesus' day there was no uniform conception of what resurrection-life would be like; his reply, therefore, is not pitted against a consensus that marriage and family life would be expected. D. S. Russell in *The Method and Message of Jewish Apocalyptic*, pp. 374 ff., rightly says that the nature of the resurrection body corresponds to the overall kind of future envisaged; when an earthly eschaton is in view (the Messianic Age), the restoration of the physical body is emphasized, when the future is seen as transmundane, a "spiritual body" is in view. The expectation of restored physical existence is dramatically expressed in the story of the patriot Razis (II Macc. 14:46) who tried to disembowel himself rather than fall into enemy hands, but was in too great a hurry to succeed; surviving a leap off a wall and "aflame with anger, he rose, and though his blood gushed forth and his wounds were severe he ran through the crowd; and standing upon a steep rock with his blood now completely drained from him, he tore out his entrails, took them with both hands and hurled them at the crowd, calling upon the Lord of life and spirit to give them back to him again." II Bar. 49-51 deals explicitly with the question, "In what shape will those live who live in thy day?" The answer: there will be no change at first: "As it [the earth] has received, so shall it restore them." But after the reality of the resurrection will have been proved in this way, the condemned will be changed for the worse, the righteous will be "glorified in changes." On the other hand, Enoch 62:15-16 speaks of a resurrection body as a garment of glory that will not age. In Tannaitic and pre-Tannaitic Judaism apparently the continuity of this life's conditions was emphasized, probably, in part at least, to assert the reality of the resurrection, as in the Lukan account of the resurrected Jesus who ate fish to prove he was no phantom (Luke 24:41-42). Strack-Billerbeck point out that there is no rabbinic description of marital life in the resurrection-time; the few passages that speak of begetting children appear to have in mind the Messianic Age, not the post-resurrection-time.

Jesus attacks the Sadducees' premises by an *ad hominem* argument: You do not know the Scriptures nor do you know God's power; therefore you do not know how to put the question. Second, he speaks about God's power: Resurrection does not mean continuation, a resumption of life as we know it; rather it means transformation of existence in which sexuality and marriage will have no place at all. God is not trapped by the law in Deuteronomy, for apparently that does not apply in the new age of resurrection. Resurrection-time will not simply be a return to paradise, to the original sinless state of man and woman in Eden, but will be something even more radical in which (bi) sexual existence as such will be no more.[11]

Should we treat Jesus' reply seriously as teaching something about resurrected status, or should we regard it as teaching that nothing whatever can be taught about resurrected existence except negatively? After all, to say that one will have an angelic existence clarifies the matter only if one first knows what angels are like. It appears, then, that this reply has the effect of saying: We can only say what that existence will *not* be like—resumption of the present. Sadducee-like questions are therefore out of

[11] The dissolution of sexual differences was an important theme in gnostic Christianity of the second and third centuries. For example, the recently found Gospel of Thomas, Logion 22, reads: "They said to Him: Shall we then, being children, enter the Kingdom? Jesus said to them: When you make the two one, and when you make the inner as the outer and the outer as the inner and the above as the below, and when you make the male and the female into a single one, so that the male will not be male and the female (not) be female . . . then shall you enter [the Kingdom]." Clement of Alexandria reports that the Gospel of the Egyptians contained a word of Jesus, "When you have trampled on the garment of shame and when the two become one and the male with the female (is) neither male nor female," then Salome will know salvation fully. Clearly, this line of thought wrestles with the bifurcation of man into male and female as a tragic division of existence which must be overcome if salvation, as restoration of the original (androgynous) state, is to be real. The issue in Jesus' mind, however, is quite different.

order and must not be used to discredit the hope of resurrection itself.

The second answer nevertheless argues that resurrection will occur. Like the Pharisees, Jesus appeals to the Pentateuch in such a debate because the opponents, the Sadducees, regarded that as authoritative; an appeal to Psalms or Daniel or Hosea would have had no weight. Jesus used the story of the call of Moses in Exod. 6. Here God identifies himself, "I am the God of Abraham, Isaac and Jacob." What has that to do with resurrection? To see the point, we need to see also the assertion in vs. 27: "God is not the God of the dead but of the living." This formulates a view that underlies much Old Testament teaching—that those in Sheol are cut off from a significant, even if not total, relation to God.[12] Now in typical rabbinic fashion, Jesus joins two opposing views: One says that God is God of the living, the other that God himself says he is God of the patriarchs who had died years before Moses was born (like the rabbis, Jesus sees that the text does not say, "I *was* their God," but "I *am* their God"). Rather than use one statement to cancel the other, Jesus draws a third conclusion: The patriarchs are alive (or will be). Only if they are not finally consigned to Sheol will it be possible for both statements to be true at the same time. *When* the patriarchs live is not so important as *that* they live. Moreover, this argument rests on the unspoken assumption that the resurrection-hope is finally grounded in the indestructible relation of God to his own, a theme to which we shall return.

Clearly, an attempt to justify belief in resurrection by such use of Old Testament texts does not impress us. It is, however, fully at home in rabbinic dialectic. In fact, it is precisely its subtlety, its sophisticated dialectic, its imaginative use of Scripture that persuades many scholars

[12] See Chap. I.

that at least vss. 26-27, if not the whole, are not from Jesus himself but from an early Christian scribe.[13] Characteristically, Jesus appeals to the will and nature of God and does not build his case on such a use of Scripture. But if at least the first part of the reply is genuinely from Jesus, then it is clear that he understood resurrection as transformation of existence.

Summary. (a) Jesus stands within the apocalyptic theological tradition which assumes resurrection, judgment, Gehenna, etc., but does not make these things the themes of his preaching. Rather, his message is the nearness of the Kingdom and the consequent call to receive it by following him, cost what may, even death. When he speaks of death, judgment, and Gehenna he does so to underscore the seriousness of his message. These themes function as sanctions for his appeal and set his message in the context of ultimate questions. As we shall see, this horizon is in tension with that provided for Jesus' message in the Fourth Gospel.

(b) Jesus did not regard death as an obstacle to faith in God or as the crucial dimension about man that must be overcome. Death is a qualifier of man's existence, and as such makes life so precious that there is no equivalent for it: What will a man give in exchange for his life? The answer is clear not because Jesus believed in the "life-principle" or because he believed in the immortality of the soul but because he saw that life was bounded by inevitable death. The insecurity of life, which the ever-present possibility of death represents, should lead to repentance, to a Godward turning of one's life. This is

[13] E.g., Bultmann, *History of the Synoptic Tradition,* pp. 26, 40, 49-50; Sherman Johnson, *A Commentary on the Gospel According to St. Mark* (New York: Harper & Row, 1960), appears to agree; on the other hand, Vincent Taylor in *The Gospel According to St. Mark* (London: Macmillan & Co., 1957), regards it as authentic primitive tradition from Jesus.

why he can speak of death in various ways when he wants to give urgency and ultimacy to his call.

(c) Jesus refused to speculate about the death of those whose life was snuffed out, just as he refused to speculate about the nature of post-resurrection existence. He did not use resurrection to undercut the importance of this life as if to say, "Oh, well, they will be resurrected anyway." In the same way, he refused to use accidental death as an index of man's relation to God, thus implying that no direct line can be drawn between the manner of a man's dying and God's verdict on his life. In short, what Jesus *refused* to say about death and life afterward is an important dimension of his understanding of man. Perhaps nothing he said is more important than what he refused to say.

(d) Finally, we cannot ignore altogether Jesus' understanding of his own fate because Jesus called men to follow him, a man who with eyes wide open walked toward death because of his commitment. Cullmann has argued that certain passages, such as the Gethsemane scene, show that Jesus dreaded death.[14] Our question, however, is not whether Jesus was afraid to die (in contrast with Socrates!) or what sort of theological meaning he saw in his death-bound life; rather, our question is whether his own agony in the face of death (Gethsemane and the cry of dereliction) was consistent with what he had taught. If Jesus' words about not fearing those who can only kill the body mean that one may have no emotion of fear and trembling in the face of execution, one might infer that he did not fulfill his own words. But this is not what the saying means, for this "fear" means ultimate regard rather than an emotion of fright or terror. In the same way, "the fear of God" does not mean fright with respect to God but acting in light of God's ultimate and abso-

[14] Cullmann, "Immortality or Resurrection of the Dead?" pp. 12 ff.

lute claim. Actually, then, Jesus was consistent with his own teaching because, despite his horror of dying, he overcame his fear of death by his fear of God.

Earliest Christianity

1. Earliest Christian understanding of death stands within the apocalyptic theology and modifies it.[15] Three considerations will indicate this.

First, the earliest Christians stood with apocalyptic and with rabbinic Judaism in believing that there was to be such an event as resurrection. We know of no Sadducean Christians. But the decisive point is that for this Jewish theology, resurrection was not an event all by itself, an isolated occurrence that stretches credulity to the breaking point. Rather, resurrection was to be part of a whole drama of the End-time, which included judgment, the defeat of Satan, the vindication of God's pledge to Israel, and punishment or reward. There was no uniformity in what was expected to happen, nor in what order nor even in regard to the participants (some schemes had no Messiah at all); and not every apocalyptic writing hoped for resurrection.[16] Nevertheless, characteristically resurrec-

[15] I am well aware that this is a controversial position. Ever since Albert Schweitzer's New Testament studies compelled us to reckon with apocalyptic as the matrix of Christianity, various escape routes have been sought, largely because Jewish and early Christian apocalyptic taught that the end of history was imminent whereas nineteen centuries have proved this to be wrong, and partly because apocalyptic has a much more cynical view of history's fulfillment than modern Western man, even in a century of war, prefers to believe. The three major escape routes are: an effort to separate ethics from eschatology so that the timeless core is the ethic of love, an existential interpretation of eschatology in which one understands his own world to come to an "end" when he is judged by the grace of God, and an outright denial that Jesus or Paul were apocalyptically dominated (on this basis the later church ascribed its own views to Jesus [e.g., Mark 13] and to Paul [II Thess.]). Much of the confusion would have been avoided had we had a clearer understanding of apocalyptic.

[16] While resurrection of the person is the fundamental view of apocalyptic, Jub. 23:31 states another view of the individual's future:

tion was part of the drama of the End, and would occur only in this context. We will never understand early Christian views of resurrection so long as we begin with our ideas of resurrection as a miracle par excellence; for them, the resurrection was a moment in the sequence of eschatological events in which God definitively asserted himself to rectify creation or even to replace it. For earliest Christian theology resurrection was unthinkable and unbelievable apart from such a network of end events. This is why stories of people's being restored to life were never confused with resurrection.

Second, as a result, once the disciples became convinced that Jesus had been resurrected[17] they could not avoid the conclusion that the end of the old age and the beginning of the new was here. In contrast with us who may doubt that such a thing as resurrection is possible, let alone relevant, they had no doubt that there was such an event as resurrection. What they needed to know was whether it had occurred or was yet to happen. If resurrection had taken place, then they lived at the shift of the ages. This is, in fact, what the disciples claimed. Convinced that Jesus had been resurrected, they believed that the new age had dawned and that the drama of the Endtime was under way. In other words, the first consequence of believing that Jesus had been resurrected was not an argument over the possibility of immortality but a revolution in the way one regarded the present.

Third, believing that Jesus' resurrection had occurred brought a thoroughgoing revision of theology because

---

The spirits of men will enjoy everlasting bliss while the bones remain in the earth. In the Apocalypse of Abraham (12, 14, 21) immediately after death the righteous go to their reward, as do the wicked.

[17] It was the appearances of the risen Lord and not the news of or sight of the empty tomb that persuaded the disciples that Jesus had been resurrected from the land of the dead. The old tradition, used (and modified) by Paul in I Cor. 15:1-11, shows this clearly.

Jesus' death appeared to contradict common expectations of what God was doing. For one thing, if Jesus was resurrected and no one else, then surely *he* must be the Son of man, the Messiah, God's regent, despite the fact that his life ended in humiliation. Consequently Christians applied titles to Jesus which had been used to talk about the eschatological figure expected at the End. Moreover, early Christians had to square this conviction about Jesus with the fact that apparently history went on as before. Only Christians believed that Jesus was resurrected and installed into messianic office. In rapid succession, and perhaps simultaneously as well, many answers were worked out. Acts 3:20-21 may be among the very earliest: the resurrected Christ is a latent Messiah, waiting in heaven until the next act in the End-time drama when he will come earthward in power.[18] Acts 2:32-36 puts it this way: God has already made Jesus Messiah at the resurrection and hence he already reigns in heaven at the right hand of God. With the help of Ps. 110, which originally celebrated the enthronement of Israel's king, early Christians said that the Messiah's reign is not postponed but is already inaugurated in heaven and in the church. The church knows that a new regime has been established and already lives by the new order amid the old one which has no more future. Here a problem emerges which runs through early Christian thought: What aspects of the new age are already open to the believer in Jesus' resurrection, and what is yet to come? Moreover, if the eschatological events have begun, how long will it be before the

[18] This is the view of J. A. T. Robinson, "The Most Primitive Christology of All?", reprinted in his collected essays, *Twelve New Testament Studies* (Studies in Biblical Theology No. 34; Naperville, Ill.: Alec R. Allenson, 1962), Chap. 10. Reginald Fuller in *The Foundations of New Testament Christology* (New York: Charles Scribner's Sons, 1965), pp. 158 ff., agrees that the Christology of Acts 3:12-26 is more primitive than that of Acts 2:36 but does not regard it as "the most primitive of all" because he thinks the Son-of-man Christology was.

consummation (epitomized by the coming of Christ in power) occurs?

A third thing concerns directly the question of death. If Jesus has been resurrected from the realm of the dead, then that abode has been ruptured. With the help of an ancient idea of death as an enemy, early Christians saw Jesus' resurrection as the defeat of a tyrant. But if death has been defeated, why do people (including Christians) still die? [19] In other words, how are Jesus' death and victory related to the dying and destiny of individual men? It is questions such as these which run through the New Testament literature even though in many places there is no explicit discussion of death as a problem.[20] These considerations suggest that what the New Testament says about death is grounded in a particular perspective which many people today no longer share.

The New Testament never totally abandoned apocalyptic views; the pluralism of the church in New Testament times is shown by the fact the same decade saw two books emerge with fundamentally different attitudes toward apocalyptic theology, both sailing under the flag of John: the Fourth Gospel and the Revelation. In a mediating position we find Matthew, while a generation later Jude and II Peter advocate vigorously an outright apocalyptic view, as does II Thessalonians.[21] It is instructive to note briefly how Revelation deals with the issue of death.

2. Written in a persecution situation, Revelation aims to undergird those facing death because they would not compromise their allegiance to Christian faith. The prob-

[19] This is a basic issue in I Thess. 4:13-18, where Paul uses apocalyptic ideas to answer the question, which apparently arose on specifically Hellenistic presuppositions about sacraments (though this is not explicit in Paul's response).

[20] E.g., Phil. 3:17-21; Eph. 2:1-7; II Tim. 1:8-10; I John 3:2.

[21] Although many scholars regard II Thessalonians as genuine, I hold it to be a post-Pauline apocalyptic document.

lem of a martyr's death runs through the book (e.g., 7:13; 14:13; 20:4-6). If Jesus has been raised as victor from the realm of the dead (1:18; 17:14), how is the believer's plight to be understood in light of history as a whole? The author shows that the present catastrophe for believers will not destroy them because the last word is God's. The writer includes a vision of the souls of the martyrs under the heavenly altar (6:9-11) to assure the living that beyond their impending martyrdom they are secure until the day when God would rectify history, and so avenge them. Where he thinks the rest of the dead are is not clear because he is not writing an essay on this subject. Moreover, there are to be two resurrections and two deaths (chap. 20). The first is a reward for the martyrs, who then will reign with Christ for a thousand years. At the end of this millennium (the only place the Bible speaks of it) Satan is again unleashed and will deceive nations (where they come from is no more his concern than the question over whom the saints will "reign" during the millennium). This will be followed by the second resurrection, this time for all men. The lake of fire [22] (20:10, 14-15) awaits all those who will be punished, including Death and Hades. Those vindicated by the Judge will inherit the entirely new heaven and earth in which there will be no more death or sorrow (21:1-5).

In this work natural death is an enemy to be overcome because the author assumes that sorrow, sickness, and death are consequences of sin, instigated by Satan. But natural death is not his main concern. Rather his theology is dominated by the problem of the innocent suffering of the saints at the hands of the drunken whore, Rome (17:6). Hence he combines two resurrection-traditions: The first is a special reward for faithfulness, the

[22] That the place of torment is to be fiery is an idea common in Jewish apocalyptic. That the locale is to be a lake is common. The idea of a flaming lake is found also in the Apocalypse of Peter.

second is a way of including all men, Christian or not, in the final settling of accounts. The entire theological interpretation of death and of martyrdom is dominated by the problem of faithfulness to God in a history which is pitted against God. This literature, therefore, should not be mined for verses to be fitted into a systematic biblical "answer" to the question, "What happens to us when we die?" Rather, it should be brought into any discussion of the enigma of unwarranted suffering at the hands of evil powers and wicked men. Its theme is the ultimate vindication of God's integrity and God's ultimate vindicating of the righteous. The question Revelation puts to us is whether apocalyptic theology deals adequately with this issue.

3. Early Christian preaching announced that by the resurrection of Jesus, God had acted decisively to inaugurate the New Day. This was the heart of the Good News. Implicit, if not always explicit, in this announcement was an evitable apocalyptic understanding of the present as the turning point of the Ages. Despite wide divergence in today's interpretations of "resurrection," there is virtual unanimity that this was the core of early Christian preaching and theology.

It was not long, however, before this message was taken to Jews outside Palestine and to Gentiles of all sorts. The decisive question then became, How will Greeks, who had different ideas of life and death and man's existence, understand this news about Jesus? What questions will they press for some answer that makes sense in a setting in which apocalyptic perspectives cannot be taken for granted? The letters of Paul, who faced these questions and dealt with them profoundly, disclose the struggle for interpretation. But we cannot grasp Paul's answers before we hear the questions; this is why we must next note certain Hellenistic views of life and death.

Some Hellenistic Views of Death[23]

The Christian gospel moved into a highly complex culture in which it is impossible to speak of "the Greek view" of death (or of anything else). Old and new ideas existed side by side as well as in various combinations. As a matter of fact, there never was a single Greek view of death, even in the classical period.

It is useful to note briefly both the development and the diversity of these Hellenistic views of death in the New Testament world.[24] To begin, probably the oldest notion was that the dead somehow continued to exist in their tombs or graves, or near them. For this reason, graves were honored and the dead buried. Periodically the family or clan would eat a meal at the place of burial (in the presence of the dead), partly to provide the departed with food, partly to humor them lest they harm the living. This custom persisted for centuries alongside views which

[23] The term "hellenistic" designates that period of Greek culture which began with the death of Alexander. With Alexander's conquest of the world between Greece and India a new culture emerged in the East—the international, cosmopolitan civilization in which Greek was the language of commerce and in which new cities with sewerage, baths, theaters, and academies spread Greek culture. One can speak of the Hellenization of the Orient just as one can speak of the Americanization of vast parts of the world after World War II. When the Romans replaced the Greeks as the administrators of this world, they perpetuated Greek culture which they admired deeply. The New Testament falls in this second phase of Hellenistic civilization, sometimes called Graeco-Roman, which began with Augustus, in whose reign Jesus was born. In this era the tide turned, and Oriental ideas and religious traditions began moving westward rapidly. W. W. Tarn's *Hellenistic Civilization* (3rd ed. [rev. 1952]; Cleveland: World Publishing Co., 1927) describes the first phase, while F. C. Grant's *Roman Hellenism and the New Testament* (New York: Charles Scribner's Sons, 1962) distills his vast knowledge of the second.

[24] The most important single book on the subject is by Franz Cumont, *After Life in Roman Paganism* (New Haven: Yale University Press, 1923). Werner Jaeger's contribution to the essays collected by Stendahl (see note 1, p. 34), "The Greek Ideas of Immortality," is concerned with classical views and their forerunners.

were logically inconsistent with the practice.[25] Later it was believed that the dead go to the subterranean realm of the dead, Hades, which corresponds to the Hebrew *She'ol.* Originally the inequalities of earthly life were simply continued,[26] each man resuming his status in society.[27] Under Orphic influence[28] this existence was differentiated into areas for rewards or punishments. The idea that the dead are judged according to their deeds in life is not originally Greek, though it had long been firmly established in Egypt. Cumont thinks that this "infernal theology" was developed in the East and taken up in Greek thought at an early stage. Once this notion took root it persisted until it was taken up by Christian thought. Cumont has characterized the matter as follows:

When the souls, or rather the shades, descend to the depths of the earth, they reach first a provisional abode where they await a decision as to their lot, an intermediate region through which all of them pass but in which some are kept for a considerable time. They then cross the Styx, and a road which is also common to all of them leads them to the court which determines their lot. . . . Infallible judges, from whom no fault is hid, divide into two companies the multitude of the souls appearing before them. The guilty are constrained to take the road to the left which leads to dark Tartarus, crossing its surrounding river of fire, the Pyriphlegethon. There those who have committed inexpiable crimes are condemned to eternal chastisement. But the road to the right leads the pious souls to the Elysian Fields where, among flowered meadows and wrapped in soft light, they obtain the reward of their virtues, whether, having attained to perfection, they are able to dwell for ever with the heroes, or whether, being less pure,

[25] For these very early views, see Cumont, *After Life in Roman Paganism,* pp. 44-58 and the first chapter of Martin Nilsson's *Greek Folk Religion* (New York: Harper & Row, 1965, reprint of 1940 ed.).

[26] Cumont, *After Life in Roman Paganism,* p. 72.

[27] Contrast Job 3:17-19!

[28] Cumont, *After Life in Roman Paganism,* p. 171.

they are obliged to return later to the earth in order to reincarnate themselves in new bodies after they have drunk the water of Lethe and lost the memory of their previous existence.[29]

With the rise of critical philosophy, such views came to be severely criticized, rejected outright, or reinterpreted. The central term in this development was *psyche,* commonly translated "soul." For Homer, psyche was the shade (*eidolon*) of the whole man which went to Hades.[30] But a different idea of psyche emerged between the time of Homer and that of Plato—that it was an invisible, eternal element, a divine component,[31] distinct and separable from the body, indeed alien to it. Apparently this view of man was fed into the Greek stream by the Orphic mystery tradition.[32] To the Orphics this eternal element was in the body as a prisoner; they coined the phrase *soma-sema*—the body (*soma*) is a tomb (*sema*) for the soul. For Orphics, suffering in Hades purified the soul so that it could be born again into another body, perhaps into a more noble one, though some were condemned to eternal punishment.[33] The most prominent form of punishment was fire.[34] Thus we have a theology according to which the soul falls into its body-tomb, whence it goes to Hades to be chastised and purified,

[29] *Ibid.,* p. 76.

[30] For a discussion of the classical and pre-classical Greek views of psyche, see Jaeger, *The Theology of the Early Greek Philosophers* (London: Oxford University Press, 1947), Chap. 5. Jaeger's discussion critically assesses the older classical work by Erwin Rohde, *Psyche,* trans. from the 8th ed. by W. B. Hillis (New York: Harper Torchbooks, 1966, 2 vols.; first published 1893, revised 1897).

[31] Jaeger says flatly, "There is nothing so un-Homeric as the idea that the human soul is of divine origin; no less strange to Homer is the dualistic division of man into body and soul which this theory presupposes." *The Theology of the Early Greek Philosophers,* p. 76.

[32] Jaeger holds the theory of the divinity of the soul to mark a turning point in the philosophical idea of God. *Ibid.,* p. 88.

[33] Cumont, *After Life in Roman Paganism,* p. 172.

[34] *Ibid.,* p. 175.

then reborn only to repeat the cycle until it attains sufficient purity to be freed altogether from the cycle and to return to its ultimate origin. In the Roman period, because the soul came to be understood as coming from a heavenly origin, Hades was relocated to a celestial place, so that there is a perpetual cycle of descent to earthly bodies, ascent to Hades (or release to the Beyond). This celestial cycle may reflect oriental astrology's influence on Greek thought.[35] In the long run celestial immortality came to be the dominant view, with the result that the old underworld gods became solar deities.[36]

The greatest interpreter of the soul was Plato. (His teacher, Socrates, does not appear to have had firm convictions about life after death. When he was about to drink the poison, his friends inquired how they should bury him. His reply: "Any way you like, if you can catch me!"—that is, the real Socrates is not in the corpse; yet he did not say where he was or even if he still "was.") Plato developed logical "proofs" for the old Orphic (and Pythagorean) [37] view that man's soul is an eternal alien in a temporal mortal body. Because it pre-exists, it is subject to the cycle of birth and death and rebirth. Death is therefore no enemy, but a friend who releases the soul from the body; the enemy, if one is to speak this way at all, is the cycle of life.

[35] *Ibid.*, p. 95.

[36] *Ibid.*, p. 39.

[37] The Pythagoreans were brothers in a religious and ethical society. They shared with Orphics the doctrine of transmigration of souls and ascetic practices designed to purify the soul. For a discussion of the relation of these two traditions, see Frederick Copleston, *A History of Philosophy* (London: Burns Oates and Washbourne, 1946), Vol. I. Chap. 4. Years before, R. M. Cornford, *From Religion to Philosophy* (New York: Harper Bros., 1957; orig. pub. 1912), pp. 194 ff., had argued that Pythagoreanism was a revival and reformation of Orphism, which itself had been a reformation of Dionysiac religion. He called this the "mystical tradition" in contrast with the "scientific tradition." He reckoned Plato with the former because of his "conversion" to Pythagorean ideas between the writing of the *Apology* and the *Phaedo* (pp. 242-49).

At the opposite end of the spectrum stood Epicurus, who insisted that at death the soul, made of atoms like everything else, disintegrates and ceases to exist altogether. This was the sharpest philosophical attack on the whole idea of existence beyond death. For Epicurus, this view was liberation from superstition and bondage to false views of the gods and of man, not a sorrow-laden conclusion. Of all the Greek philosophical views of man, this appears in many ways to be nearest that of modern "secular man," allegedly content with proximate values and moderate satisfactions that require no justification or adjustment beyond the grave.

A third philosophical tradition, dominant in the Hellenistic period among certain intellectuals at least, was the Stoic view[38] according to which the soul is material like the body. The soul dissolves into the primal stuff out of which all things were made (fire) and will be made again. There is only one ultimate substance, not two worlds as Plato had said. Through this whole monistic cosmos Reason (Logos) moves to make it cohere rationally. Consequently, the rational Law of the universe is also the law of the self. For the Stoic, then, there was no personal destiny after death but only reassimilation into primal matter. Individuation was only temporary, as was everything else. What concerned him was duty, reconciliation to fate, and manly dying—fearless dignity in the face of death, natural or catastrophic.

Alongside this variegated theoretical interpretation of life and death there existed a cultic tradition which also interpreted man's existence, though without placing a premium on logical reflection. This centered in the mystery cults. Even more than gnosticism (see below), these cults (such as that located at Eleusis or the Dionysiac

[38] One should guard against speaking too strongly of the "Stoic view" since Stoicism underwent a five-century-long development in diverse directions, including a distinctive Roman coloration.

which had no central shrine) go back to primordial times. The cults offered intense religious experience of the irrational; frenzy and mania were signs of divine possession. For the more sophisticated cults, such as Isis, seeing the mystery-rites served to make the divine present. Aristotle's observation was apt: the cults do not teach something but allow one to experience a power and to be put into a state of mind. In Graeco-Roman times the cults from the East and from Egypt rapidly moved westward: Isis and Osiris, Serapis, The Great Mother, and Mithra: Each had its own priesthood, rites, and promises. Organized as brotherhoods, they were for many the main form of personal religion.[39] The exact relation between these cults, with their mysterious rites, and gnosticism (see below) is not clear, but Bultmann may be right in regarding gnostic theology as the theoretical statement of what was celebrated in the cults.[40]

The cults were developed on the assumption that immortality could be acquired by participating in the life of the deity.[41] Because most of the mystery gods were dying and rising deities, they had themselves overcome

[39] A. J. Festugière, *Personal Religion Among the Greeks* (Berkeley: University of California Press, 1954), p. 40 sees this too. The traditional religions of the city-states were civic affairs, not personal faiths. Especially the Romans regarded civic religion as a program of the state to assure prosperity and power. Hence the empire resisted the cults as long as possible, but eventually could not succeed in repressing them any more than it succeeded in destroying Christianity. For a brief account of this process, see R. M. Grant, *The Sword and the Cross* (New York: The Macmillan Co., 1955).

[40] Rudolf Bultmann, *Primitive Christianity in Its Contemporary Setting*, trans. R. H. Fuller (Meridian Books: Cleveland: World Publishing Co., 1958), p. 169.

[41] When F. C. Grant, *Roman Hellenism*, p. 78, says that cults offered *blessed* immortality because it was almost universally assumed that there was some sort of continuity of existence after death, he appears to confuse mere continuity with immortality; it is not evident that "immortality" was used so loosely. Rather, a subtle distinction appears to have been made between sheer continuity and immortality. This is rightly emphasized by Bultmann's article Θάνατος in Kittel, *Theological Dictionary of the New Testament*, Vol. III.

death and could confer their power on those who were initiated. The rituals, such as eating raw flesh torn from living animals or frenzied dancing sometimes accompanied by self-mutilation (including castration as an act of overcoming the flesh) or drinking the fluid of the gods —wine, were designed to do this.[42] A. D. Nock formulated the appeal of the mysteries as follows:

> We (the mystery priests) assume from the fact of your approach to us that you are not in too bad a state. We will of course give you a preliminary rite or rites of disinfection which will ensure the requisite ritual purity. That is to be followed by our holy ceremony, which will confer on you a special kind of blessedness which guarantees to you happiness after death.[43]

In the Orphic mysteries, on the other hand, the rituals were designed to provide a means of escape for the eternal soul now trapped in a mortal body.

Given the eclectic character of the Hellenistic period, the apostles did not encounter any of these views in their "pure state." Rather, they met partly a mood, partly a cacophany of inconsistent views held together by the allegorical method which allowed one to give new meanings to old myths, partly a variety of options among which one could choose. The cities of the Graeco-Roman world contained as heterogeneous an assortment of views of death as do our own. Given the character of the New Testament, moreover, only certain aspects of this milieu are reflected in the canon, namely those ideas which challenged the understanding of man and his salvation as taught in the

[42] A. D. Nock wrote that only in Orphism and in the Eleusinian mystery were the rites actually requisites for immortality; elsewhere he believed them to be rites of assurance. *Conversion* (London: Oxford University Press, 1933), p. 13. The standard treatment of mystery religions remains Harold Willoughby's *Pagan Regeneration* (Chicago: University of Chicago Press, 1929; repr. 1960).

[43] *Conversion,* p. 12.

church. Moreover, we do not know what Paul, for example, said to the Stoic or Epicurean[44] view of man's soul or of his dying. Likewise, the New Testament does not allow us to see clearly how Christians met the mystery cults, though some clues can be found.[45] This means, then, that we must locate that aspect of the Hellenistic scene which is actually dealt with in the New Testament. In general, this is identifiable as a form of gnosticism or proto-gnosticism.

Some scholars are unhappy about efforts to relate the New Testament to gnosticism because we do not have gnostic documents from pre-Christian times.[46] Others are persuaded that this fact must not mislead us into thinking that gnosticism exists only as a parasite on Christian theology, because the Christian element can be removed from many Christian gnostic systems without disrupting the system itself; in these, the Christian stratum is simply the latest item absorbed into the eclectic, syncretistic system. Moreover, parts of the New Testament (such as Colossians) make more sense if we work with the hypothesis that at least a proto-gnostic movement was "in the air" even if it was not yet organized into cults and systematized into explicit theology. Consequently, while the paragraphs that follow are a composite portrait drawn from details in diverse gnostic systems later than Paul, it is likely that they represent the sort of thing his letters grapple with.[47]

[44] Interestingly, the response of the Epicureans who are said to have heard Paul preach in Athens is not given (Acts 17); presumably they joined in the mockery with the Stoics, with whom they otherwise disagreed.

[45] See Grant, *Roman Hellenism*, pp. 77 f.

[46] E.g., R. McL. Wilson's essay in *The Bible in Modern Scholarship*, ed. J. P. Hyatt (Nashville: Abingdon Press, 1965), pp. 272-78. Wilson refers there to R. P. Casey's vigorous dissent from continental research on Gnosticism.

[47] I want to record my long-standing indebtedness to Hans Jonas' work on Gnosticism, marked by his pulling together diverse materials from widely separated times and places in order to lay out the underlying rationale of the phenomenon, as well as by his use of Heidegger

Hellenistic gnostic views of man, elaborated in a seemingly infinite number of variations, were at bottom a reassertion of the Orphic view of man, though modified in significant ways. The gnostics drew on many ancient traditions (and invented new ones) to talk about the eternal alien buried in man: It was the divine spark, the ray, the essence, the seed, etc. Man's existence is a tragic bondage of the eternal in the mortal. The gnostics could agree with the Stoics that man's body and soul were part and parcel of the cosmos; but whereas this conviction made the Stoic feel at home in the wide universe, for the gnostic it underscored his strangeness because his true self, his transcendent essence, was at home in a totally different world, the realm of light. Moreover, the Stoic regarded the orderly movement of the planets and of earthly nature as evidence of a cosmic law which governed also his own life; this providence assured him that the whole operated according to the rational principle (Logos). Therefore his life "made sense" if he lived according to reason. But the gnostic regarded the cosmic order not as providence but as fate, a law-abiding, inescapable tyranny of malign powers residing in the planets. For him, the harmonious working of the celestial bodies attested the coherent tyranny of the material over the eternal spirit within the cosmos. The Stoic could gaze at the stars and give thanks for providence, but the gnostic could only curse his bondage to the world.

Unfortunately, before a man becomes a gnostic he does not even know that this is bondage! And when he becomes

---

to interpret the structure of existence which the various forms of Gnosticism expressed. His views are summarized in *The Gnostic Religion* (Boston: Beacon Press, 1958). Bultmann's delineation of Gnosis leans heavily on Jonas' work. See Γνῶσις in Kittel, *Theological Dictionary of the New Testament,* Vol. I, as well as Bultmann, *Primitive Christianity,* pp. 162-71. R. M. Grant, who does not approach Gnosis in the tradition of Jonas, has compiled a useful handbook of gnostic documents, Christian and non-Christian. *Gnosticism* (New York: Harper & Row, 1961).

a gnostic, he is no longer bound. The gnostics believed that the material world and its personalized manifestation, the body, exerted a malign influence on the eternal spirit or soul, made it drowsy, drunk, forgetful, ignorant, etc. Thus the situation of unknowing marks the plight of the divine element. Hence the soul (or spirit) needs revelation to be saved. A second-century Christian gnostic formulated it aptly:

> Until baptism . . . Fate is real, but after it the astrologists are no longer right. But it is not only the washing that is liberating but the knowledge of who we were, and what we have become, where we were or where we were placed, whither we hasten, from what we are redeemed, what birth is and what rebirth.[48]

Armed with this knowledge, the divine in man could free itself of the material influence now, and at death escape the cosmos altogether in order to return home to the transcosmic world whence it came. Without this knowledge (gnosis) the spirit (soul) was destined to be reborn endlessly. This revelation occurred because a savior figure bootlegged knowledge into the cosmos; receiving the revelation was possible because the savior and the saved were both of the same eternal substance. In such a perspective the "fall of man" was not merely the tragedy of the primal man but occurred every time an eternal spirit was born into a body. Salvation consisted in escape, radical abandonment of the world, flesh, matter, and body altogether. Whereas Jewish apocalyptic traced man's mortality to Adam's sin, thus making man (generically) responsible for mortality (by regarding mortality as an event rather

[48] From the *Excerpts of Theodotus* 78. Theodotus was a Valentinian whose work was studied by Clement of Alexandria. R. P. Casey edited, translated, and commented on these materials in *The Excerpta ex Theodoto of Clement of Alexandria* (Studies and Documents 1; London: Christophers, 1934), from which this quotation is taken.

than as an ontic flaw in existence per se), gnostics traced sin and mortality to existence itself, thus making the Creator responsible for man's plight and making man the innocent, tragic victim of fate. This is why gnostics invariably separated the Creator of the world from the highest god who had no responsibility for creation at all, but who did intervene to rescue the divine sparks within it.

Even this terse outline of selected features suggests several important issues. First, it is apparent that the gnostic understanding of man and his fate leads directly to a doctrine of God. Consequently, early Christian creeds insisted, as a battle cry, "I believe in God the Father Almighty, maker of heaven and earth, and in Jesus Christ his only Son." Here the church refused to separate the Creator from the Savior. Second, while the church won the battle it did not annihilate gnostic theology, for today it survives in even the most conservative theologies. It is found, for example, wherever it is assumed that the gospel awakens an eternal soul from its error or slumber and thereby saves it for its eternal home. (One gnostic idea which has not perpetuated itself widely is the old view of the transmigration of souls.)

Much of the current confusion about death, immortality, resurrection, eternal life, "soul's salvation," etc., stems from the fact that this gnostic language, grounded in ancient Orphism and other traditions as well, has been perpetuated alongside views of man with which it is in conflict. Our contemporary outlook is more akin to the Hellenistic situation than one might at first suppose.

We can see how the stage was set for a lively and exciting encounter when the apostles claimed that there is salvation for those who believe that the crucified Jesus has been resurrected from the realm of the dead. Would such a message even be understood? How would it have been interpreted? Acts 17, which Luke regards as the epitome of Paul's preaching to the gentiles, is not encouraging. His first attempt was a total failure because the audience took "resurrection" to be the goddess (*anastasis,* resurrection, is a feminime noun) who appeared with Jesus, while his second sermon, recast along Stoic lines, was interrupted precisely when Paul mentioned the raising of Jesus from the dead. Yet some Greeks did receive this announcement as the Good News. But what did they understand by it? That is the overarching question of the next section.

Paul

1. Because Paul's letters emerged in particular confrontations of the gospel with Hellenistic theology we need to delineate briefly the contours of that debate, seen most clearly in the Corinthian letters, especially in I Cor. 15, which will be the center of our analysis.

First, the news of Jesus' resurrection constituted the center of earliest Christian preaching to Gentiles just as it did to Jews. Thus Paul's earliest letter says the readers have come to "wait for his Son [God's] from heaven, whom he raised from the dead, Jesus who delivers us from the wrath to come" (I Thess. 1:10). Likewise, Paul's most complete exposition of the resurrection, I Cor. 15, begins by reminding the readers that they had accepted his preaching of the death and resurrection of Jesus. As we saw in Acts 17, Luke shows that it was the news of Jesus' resurrection that offended Athenians. The fact that Paul can say that he preached only Christ crucified (I Cor. 2:2) does not mean that sometimes Paul omitted the resurrection from his preaching but rather that he so closely linked cross and resurrection that he could refer to the cross alone as a symbol of the whole complex.[49] In short,

[49] Paul can also mention only the resurrection (e.g., I Thess. 1:10 or Rom. 8:11) without excluding the cross, since for him they together

Paul treats the problem of death and resurrection as an issue within the church, as a believer's issue. Paul's letters do not give us his way of making resurrection credible to Greeks in general, but rather express his way of regarding the matter "from faith to faith." How Paul first presented the resurrection-news to gentiles is another matter.

Second, this intra-faith discussion has a sacramental dimension. In Rom. 6 Paul discusses Christian baptism (also in I Cor. 10). Yet Rom. 6 does not outline his doctrine of baptism but picks up those aspects which were common stock among early Christians and builds on them his distinctive argument. That is, he points out the meaning of what was already believed to be true, and of what accepted sacramental action implied. Paul reminds the Romans that in baptism the believer is buried with Christ, and has been baptized into participation with him. Here Paul makes a subtle but decisive point: While in baptism we have been "buried with Christ" we have not yet been raised with him in the resurrection.[50] Instead, baptism made us partners in his death "so that we might walk in newness of life." For Paul, the present-time participation in Christ's resurrection is a new ethical life, not a present immortality. Almost as if he had the mystery rites in mind, Paul says in effect that sacramental action does not confer immortality even if we are made partners with Christ's death and resurrection.[51]

---

constitute one saving event. See Rudolf Bultmann, *Theology of the New Testament,* trans. Kendrick Grobel (New York: Charles Scribner's Sons, 1954), I, 292-93.

[50] This is one of the differences between Paul himself and the post-Pauline tradition in which this nuance is eliminated. See Eph. 2:4-7; Col. 2:12; 3:1.

[51] Ernst Käsemann has shown that the same theological position underlies Paul's discussion of the Lord's Supper. "The Pauline Doctrine of the Lord's Supper" in *Essays on New Testament Themes,* trans. W. J. Montague (Studies in Biblical Theology No. 41; Naperville, Ill.: Alec R. Allenson, 1964). The relation of Paul's understanding of

Paul wrote Romans after his struggles with the Corinthian church had been more or less resolved, and he probably formulated a conviction that had been fought over with that church. To oversimplify, the Corinthians evidently believed that being baptized into Christ's death and resurrection made them immortal victors over time and space and flesh. Moreover, their ecstatic moments, speaking in tongues and other forms of intense religious experience, were held to confirm their freedom from the body. In ecstasy they escaped the body and spoke "the tongues of angels." This is why Paul taunts them, "Already you are kings!" (I Cor. 4:8-9).

Consequently, in the third place, when Paul writes to the Corinthians about resurrection, he deals with a misinterpretation of what he had previously preached. But how could such a misinterpretation arise on so basic a matter? In I Cor. 15:12 Paul addresses those Christians who believed the news of Jesus' resurrection and yet say there is no such thing as resurrection. These are not Epicureans for they baptized the living for the sake of the dead.[52] Rather, they were Christians who understood the gospel in a gnostic way.[53] In II Cor. 11:4 he taunts the church for receiving those who preach another Jesus,

---

baptism to the Hellenistic cults has been discussed continually for two generations. The issues, hypotheses and relevant materials can be studied easily in Günther Wagner, *Pauline Baptism and the Pagan Mysteries,* trans. by J. P. Smith (Edinburgh: Oliver & Boyd, 1967; German ed. 1962).

[52] It is impossible to know with certainty the precise significance of this rite, reported only here in the New Testament. Apparently it was a sacrament by which the living sought to secure blessedness (if not immortality) for the departed. This obscure passage has generated many equally obscure interpretations, some of which are cited in Jean Héring's commentary *The First Epistle of St. Paul to the Corinthians,* trans. A. W. Heathcote and P. J. Allcock (London: Epworth Press, 1962; orig. French ed., 1948). For a useful statement of the issues involved, see G. R. Beasley-Murray, *Baptism in the New Testament* (London: Macmillan & Co., 1962), pp. 185-92.

[53] Whether they had gnostic perspectives before they became Christians or were persuaded by Christians preachers of this outlook is neither clear nor decisive for our discussion. What is important is to

who offer another Spirit and another gospel. Clearly this was Paul's way of "reading" those he called "false apostles" (II Cor. 10:13); they themselves did not appear in the church saying, "We have another Jesus." On this basis they would scarcely have gotten a hearing. Rather, they said in effect, "We know the true meaning of what you already believe. Paul does not really understand the matter correctly." This is why Paul defended his integrity and his gospel at the same time.

How, then, did the opponents interpret the gospel? If they said, "There is no resurrection of the dead," they did not mean to say, "There is no hope for the future," or "You have been deceived because there is no truth to the gospel." Rather, for them, "There is no resurrection" was a "triumphant message" of release from the body—any body—altogether.[54] These gnostics regarded themselves as essentially, ontically "spirit"; their spirits, now trapped in mortal bodies, were through Christ and the sacraments assured of release from everything that enslaved them. But if they accepted the news that God had resurrected Jesus, how could they deny the resurrection? Unfortunately, we do not know. We may infer, however,

---

recognize that these Christians probably had a coherent theological perspective and were not guilty of "muddled thinking" as M. E. Dahl says. *The Resurrection of the Body* (Studies in Biblical Theology No. 36; Naperville, Ill.: Alec R. Allenson, 1962), p. 76. Rather, in light of the Corinthian penchant for "wisdom," they probably regarded Paul's steady effort to relate apocalyptic theology to Corinthian questions as muddled.

[54] This has been seen clearly by Walter Schmithals, whose important book *Die Gnosis in Korinth* (F.R.L.A.N.T. 66; Göttingen: Vandenhoeck & Ruprecht, 1956) has not been translated. While both his views and his methods have been severely criticized (because, e.g., he uses post-Pauline gnostic texts to interpret Paul's opponents and insists that Paul fought but one issue in all his gentile churches, some form of Gnosticism), there is no doubt that he has put the discussion of the Corinthian letters on a new plane. I suspect that many views expressed here are the result of suggestions made by Schmithals, though I can no longer trace their lineage.

that they regarded it as no resurrection at all, but as his release from the body.[55]

Consequently, Paul's discussion in I Cor. 15 is no leisurely consideration of alternatives or a reflective summary of what a modern man in the first century can believe. Rather, it is a polemical statement sweated out of controversy with his own church over the meaning of his own (and their own) gospel-faith. For Paul, everything is at stake here. We do not understand Paul at all unless we see the struggle that prompted the discussion.

2. It is helpful to see the scope of the argument as a whole. (a) I Cor. 15:1-11 states the tradition which Paul received and transmitted, with some typical Pauline modifications.[56] He does not begin with the nature of

[55] The problem of the gnostic interpretation of Jesus' resurrection is an exceedingly complex one. One Valentinian tradition, which had clearly distinguished the human Jesus from the heavenly Christ, said that at baptism the divine Christ came upon Jesus and was then withdrawn from him at the end so that death could work its power; afterward the corpse of Jesus was raised again. This was an attempt to keep the tradition of the resurrection while at the same time preserving the divine essence from the experience of death. *Excerpta ex Theodotou* 61. The Ophites known to Irenaeus held the same view (*Adv. haer.* i 30:13). Basilides, according to Irenaeus (i 24:4), held that the divine Son of God did not die because by last-minute deceit he managed to have Simon of Cyrene look like Jesus, while Jesus was made to look like Simon, so that it was really the Jesus-appearing Simon who was crucified, while the Simon-appearing Jesus stood by and laughed derisively. Whoever did not believe this to be the truth of the matter revealed his continuing bondage to the world. In the *Acts of John,* Jesus himself insists (referring to the Passion), "What they say of me, that befell me not, but what they say not, that did I suffer." Here the Passion is understood as the process of "separating off the manhood" (98 ff.). The ascension occurred apparently during the crucifixion, as appears to be the case also in the *Gospel of Peter* in which the crucified and abandoned Jesus cries, "My power, my power" instead of (viz., as an interpretation of!) "My God, why hast thou forsaken me?"

[56] That Paul added vs. 6b (indicating that of the five hundred who saw the risen Lord some are still alive) as well as 8-11 is clear. Far from clear is whether the tradition was first formulated in Aramaic-speaking Jerusalem Christianity or in Hellenistic Christianity. Nor is the original purpose of this summary evident. Fortunately, our analysis does not depend on a solution to these vexing questions, because we are concerned with the use of the tradition in Paul's argument. Bult-

the soul or of the body or of death or of life beyond the cosmos, but with common Christian tradition about Jesus' death and resurrection—as if to say, "We do not begin this discussion in mid-air or on first principles, but at the concrete place where we both find ourselves: recipients of a believed tradition about Jesus' resurrection." (b) I Cor. 15:12-19 then joins the issue: Some of you who believed this with me now proclaim there is no resurrection. What is at stake in our dispute? Nothing less than the integrity of the gospel and of faith based upon it. (c) I Cor. 15:20-28 responds to the issue by outlining an answer which links inseparably the resurrection of Jesus and the resurrection of the Christian. (d) I Cor. 15:12-34 doubly supports the arguments, the first (baptism for the dead) is grounded in the practices of the readers as if to say, "You are not even consistent"; the second comes from the life of Paul.[57] These two considerations show that the question is not simply one of speculative ideas which one may or may not hold but one which impinges directly on the way writer and readers live. (e) I Cor. 15: 35-57 then answers the question, "How are the dead raised?" That this "How?" does not concern the *means* by which resurrection takes place is clear from the next question, "What kind of body?" Here Paul explains what

---

mann has been critical of Paul's reference to the living witnesses, because this appears to make the resurrection a "visible fact in the realm of human history." *Theology of the New Testament,* I, 295.

[57] Paul has often been criticized for this line, not simple for transmitting as a serious theological argument a popular misinterpretation of Epicurean ethics, but for trying to strengthen the case for resurrection by appealing to its role in justifying (compensating?) his personal danger. But this criticism usually bypasses Paul because it is aimed from a quite different standpoint. Behind Paul's argument is a simple conviction: If salvation is for the eternal soul only and if the body is to be discarded, why should one risk his body for the sake of his convictions? (Ignatius, *Trall.* 10, draws the same conclusion.) On the gnostic basis there is really nothing at stake any longer—quite the opposite of Paul's view in I Cor. 10! Much later, one of the accusations hurled against gnostics and docetists was in just this vein—they produced no martyrs.

he means by resurrection. He does not describe resurrected bodies at all, but shows what resurrection is all about. Not until this is clear can we see why Paul argues for resurrection with so much passion.

3. Our analysis concentrates on I Cor. 15:20-28 and 51-57.

I Cor. 15:20-28. The whole argument rests on the assumption that resurrection is not something restricted to Jesus; rather, his resurrection is the first and primal one which will include Christians as well. This is why Paul says Christ is the "first fruits of the dead." First fruits are a pledge that represents the whole harvest. As we have already seen, this reflects the apocalyptic way of understanding the resurrection of Jesus—as a signal that the End events are now under way.[58] That Paul is operating within this perspective is clear from the outline of the End events in vss. 23-28: Christ the first fruits, then the whole harvest ("those who belong to him") at the Coming, the Parousia. This is the same view Paul states in I Thess. 4:13-18.[59] In I Cor. 15:28 he says that at the End Christ

[58] Paul uses "first fruits" (ἀπαρχή) in more than one sense. In Rom. 16:15 and I Cor. 16:15 it is used of first converts; in Rom. 8:23 of the Holy Spirit. It appears that when Paul has in mind the overall Heilsgeschichte, Christ is the first fruits; when he has the Christian's existence in history in view, the first fruit is the Holy Spirit. In both cases, the term functions as a way of maintaining the tension between the already and the not yet. Paul uses another term, down payment (ἀρραβών), to make the same point. Thus II Cor. 1:22 says the Spirit is the down payment for future salvation.

[59] The discussion in I Thessalonians addresses a somewhat different issue: fear that the dead will have forfeited their participation in the consummation. (This interpretation implies that "shall not precede" [οὐ μὴ φθάσωμεν] means in effect "shall not even precede" and rests the case more heavily on vs. 13 than on the stated sequence of events.) The more common view, that the Thessalonians were distressed lest the living have advantage (one of sequence!) over the dead at the coming, is not a compelling interpretation of a real problem. Interestingly, in I Thessalonians, Paul does not say, as he does in I Cor. 15:52, that at the Parousia both the living and the dead shall be changed. I Thessalonians also differs from I Corinthians in that it speaks of meeting the Lord in the air. I Thes. 5 goes on to say that the day of the Lord

will transfer his regency, begun at the resurrection, to God so that the Father will be the sole sovereign. In developing this point Paul appeals to Ps. 110, which Christians had already interpreted to refer to Jesus as exalted Lord.[60] Ps. 110 was originally a hymn that celebrated the king's power and rule in God's name. It begins:

> The Lord [God] says to my lord [the king]:
> "Sit at my right hand,
> till I make your enemies
> your footstool." (RSV)

It goes on to promise victory over the king's enemies. Paul also uses Ps. 8, which celebrates the dignity of man as sovereign over creation:

> What is man that thou art mindful
> of him
> And the son of man that thou dost care for him?
>
> Yet thou hast made him little less
> than God,
> and dost crown him with glory
> and honor.
> Thou hast given him dominion over
> the works of thy hands;
> thou hast put all things under his feet.

---

will come as a surprise ("like a thief in the night"). II Thessalonians, which I regard as not from Paul, addresses a still different issue—that one must not suppose that the Parousia has already occurred (II Thess. 2:2 ff.), a view akin to that of II Tim. 2:18.

[60] Important analyses of early Christian uses of the Bible (later called "the Old Testament") are found in C. H. Dodd's *According to the Scriptures* (London: Nisbit, 1952) and in Barnabas Lindars' *New Testament Apologetic* (Philadelphia: Westminster Press, 1962) and in Chap. 4 of C. F. D. Moule's *The Birth of the New Testament* (New York: Harper & Row, 1962). It is clear that Paul depends on an established, traditional use of Ps. 110.

Now what have these Psalms, one about the Israelite king and the other about man in general, to do with the coming of Christ and the conquest of death? As far as their original scope of ideas is concerned, the answer is "Nothing." But neither Paul nor any other Christian in his day was interested in adhering to the original meaning of the Old Testament. Rather, they read it in light of faith centered in Jesus. This means that for early Christians, Ps. 110 referred not to Israel's ancient king but to the Messiah, as also current Jewish interpretation held. Since the Christians believed that the Messiah was Jesus, the Psalm had to refer to him. And since it did not describe the life of Jesus or the present empirical state of the world, it must predict his role at the End Time; that is, it promised that at the Coming he would defeat all his enemies. Ps. 8 was read in the same way, and this interpretation was aided by the fact that it spoke of the son of man. The phrase "son of man" has various meanings in the Bible. The original meaning in Ps. 8 is simply "man," as the parallel lines show. In apocalyptic, Son of man becomes God's agent who at the End time will execute God's will over creation. Early Christians believed Jesus was the Son of man.[61] While Paul never calls Jesus the Son of man, it is clear that his use of Ps. 8 depends on this usage, for it mentions the (future) dominion of the Son of man over all creation.[62] But who are the enemies? Clearly,

[61] We can leave aside the question of Jesus' own understanding of this figure. See H. E. Tödt, *The Son of Man in the Synoptic Tradition,* trans. D. M. Barton (Philadelphia: Westminster Press, 1965), and A. J. B. Higgins, *Jesus and the Son of Man* (Philadelphia: Fortress Press, 1964).

[62] That Paul knows the Son-of-man tradition in some form is clear from his reference to the "man from heaven" in I Cor. 15:47-49. But here he does not use the concept to speak of Christ's lordship but to argue for our participation in his state just as we now share Adam's. Clearly, Paul uses the ancient myth of the primal man. The relation between the apocalyptic Son of man and the primal man is far from clear. The question has been explored recently by F. H. Borsch, *The Son of Man in Myth and History* (Philadelphia: Westminster Press, 1967).

they are not earthly powers, such as Rome, but cosmic forces, the "principalities and powers" [63] that reside in the planets. The ultimate enemy is death. This is also the primal enemy, since in Adam all die. Neither the origin of these ideas nor the details of the Pauline interpretation of them must deflect us from the main point here—that Paul regards the resurrection of Jesus as installing him in an office in which he extends his sovereignty over all creation (I Cor. 15:25-26), a process which is the background to Paul's sense of mission. I Cor. 15:51 continues the outline of the consummation, begun at vs. 24: Jesus' resurrection will be consummated by the final triumph over death.[64] In this way the resurrection of Christians will complete the inaugurated triumph of Christ's resurrection. In this scheme the roots in apocalyptic theology are evident.

I Cor. 15:35-50. Here Paul argues that there is such a thing as a "spiritual body" [65] though he says not a word about its nature. His only concern is to insist that there is such a thing. This is why he compares burying the dead with planting a seed: Just as a brown seed becomes a green plant, different in every way yet mysteriously continuous with its antecedent,[66] so a perishable body

[63] See Heinrich Schlier's *Principalities and Powers in the New Testament* (Quaestiones Disputatae No. 3; Edinburgh and London: Thomas Nelson & Sons, 1961).

[64] In vss. 54b-55 Paul alludes to Isa. 25:8 (in a modified wording) and Hos. 13:14. The latter mentions Sheol (Hades), which Paul replaces with death. Here too Paul discovers new meanings in the Bible.

[65] The phrase "spiritual body" is difficult to understand, partly because this is its sole New Testament occurrence, partly because in our common parlance anything "spiritual" is almost by definition incorporeal, ethereal, and having to do with attitudes more than with "entities." Paul contends that the resurrected man will be of the same order as the exalted and transformed Jesus—Spirit (in II Cor. 3:17 Paul says "the Lord is the Spirit")—as Phil. 3:21 shows: Christ "will change our lowly body to be like his glorious body."

[66] Bultmann, *Theology of the New Testament,* I, p. 192, thinks, wrongly I believe, that Paul was misled by his opponents into using an illustration which implies continuity of body-form despite change of

becomes an imperishable body, a spiritual body. Why is this important for Paul? The reason is stated in vs. 50: Flesh and blood cannot inherit the kingdom of God, and the perishable does not take over the imperishable. That is to say, the destiny of man cannot be reached by persons with bodies that die and decay; moreover, the transition from "mortal" to "immortal" is not a natural one. It must not be overlooked that on this point Paul and his gnostic opponents would agree completely. What separated them was the conclusions they drew from the same premise. The gnostics concluded that because flesh and blood cannot inherit the kingdom, salvation requires abandoning flesh and blood altogether, categorically, so that the soul could be saved. Paul, on the other hand, cannot conceive of disembodied existence as the *sine qua non* of salvation, for the body is the manifestation of the self. Therefore he argues for resurrection, not release. But what does "resurrection" mean for Paul? The penultimate paragraph discloses what Paul has in mind.

I Cor. 15:51-57. Paul begins by pointing out that he is about to disclose a "mystery"—not in the sense of the initiation cults but in the sense of a disclosed clue to what transcends comprehension. He is not now at last giving esoteric information about the soul; consistently,

---

substance. Rather, Paul is thinking concretely, not in sophisticated philosophical terms. "Body" is the concreteness of the whole self. The fact that actually a seed does not die when it sprouts is an agricultural datum that is beside Paul's point. Paul is using a common sense illustration (a brown seed is buried, a green shoot comes up), not developing an exact analogue to eschatological transformation of the body-self. J. A. Schep, *The Nature of the Resurrection Body* (Grand Rapids: Eerdmans, 1964), p. 194, though disagreeing with Bultmann, operates with the same erroneous conception in order to argue that Paul teaches the "substantial continuity between our present body . . . and the resurrection-body. . . . *This* body of flesh will be raised." J. A. T. Robinson has argued that Paul has in mind the corporate body of Christ, the church. This reflects his unjustified use of Ephesians to interpret Paul. *The Body* (Studies in Biblical Theology No. 5; Naperville, Ill.: Alec R. Allenson, 1952), especially pp. 80 ff.

he adheres to his eschatological outlook and concentrates on "what will happen" at the Coming. The point is simple enough: both the living and the dead will be "changed"—that is, utterly transformed. This is what resurrection means with respect to man's existence. The mortal becomes immortal. Precisely this transformation constitutes the triumph over death. (Jeremias observed that this view of resurrection as transformation is a distinctively new teaching of Paul's vis-à-vis certain Jewish ideas of resurrection as restoration.) [67] Then is when the Old Testament lines will come true:

> Death is swallowed up in victory.
> O Death, where is thy victory?
> O Death, where is thy sting?

But what is the "sting" of death? For Paul, it is not pain, or sickness, or sorrow, or fear of dying. For him, the sting of death is sin. Once again, Paul connects death and sin.[68] Death for him is not merely a physiological fact; it is primarily a moral fact, traced to the consequence of Adam. This also means that for Paul sin is a form of death, a power which separates man from God's effectiveness. This inner connection between sin and death permits Paul to say in vs. 17 that if there is no resurrection (that is, if Christ has not been resurrected and if Christians must not expect any) we are still in bondage to sin,[69] for to him the bondage to sin and the bondage to death go together. Probably no line in the

[67] "'Flesh and blood cannot inherit the Kingdom of God' (I Cor. 15:50)," in his essays, *Abba* (Göttingen: Vandenhoeck & Ruprecht, 1966 [orig. pub. in 1956]), p. 307. Jesus' reply to the Sadducees agrees with this (see previous section).

[68] As in Rom. 5:12 ff.; 6:23; see Bultmann, *Theology of the New Testament,* I, 246-49.

[69] This is also why Paul regards baptism as the point at which one's participation in Christ must be marked by a break with sin; see Rom. 6:1-14.

whole chapter is more offensive to us today than just this contention, for many believe they are freed from the tyranny of sin by faith in Christ whether or not they believe in resurrection, his or theirs. We cannot discuss this issue here, but we can point out that honesty may compel some to take issue with Paul.

4. It is one thing to trace Paul's argument, another to grasp what is happening as he develops it.

First, it is obvious, as it surely must have been in Corinth, that Paul meets the gnostic problem with the resources of Jewish apocalyptic modified in light of Jesus' resurrection.[70] What are we to make of this way of meeting the issue? Are we to conclude that Paul was poorly informed about the issue and that he gave, in effect, the wrong answer?[71] I do not believe this to be the case. But if he saw the issue rightly, did he reach for the wrong solution anyway—is Paul's "answer" beside the point? This too is a premature conclusion, for apocalyptic and gnostic theology are not utterly incommensurate perspectives. Both agree that mortal man cannot attain his destiny because of the tyranny of history, and both see man as delivered over into bondage to malign powers, whether Satan (as in apocalyptic) or cosmic rulers (as in gnosticism).[72] The question, then, is how this enslavement of man is to be overcome. Moreover, Paul's is a modified apocalyptic in which the Messiah's victory is not political, in which there is no Messianic Age (or mil-

[70] There is no convincing evidence that Paul moved away from apocalyptic theology as a result of his encounter with Greek thought, as W. L. Knox, for example, held in *St. Paul and the Church of the Gentiles* (London: Cambridge University Press, 1939, repr. 1961).

[71] Bultmann, *Theology of the New Testament* I, p. 169 suggests this, and Schmithals, *Die Gnosis in Korinth,* emphasized it repeatedly.

[72] Because Greek thought had no Satan-figure, gnostic theology traced man's plight to the creator; conversely, because Jewish theology could not indict the creator, apocalyptic theology was increasingly concerned with Satan and the "fallen angels." One sees this not only in Enoch but in the literature from Qumran (where Satan is called Beliar).

lennium), in which the kingdom of God is not an earthly kingdom at all.

Actually, Paul uses apocalyptic to deal with existential issues of sin and death, powers that enslave the self and mankind. Nevertheless, Paul emphasises the defeat of these enemies rather than escape from them, because Paul regards the present state of man as "historical"—as stretching between the first and second Adam. Paul does not view the problem of sin simply in personal or existential terms, nor primarily in metaphysical ones but rather in "historical" terms (Heilsgeschichte) which compel him to see sin as having a beginning and an end at the End—basically the apocalyptic perspective. Hence Christ is for him not a timeless example of what happens to the individual at death, as the gnostics apparently viewed him, but the historic event that triggered the eschatological chain reaction of the End-event drama. But is this really an appropriate way to answer the gnostic theology? To see this requires us to note other considerations.

Second, why does Paul insist that there must be some sort of bodily existence? Here the answer lies on two levels. The first is a cultural one—Paul was a Jew, nurtured by the Old Testament and by the synagogue and by apocalyptic themes as well. This tradition simply could not conceive of any existence worth talking about that was not corporeal. Because the body is the expression of the self and not primarily the obstacle to the self's expression, restoration of the self beyond dissolution of the body required some sort of bodily existence. But it would be selling Paul at too great a discount if we conclude that he is simply manifesting his Jewishness—though doubtless the Corinthians viewed him thus, as too unsophisticated to see the real problem.

The other level was the theological issue: man's salvation. If salvation from man's deepest problem lies in escape from body categorically, then the conclusion is clear: God created something that cannot be saved but must be discarded. On this basis, the human problem must be traced to the Creator because he made man mortal. But Paul refuses to indict God in order to talk about the innocent immortal soul victimized by the mortal body; this the Gnostics did who said: The Creator was either ignorant or immoral (or both) when he made this jerry-built man. Far from thinking that Paul stumbled onto a problem unprepared and gave an answer that missed the point, I am convinced that years of experience in the Hellenistic world taught him precisely what the issue was, even if he does not put it into words. For Paul, the problem with which man is beset is not that God put him together wrongly but that man himself went wrong. Man's deepest problem is not substance but sin; death is the pay-off,[73] not the cause. This is why, perhaps, Paul does not discuss the "nature" of the soul, or of the body or of the "spiritual body." Paul apparently believed that because the gnostic questions are wrong, they must be met by a fundamentally different way of regarding the actual situation of man.

Third, if Paul thinks in terms of an originally good creation which subsequently came under the tyranny of sin and death, then much more is involved than the existence of man. The whole creation is subject to death: Everything that lives, dies. Because Paul sees all death on the same horizon, because he does not regard man's dying as a neutral physiological datum but as a theologically significant dimension of existence, it is inevitable that "nature's death" too comes within the scope of Paul's theological reflection. The principalities and powers that tyrannize man are not eternal enemies, of course, because they too were created. Hence they are somehow rebel-

[73] Rom. 6:23: "The wages of sin is death."

lious creatures, though Paul nowhere shows any interest in retelling the story of their "fall."

Rom. 8:18-25, 35-39 shows how this cosmic sweep of Paul's thinking about death appears. (a) When Paul speaks of creation's having been "subjected to futility," he refers to the curse on the ground reported in Gen. 3. At the same time, the "historical" character of "nature's" condition is disclosed in the assertion that creation was subjected in hope—that is, with an eye to final redemption. Not to have said this would have suggested that the consequences of Adam are irreparable. (b) Both the cosmos in general and the believer in particular long for redemption. What is not clear is how nature's "groaning" is related to the Christian's, whose inner longing is set in motion by the Spirit's presence as intensifying, and perhaps raising to consciousness, the longing for redemption of our bodies. (c) In the Hellenistic world it is decisive that Paul does *not* say we long for *release from* our bodies but for the *redemption of* the body. (d) The powers over history and the empirical world (principalities and powers), like forces within it (famine, distress, etc.) are unable to separate the believer from Christ Jesus because Christ's resurrection established his victory.

What is at stake in the resurrection, then, is the Creator's relationship to what he has made. Paul can think of nothing that is ultimately to be classed as unredeemable, as nothing but disposable slag. For Paul, what God created, he will redeem—all of it. This may explain why Paul does not speak of the ultimate punishment of the hostile powers or of those who reject God's act in Christ. Paul's universalism is stated baldly: "For as in Adam all die, so also in Christ shall all be made alive" (I Cor. 15:22). In the same vein, when wrestling with the theological meaning of the conviction that God must keep his word to Israel even though Israel rejects the gospel, he must conclude that ultimately "all Israel will be saved."

(Rom. 11:26). These statements do not come from speculation about man's potential or about a "second chance" after death, but solely from the logic of Paul's conviction that God has made Jesus Lord; that lordship is not in full effect so long as it is anywhere resisted. Moreover, for Paul, that lordship functions as God's instrument of reclaiming his sovereignty over all creation. When that is achieved, and the Son is himself subordinated to the Father, the process will be complete and God will be "everything to everyone."

Fourth, it is important to see that Paul finally does not reject completely the traditional Greek way of regarding the problem of death. As we have seen, the apocalyptic tradition emphasized death as a power that subjects everything that lives. But the Greek tradition viewed death more as the tyranny of an inbuilt structure. It is instructive to see how Paul finally comes to terms with this view which spoke of mortality rather than of death. In the closing lines of I Cor. 15, Paul subtly shifts to mortality-immortality terminology. "For this perishable nature must put on the imperishable, and this mortal nature must put on immortality," etc. (I Cor. 15:53-54). Only after these lines does he go on to speak of the victory over the power death. Paul grants that this Greek way of regarding man's death is legitimate, in fact inescapable. Yet he does not speak of shedding the mortal to free the immortal (a point which he carefully avoids making in II Cor. 5:1-5 as well).[74] That would have conceded too much—that the immortal essence had been

[74] This is an exceedingly important passage because here Paul clearly expresses his alternative to the Hellenistic idea of stripping off the body in order to leave the eternal essence free ("naked"). In keeping with Jewish modes of thought which regard ultimate realities as already existing in heaven waiting to be revealed instead of emerging in the course of time (thus being subject to history), Paul says this new bodily existence already exists in heaven. The comment that this "tent" is not made with human hands expresses the closely related idea: it is strictly God's alternative to humanly procreated bodily existence.

there all along, longing in agony for release. No, he talks about immortality as an event that happens to mortal man, as a gift of God at the coming of Christ. In other words, whereas the old Greek tradition began with immortality as the given and regarded existence (epitomized by mortality) as a tragic crime against the innately immortal soul, Paul began with the good creation and saw history, sin, and mortality as a long tyranny to be overcome by the Creator himself. Of this victory, Jesus' resurrection is the first fruits. For Paul, immortality is not man's original nature prior to existence but God's final gift. In other words, Paul "solved" the Greek problem of mortality, of a quality of existence, within the mythic framework of creation and redemption on the horizon of apocalyptic theology.

5. Our discussion of Paul has bypassed very important passages, such as II Cor. 4:7-12; 5:1-5; and Phil. 1:19-26. In these we see not so much Paul's ideas about death (as a theme for discussion) as his way of building into his life the import of his way of regarding Jesus' life and death. A more important omission from the discussion concerns the potential of Paul's perspective for us. That is, stating the logic of Paul's thought has not yet made him credible. In fact, we have already hinted that we might disagree categorically with him. Again this theme cannot be discussed here, or even focused. Nevertheless, we can locate two points where the issue will probably be joined.

First, Paul has argued for resurrection as actual transformation of bodily, empirical existence. To him, resurrection is not restoration to life, not even an improved one. At the same time he refused to say anything at all about that eschatological existence in a spiritual body, just as he did not say what sort of corporeal existence the resurrected Lord had, much as the curious of today might wish it otherwise. Yet many serious believers today find Paul to be utterly incredible and quite irrelevent. For them, the resurrection of Jesus is a mythological way of regarding the new understanding of Jesus' death, a new self-understanding in which the ultimate significance of Jesus for the self is grasped.[75] On such a view the resurrection of Jesus is not an event that "happened" to Jesus at all but a way of expressing the source of what "happened" to the believer himself. Older pietists used to put it this way: Christ is not really raised until he is resurrected in your heart. In the same vein some persons do not expect resurrection for themselves, though they might hope for some sort of continuity of consciousness beyond death. There is nothing to be gained by hurling epithets at one another, "Disbeliever!" or "Unliberated biblicist!" Rather, germane discussion can proceed only if it is agreed what the issue is. As we have seen in various ways, the issue is whether one thinks ontically about man, whether man's being mortal is itself a problem to be overcome, and whether man's dying is a pivotal aspect in that being. If it is, then resurrection as transformation may make sense; if not, then it is an answer to an unreal question.

The second issue concerns Paul's linking sin and death. Must one see death as the tragic consequence that marred an originally perfect (i.e., deathless) creation? If death is a tragic event that overtook existence, then it poses a theological issue that must be overcome by another event. But suppose one views death as a neutral process, as simply the end of a series of physiological changes in the

[75] The reader will scarcely miss this allusion to Bultmann's interpretation of the resurrection in which he seeks to restate the intent of the mythological form in which the New Testament states the meaning of Jesus. Bultmann's position is clearly stated in "New Testament and Mythology" in *Kerygma and Myth,* ed. H. W. Bartsch, trans. R. H. Fuller (Torchbooks; New York: Harper & Row, 1961). Bultmann restated his views in *Jesus Christ and Mythology* (London: S.C.M. Press, 1960).

organism? Or suppose death is no enemy but a friend who ends the hard life of all living things? With such presuppositions news of Jesus' resurrection and victory over the enemy death sounds unintelligible, for those concepts are grounded in the biblical idea of creation and fall and consummation. If one does not hold that sin and death are related tyrannies, what are the alternatives, and how adequate are they to interpret the nature of man? [76] Or must one contend that the biblical horizon is essential, however it be translated into new conceptions?

That we are not the first to find the biblical-apocalyptic perspective problematic is disclosed in the New Testament itself—in the Gospel of John.

The Fourth Gospel

In addition to future-oriented apocalyptic theology there developed another which emphasized the presence of eternal life now. Our sources do not allow us to trace the development of this second line, but we can safely assume that both negative and positive factors were at work. The negative reason centers either in the disappoint-

[76] For John Knox the resurrection of Jesus is a reflex inference by the church which had discovered his presence, and the objective event of the resurrection is the emergence of the church. Hence Knox is unwilling to speak as Paul does about the resurrection; to oversimplify, Knox thinks theologically about the historical phenomenon of the church and its life as the central datum, whereas Paul thinks mythologically about the life and death of Jesus. Hence Paul deals with the tyranny man experiences in a way in which Knox cannot, since the latter must insits that the church "is the locus, the only locus, of the Event." The historicism is evident when he writes, "If the intention of God's action in Christ was not the bringing of this community into being, then we must say either that his intention failed or that twenty centuries of history have not provided the slightest clue to what that intention was." These views are argued in *The Church and the Reality of Christ* (New York: Harper & Row, 1962), p. 106. Also in his earlier book *The Death of Christ* (Nashville: Abingdon Press, 1958), Knox argued that the "story" of Christ's victory (his expression for the mythic narrative), like that of his sacrifice, was created to express the meaning of the life of the church. See esp. Chap. 7.

ment over the fact that Lord did not return[77] or in the conviction that this expectation was inadequate to start with. The positive factor was the Christian experience of a new dimension of life here and now because one believes in Jesus and is a partner with others in the church. In Hellenistic churches (such as Corinth) doubtless the sacraments encouraged this conviction that eternal life is present now. The most important writer who emphasized the presence of eternal life was the author of the Gospel of John.[78]

1. This gospel is so different from the others, and from the whole New Testament as well, that we must first scout the landscape to discover how the treatment of death and resurrection fits into its theology as a whole.

First, John insists that to know Jesus properly one must know who he is with respect to God and the world. Therefore he begins by quoting a hymn to the Logos.[79] The Logos was an old and varied concept in Hellenistic philosophy and theology.[80] But for our author he is the

[77] It is not clear that adjusting to the delay of the parousia (or the disappointment) was the dominant factor in early Christianity's development, as Albert Schweitzer argued. Bultmann's interpretation of John (*Theology of the New Testament,* Vol. II), by far the most penetrating in recent decades, does not emphasize this issue.

[78] Who this writer was we have no sure way of knowing. The tradition that he was the unnamed "disciple whom Jesus loved" (13:23; 19:26; 20:2; 21:7, 20), i.e., the apostle John, cannot be established. I do not believe that the same man wrote the Fourth Gospel and the Epistles or the Revelation. In this discussion "John" refers to the author of the Fourth Gospel, whatever his name might have been.

[79] That John 1:1 ff. incorporates a hymn (or a hymnic piece) is virtually certain; far from certain, however, is its present extent (does it end at vs. 14, at vs. 17, at vs. 18?) and the author's reason for inserting references to John the Baptist (1:6-8, 15) into it. Nor is the original home of the hymn evident, as critics' disputes reveal. For a useful survey of the issues, see Raymond Brown, *The Gospel According to John* (Anchor Bible) I, 3-37, where important literature is cited as well.

[80] See the article "Logos" in Kittel's *Theological Dictionary of the New Testament,* Vol. IV. Some scholars prefer to relate John's Logos rather to Hebraic (or at least to Hellenized Jewish) theology. Among them is C. H. Dodd, *The Interpretation of the Fourth Gospel* (London:

Creator through whom all things came to exist, "and without him, was not anything made that was made." And this Logos became Jesus. Because Jesus was nothing less than the divine Creator enfleshed, whoever meets Jesus, meets his Creator and Judge embodied. Whereas the oldest Christology saw Jesus as the man from Nazareth whom God took to heaven to wait until the last day when he will send him back as Judge, John viewed Jesus as the Logos-Creator in the flesh to start with.[81]

Consequently, the words and deeds of Jesus before his death are revelatory. On this basis Jesus' life was not a lowly prelude to victory (as in Phil. 2:5) but was the locus of God's encounter with the world. No future confrontation between God and the world can surpass this one. It can only confirm it. As a result there is a timeless quality in John's gospel which emphasizes the ever-present now. Now is judgment, now is salvation. There is no "is, was, or shall be" in the presence of the Creator (e.g., 8:58). It is always now. Nothing more decisive can possibly happen than has already happened.

Third, on this basis John transforms some traditional beliefs and pushes others to the edge. For example, the return of Christ after death is reinterpreted to be the coming of the Spirit.[82] There is no Pentecost seven weeks

---

Cambridge University Press, 1953), pp. 263-85. Bultmann rightly criticizes him for ignoring the mythological background of the logos speculation in Hellenism which had influenced Jewish wisdom theology in pre-New Testament times. Bultmann's review, originally published in *New Testament Studies* 1 (1954/55), pp. 77-91, has been translated and published in the *Harvard Divinity Bulletin* 27 (1963).

[81] It is characteristic of John that he can assert the incarnation in 1:14 without appealing to a narrative describing it. The later church combined the traditions to say what no one in the New Testament says, that the Logos was incarnate in the womb of Mary.

[82] John's word for the Holy Spirit, *parakletos,* is difficult to translate. RSV uses Counselor, NEB has Advocate, KJV uses Comforter. The Paraclete passages (14:16-17, 25-26; 15:26-27; 16:6-11) are all part of the farewell discourses. Surprisingly, Jesus' prayer for the disciples after his departure (chap. 17) does not mention the Paraclete (though perhaps 17:26 alludes to him). Evidently, by this designation John is interpreting

later as in Acts, but on Easter evening the risen Lord himself imparts the Holy Spirit to the disciples (20:19-23). Since the Spirit is now with the church, what occurred in the primal confrontation with Jesus continues in perpetuity. For John, the event of Jesus Christ is an event that keeps on happening whenever the church is faithful to the words of Jesus. One conviction pushed to the margin is the future resurrection. The author does not deny resurrection. As we shall see, he simply does not build his case on it, or give it prominence.

Finally, given this author's freedom to remodel traditions, we are not surprised that he also recasts the life and words of Jesus. Instead of short simple sayings, as in the Synoptics, John's Jesus makes long speeches or discourses. Instead of a great variety of miracles he had only seven, and he regards these as signs,[83] manifestations of who Jesus is and what he means for the salvation of *all* believers, not jut for the original participants or witnesses. Thus the healing of blindness is a sign of how Jesus heals all spiritual blindness, not just the eyes of that particular Jew (John 9:1-41). The climax of the seven signs is Jesus' raising of Lazarus from the dead.

It is not possible or necessary here to continue this

---

the work of the Spirit in order to avoid the problems of ecstasy (revealed in I Cor. 12-14) and of associating the divine Spirit with miracle-working power (as in Acts 2:1-21; 4:31; 5:12-16; 6:8) or with predictive power (as in Acts 21:7-14). John contends that the "religious experience" (to use our jargon) of the Spirit in no way minimizes the role of Jesus but to the contrary is precisely what relates the later believers to the incarnation (see 14:26; 15:26). This complements his observation that full understanding of Jesus was achieved only after Easter—after the Spirit enabled the disciples to "remember" (2:22; 12:16). Ernst Kasemann made the farewell discourses the basis of a stimulating analysis of John, *The Testament of Jesus,* trans. by Gerhard Krodel (Philadelphia: Fortress Press, 1968).

[83] Bultmann has contended that one of the sources John used was a book of signs which had already developed this view of Jesus' wondrous deeds. Our discussion does not hinge on a decision regarding this possibility. For a survey of the issues see Brown, *The Gospel According to John,* pp. xxiv-xl, where the literature is cited.

list of peculiarities. Enough has been suggested to see that we must not read John as if it were simply a revised Matthew or Mark. In this Gospel nothing is quite the same as in the others. Death and resurrection is one of the places where the ground suddenly shifts out from under us.

2. There are many occasions when the Johannine Jesus talks about life, but seldom does he talk about death. In light of what we have said, this cannot be taken to mean that John's gospel has little to contribute to the discussion. Rather, it means we must be attentive to the way he talks about our issue. After noting several passages we will look at the Lazarus story.

(a) The Johannine perspective first[84] emerges clearly in chap. 3, the discussion prompted by the conversation with Nicodemus (3:1-21). Here Jesus insists that only if one is born anew[85] can he enter the kingdom of God. Paul also said "flesh and blood" cannot inherit the kingdom of God and that a transformation of existence is needed. But whereas Paul expected this to occur at the coming of Christ, John insists that this requirement can be met here and now because the Spirit gives new life. That John is not talking about the diffusion of the divine essence into mortal flesh (like an additive) is clear from vs. 15, "Whoever *believes* in him may have eternal life." Having the Spirit's new birth and believing in Jesus are two ways of saying the same thing. Both bring eternal life. Just as the present new life is possible now because the

[84] Actually, it is mentioned in the prologue: 'In him was life and the life was the light of men."

[85] Whether the word *anothen* should be translated "anew" (RSV) or "from above" is not self-evident; actually, John may intend both meanings at the same time. Oscar Cullmann has shown that one of the characteristics of John's style is his penchant for double meanings, *Early Christian Worship*, trans. A. S. Todd and J. B. Torrance (Studies in Biblical Theology No. 10; Naperville, Ill: Alec R. Allenson, 1953), pp. 50 ff.

Source of life, the Logos incarnate, is present, so the last judgment occurs now whenever people refuse him to whom they owe their existence, "For God sent his Son into the world, not to condemn the world, but that the world might be saved through him. He who believes in him is not condemned, but he who does not believe is condemned already" (3:17-18). Eschatological judgment on his life does not wait for Judgment Day, the second resurrection, etc. "Light has come into the world, and men loved darkness rather than light" (vs. 19). Judgment has already happened, and continues to occur. On the other hand, whoever receives the Son and believes in him already has eschatological life. Therefore the chapter can end with the bald statement: "He who believes in the Son *has* eternal life; he who does not obey the Son shall not see life"; i.e., he will not have eternal life at all, even though he continues to live in time-space, for that is not real life anyway.[86]

We should note that for John eternal life is not primarily endless life. That is not excluded, of course; but what is important for John is the *quality* of existence, and not its quantity. Extension of existence is not eternal life for this theologian. To put it in different words, John believes that man's deepest problem is not that his life ends, but that it is lived in the wrong direction. The problem is not that there is not enough life, but that it is the wrong kind. Therefore John is interested in immortality only as it is a symptom of the transcendent quality of life. He is interested in what is eternal, not simply in something that never ends.

(b) John 5:19-25 is part of the dispute over Jesus' healing on the Sabbath.[87] John uses this controversy to

[86] This is implied in John's phrase "true life."

[87] Although John regards Jesus' healings as signs of salvation, he carefully insists that "the world" (represented by the "Jews" according to Bultmann: see note 91, p. 87) did not perceive them as such. Therefore

let Jesus comment on his work. The theme is the life-giving work of Jesus, or more precisely, the contention that Jesus' work is God's work and that God's work is Jesus' work. A second theme is that Jesus is not usurping God's place, not overextending himself; rather, God has given his work into the hands of Jesus. Three witnesses attest this role: John the Baptist, God himself, and the Scripture. Here we are interested only in the first theme.

Two things should be observed. First, again we hear the basic argument: Whoever receives Jesus' *word*[88] has eternal life already. Judgment Day lies behind him and he has "passed from death to life" (5:24). This is possible because the Father endowed the Son with power to confer life. Second, alongside this view is the older one: There will be a time "when the dead shall hear the voice of the Son of God, and those who hear will live" (5:25). In vss. 28-29 Jesus says that all the dead will be raised for judgment, when their destinies will be decided.

How are we to explain this? There are two major possibilities. One, advanced by Bultmann, regards all refer-

---

the sign-narratives are commonly followed by disputes over Jesus' authority. This is John's way of saying that the revelation in Jesus is not self-validating. In chap. 5 the controversy over the Sabbath differs from that of the Synoptics (e.g., Mark 2:23–3:6) despite 5:16, because 5:17 has Jesus respond with a claim about himself and his Father (God). The rest of the chapter is a polemical discourse on Jesus' relation to the Father.

[88] See also 6:63, 66. For John, Jesus' word (or words) are not merely his utterances. Rather, Jesus' word is his work, and his work is to bring his word, as passages such as 8:28 show: "I *do* nothing on my own authority but *speak* thus as the Father has taught me" (see also 14:10). Bultmann has formulated it well: John's Jesus demands "faith that understands Jesus' words as *personal address* aimed at the believer, i.e., as Jesus' 'working' upon him," *Theology of the New Testament*, II, 61. It is not Jesus' ideas, formulated in words, that have life-giving power, but for John "word" is a way of grasping the import of Jesus himself: Just as *his words* are life-giving, so *he* is "the way, the truth, and the life" (14:6). Again Bultmann puts it well: "So truth is not the teaching about God transmitted by Jesus but is God's very reality revealing itself—occurring!—in Jesus." *Theology of the New Testament*, II, 19.

ences to the future resurrection "out of tombs" as interpolations by a tradition-minded editor who added these phrases to make John's gospel more acceptable to the church.[89] The other alternative, or some form of it, holds that John has let the old view stand, but has so effectively surrounded it with his own emphasis that it is relatively unimportant. On this basis he who now passes from death to eternal life by believing in the Son will in the future also be resurrected. Bultmann's analysis, on the other hand, requires us to conclude that the author himself gave up future resurrection altogether for the sake of present eternal life.

(c) In John 6:47-59 is also a part of a long argument, this time over Jesus' sacramental role. When the crowd found Jesus the day after the miracle of the loaves,[90] he rebuked them for seeking him because they had been well fed. This sets in motion a dispute over the true bread, Jesus himself, which comes from heaven. In typical fashion John reports that the "Jews" took this literally and were offended (vss. 41-42).[91] Jesus then expounds his role as the "bread of life" (vss. 49 ff.) and as the sacramental life:

[89] E.g., 5:28-29; 6:39, 40, 44; 12:48. Bultmann also holds that the editor added sacramental views such as 1:51b-58; 19:34b. It is widely accepted that the present text of John incorporates later additions (chap. 21 is the clearest), though there is no substantial agreement about Bultmann's hypothesis.

[90] This is one story that appears also in the Synoptics (Mark 6:30-44 par.; a variant of the tradition is repeated in Mark 8:1-10). Many commentators see sacramental overtones in the Markan account also (though Mark 8:14-21 shows that Mark himself put the stories to a different use!); even so, one ought not to harmonize these accounts but allow each evangelist to make his own point by his distinctive use of the tradition.

[91] Bultmann has argued that John uses the "Jews" to epitomize the world's rejection of the revelation of the Son, *Theology of the New Testament,* II, 5, 15, 44 ff. (Hence it is misleading to speak of "anti-Semitism" in John.) John shows the "Jews" to be guilty of gross misunderstanding (e.g., 6:41-42, 52; 7:32-36) or as being divided over Jesus (e.g., 7:40-44; 9:13-17), or even has Jesus say that their "Father" is the Devil (8:44-47).

Truly, truly, I say unto you that whoever believes in me has eternal life. I am the bread of life. Your fathers ate manna in the wilderness, and they died. This is the bread which comes down from heaven, that a man may eat of it and not die. I am the living bread which came down from heaven; if anyone eats of this bread, he will live forever; and the bread which I give for the world is my flesh. (6:47-51 RSV)

When the Jews protest, Jesus presses the point even more:

Unless you eat the flesh of the Son of man and drink his blood, you have no life, in you; he who eats my flesh and drinks my blood has eternal life, and I will raise him up at the last day. For my flesh is food indeed, and my blood is drink indeed. He who eats my flesh and drinks my blood abides in me, and I in him. As the living Father sent me, and I live because of the Father, so he who eats me will live because of me. This is the bread which came down from heaven, not such as the fathers ate and died; he who eats this bread will live for ever. (6:53-58 RSV)

This is a "hard saying." John does not shrink from extreme language.

We must restrict ourselves to several observations. First, the idea of divine food which makes men immortal is very ancient and widespread. The ancient Semitic world talked about the tree of life in the garden, or of a certain plant; the Greeks had ambrosia and nectar; the Hellenistic world had its sacraments of immortality. What shocks *us* did not shock them. What offended "the Jews" was the claim that such life-giving food consisted of Jesus himself. Second, here the Christian sacrament is being reinterpreted and contrasted with the Old Testament manna at the same time. John's Gospel has no account of the Lord's Supper, having replaced it with the story of Jesus' washing the disciples' feet and with the "farewell discourses" (13:1-16:33). For John, the Christian Eucharist is not a means by which one participates in Jesus' death (as it was for Paul) but in his life—that is, in the new life for man which the Incarnation brought. Because he viewed this as true, eschatological, eternal life, he could say that those who were partakers of it by eating the Eucharist would not "die," as did the Israelites who died despite the miraculous manna. Third, here language is stretched to the breaking point. Nothing has literal meaning. Jesus is not bread, even though he says he is. No one eats his flesh and drinks the blood in his veins, even though he says they must. So also the idea of never dying, of living forever, is not to be taken literally, as if eating the sacrament provided automatic immortality. That would be precisely the view of the Corinthians. Rather, John uses this language in a dangerous, exciting way, so that the words are symbolic and analogical. By never dying he does not mean breathing in perpetuity, but not coming under the power of death, of passing from death to life here and now. He who shares that reality which makes Jesus what he is, eludes the power of death.

(d). A very well-known paragraph, especially popular at funerals, comes from the farewell discourses (14:1-7). "Let not your hearts be troubled; you believe in God, believe also in me. In my father's house are many rooms; if it were not so, would I have told you that I go to prepare a place for you?"

This entire passage too must be understood in light of Johannine theology. It begins the second half of the Gospel in which Jesus speaks only to the disciples. These discourses state who Jesus is and the destiny of the disciples after he has gone and the Counselor has come. The 14th chapter is aimed at comforting the disciples in the face of Jesus' departure from the world and their being left behind. Moreover, here we see how John understands the life of Jesus. Whereas the previous passage said he was the bread that came *down* from heaven, now he speaks of his departure (implying that he will go *back up* to the Father). John sees the life of Jesus as the earthly career of the Son of God who comes to earth, completes his task, and returns to heaven from which he came.[92]

This mythological framework for the life of Jesus includes the belief that the redeemed shall share the destiny of the redeemer. Paul had made a similar point in I Thess. 4 when at the coming of Christ the transformed believer would be with the Lord, and in Phil. 3:21 where the transformed body of the believer is expected to become like the Lord's. But John does not have in mind a coming again at the end of the world, but the coming of the redeemer to each disciple at the time of his death (14:3).[93] The place that Jesus prepares is in the Father's house—not the temple, but in the heavenly abode.[94] The concern for the *way* to the Father's home is a common concern in the Hellenistic world (see previous section), especially among those who expected that the soul of the dead would be led to the stars by Hermes or some other god. It was also a main desire among those who feared having to pass through all the regions of the portals of the heavens in order to get out of the cosmos. John uses such a view to interpret the work of Jesus with respect to the disciples. Here there is no fear of the journey, despite the world's hatred, because Jesus' death has overcome the world's hostility: "Be not afraid, for I

[92] The same descent-ascent pattern appears in 3:13. John often has Jesus speak of his being "sent" into the world (e.g., 8:42). See Bultmann, *Theology of the New Testament,* II, 33-40.

[93] According to C. K. Barrett the context shows that John thinks of Jesus' "coming" as including also his "coming" in the Spirit during the disciples' lifetime as well. *The Gospel According to St. John* (London: S.P.C.K., 1955).

[94] The King James Version has misled many readers by translating the word as "mansions" (from the Latin, *mansiones*). But the word means "abiding place"—here, not a mere stopover. This word does not imply a series of progressions from one stage to another. Actually one should not squeeze *any description* of the hereafter out of this phrase.

have overcome the world" (16:33).[95] There is apparently no place here for future resurrection. Nothing is said about the end of the world, the last judgment, or other aspects of the apocalyptic view.

(e) Just as the sayings of Jesus in this Gospel state John's view of death and life eternal, so the story of Lazarus (11:1-44) shows Jesus the giver of eternal life. Not only is this the greatest and most climactic sign that Jesus gives, but it is the immediate event that brings about Jesus' own death.[96] Jesus' greatest act is shown to bring about the greatest resistance and rejection. It is important to note that the author uses a "resurrection" story to transform the old resurrection idea.

Two things are of special importance for our theme. (1) The story is carefully focused on Jesus' teaching about resurrection; it shifts belief in a future resurrection to believing in Jesus *now*. John shows Jesus to be interested not in proving that resurrection is the right thing to believe, as in his argument with the Sadducees, but that merely believing it is unimportant. Martha complained, "Lord, if you had been here, Lazarus would not have died." To Jesus' promise, "Your brother will rise again," Martha replied, "I know he will rise again at the resurrection on the last day." Now comes John's main point: Jesus said, "I am the resurrection and the life; he who believes in me, though he die, yet shall he live, and whoever lives and believes in me shall never die. Do you believe this?" What matters is believing that Jesus is the one who

[95] John insists that those who belong to Jesus will share the same fate at the world's hands as he has, and for the same reason: they are no longer "of" the world (15:18-25). Here John echoes the apocalyptic understanding of the church in the hostile world, as does Matt. 10:16-25. It is characteristic of John's dialectic that he has Jesus announce his victory precisely at that moment when, according to worldly criteria, Jesus is about to be defeated by Pilate and the cross.

[96] John 11:45-53; 12:9-11, 17-19. The difference between the Synoptics and John at this point is well known.

brings life now, whatever may happen to the dead in the future. Martha's view of the traditional resurrection at the last day is perfectly good Jewish orthodoxy. Jesus doesn't reject it but relativizes it by his claim, "I am the resurrection. Do you believe this?" She can believe it before anything occurs at Lazarus' tomb.[97]

(2) The story of Lazarus thus becomes a symbol of how Jesus brings life to the dead. Lazarus is viewed here as a symbol of the death that characterizes all men before Jesus brings them new life. The story moves on two levels at the same time: The first concerns what happens to the body that is already decaying, and is merely the occasion to reach the second level—that Jesus brings the resurrection to those who hear this voice and obey, to the living "dead" as well. Both Lazarus and Martha are grasped by Jesus' power. There is no suggestion that Lazarus is transformed. Rather, he is resuscitated, revived, restored. He starts functioning again. Presumably he will die again. One speaks correctly of the "raising" of Lazarus, not of his resurrection. But resurrection has already come to Martha! This is John's way of saying that mere continued existence on earth is not what resurrection is all about. Restoring Lazarus to life is an unforgettable way of making that point. On the other hand, eternal life is not subject to death where it matters. Resurrection-life that counts comes by believing now in Jesus and by the presence of the Spirit.

3. The Fourth Gospel, in conclusion, represents a unique stream of early Christian thought. While sharing with Paul and the early church as a whole the conviction that in Jesus of Nazareth, God had acted decisively to rectify man's plight, John is interested neither in "correcting" Paul nor in continuing his theology (as is Ephe-

[97] This is consonant with John's general distrust of faith based on miracles; see 2:23-25; 6:26; 20:24-29.

sians, for example). Rather, John interprets Jesus in such a way that man's plight is overcome already; the present is not the down payment for future salvation as in Paul.[98] Appropriately, the death-resurrection of Jesus is not, as for Paul, the pivotal event which broke the power of sin and death over man; rather, the career of the Incarnate One as a whole constitutes the saving event.[99] Therefore in contrast with Paul, Jesus' resurrection is not the point of victory since Jesus is victor over the world when the Passion story gets under way (16:33). Consistently Jesus insists that the resurrection is not a future event for the dead but that it is a present possibility for those who believe that he himself is resurrection and life (11:25). Distinctive themes such as these should not be combined with those found in Paul or the Synoptics in order to present a single New Testament view of eternal life. Above all, one should not assume that what John means by eternal life is what Paul has in mind when he speaks of immortality, though they may overlap.

Perhaps the most significant emphasis in John is his insistence—albeit an indirect one—that man's deepest problem is not mortality and death and sin as for Paul but his not knowing the Father, not having true life now but existing in darkness—all the things that characterize the "world" for John. As in apocalyptic, the world (the human world) is in bondage to Satan (12:31; 14:30; 16:11).[100] Unlike Paul, however, John does not discuss

[98] Unfortunately, because Bultmann has not given apocalyptic theology its due in Paul's thought, he assimilated Paul to John, writing that for both "the eschatological occurrence is understood as already taking place in the present, though John was the first to carry the idea radically through." *Theology of the New Testament,* II, 10.

[99] See Bultmann, *Theology of the New Testament,* II, 52.

[100] The same apocalyptic note is struck in I John 5:19. The fact that such phrases and ideas occur also in the Dead Sea Scrolls has misled some scholars into prematurely associating John with Qumranian theology and tradition, thereby ignoring the totally different orientation in which similar phrases may appear.

the future defeat of this tyranny, for this defeat is announced by Jesus himself (16:33). Nor does John wrestle with the question, When will the world's hatred of believers (15:18–16:4a) be overcome and God be "all in all"? Moreover, Paul's concern for the redemption of the cosmos is simply not present in John and should not be read into it from 3:16. Everything is concentrated on stating the meaning of Jesus in a way that opens the choice of eternal life or continued existence as living death. So radical a change does this new life bring that he uses extreme language to discuss it: new birth, resurrection, going through judgment. On this basis, John implies that questions about what happens after death are unimportant. Whoever now has life in the Son and believes his promise that he has departed to prepare a "place" for his own knows all he needs to know to face the world.

Those close to John may well find Paul's views unnecessary; those close to Paul may find John unsatisfactory. The majesty of both exceeds that of their admirers.

The Significance of New Testament Views of Death

1. These early Christian theologians stated the meaning of Jesus for the mystery of death and life as it was perceived in the Graeco-Roman world, including Palestine. This is what the historical character of the New Testament means. One consequence is that the more clearly the milieu of the New Testament statements is perceived, the less possible it becomes to uproot them for "instant theology" or to combine them into a systematic treatment of the theology of death, resurrection, life after death, heaven, or hell. Rather than press the New Testament into a premature unity of thought, one should seek first to grasp its rich diversity, a diversity which reflects both the multifaceted tradition and the complex situation

in which the literature was written. Another consequence is that it becomes less than self-evident that the New Testament speaks directly to our ways of regarding man's dying. Because the New Testament "answers" once dealt with ancient questions they appear no longer to meet ours. The mystery of death as *we* perceive it is shaped by a different situation. On the other hand, once the New Testament's conversation with its culture is in focus, it might also be true that we have more in common with it than we had first suspected. In any case, neither the irrelevance nor the relevance of the New Testament ways of regarding death should be taken for granted. After all, the New Testament is no more historically conditioned than its modern readers.

The second feature centers in the New Testament's way of generating new questions precisely by dealing with old ones. For example, in taking up the idea of instantaneous blessedness after death while at the same time holding to the hope of the resurrection, Christians faced a virtually insoluable problem of relating these two convictions. Without historical perspective on the diverse statements, one asks, If after death the believer goes to be with the Lord in glory, why does he still need resurrection at the end? Or, in rejecting the preexistence of the eternal soul in favor of the belief that it is created with each individual and may become immortal, the question was forged: When, precisely, did the soul arrive in the body and at what point after death did it leave? (The former is of some importance in the discussion of abortion and the latter for the rite of unction.) Or, what happens to the soul between death and resurrection? The New Testament does not have ready-made answers to such questions; hence when the church canonized this literature and consequently held it to be a consistent theological norm, it had to work out the logical relationships between disparate statements and assumptions. The church inevitably did what we have said can no longer be done—developed an encompassing doctrine of death out of New Testament materials. That many nonbiblical elements entered the stream in the process is not surprising, inasmuch as the biblical statements themselves presuppose ideas shared with the ancient world. A clear example of this is the doctrine of Christ's descent to Hades, which we have omitted from the discussions for reasons of space. The point is that the New Testament generated an ongoing process of interpretation which was largely, but not completely, a process of drawing a coherent doctrine out of the New Testament. The penitential system was one of its monuments. The rise of the modern era, marked by the erosion of Christendom and the development of views of man based on social and psychological sciences, has made this systematized doctrine of death as alien to us as are its biblical roots, if not more so. At the same time, much of the old terminology continues to be used. Even in the space age some continue to speak of the soul's going to heaven (though less is said of its possible descent to hell) or of being "with the Lord." Death is a problem today partly because the language we inherited to talk about it no longer says what we think about it; we use this language because it often has residual psychological power in times of crisis and grief. It is precisely this disjuncture that calls for a theological assessment of what the New Testament, which is a major source of our inherited thought about death, says and does not say.

2. The central theological question which the New Testament views of death and life put before us is whether death and life are theological issues at all. The stream that flowed from apocalyptic springs, like that from gnostic sources as well, insists that man's dying is a theological issue, not a neutral fact (expressed in the antiseptic term "expired"). For this tradition it is not the

sheer uncertainty of life but the certainty of death that constitutes the problem. But why is it a problem? Fundamentally man's death appears to indict the Creator, for it raises the question, How did it happen that the undying Creator made life subject to death? As we have seen, the "fall-of-man tradition" serves to vindicate the Creator and his original work by connecting sin with death, just as the gnostic myth of the demiurge clears the highest God of responsibility for mortal life. In other words, behind the various ancient theologies, even those pitted against each other, stands the struggle to understand life and death in theological terms with a moral component. If today death as such poses no moral problem, then we have no more than historical interest in the New Testament or in that vast ancient tradition with which it shares this concern. If, on the other hand, we are not yet beyond grappling with the fact of death in moral terms—that is, if the fact that every form of life ends in death is still problematic and enigmatic in light of God's own deathlessness—then the New Testament views ought to be taken seriously.

For the New Testament, especially those elements more influenced by apocalyptic, the key question is not man's individual immortality; rather, it is whether the universal fact of death mocks faith in the living (deathless) God and whether the meaningless agony and dying of the innocent mock the moral integrity of God. The New Testament views of death are not at all concerned with the preservation beyond death of the identity and achievements of the middle- and upper-class individuals, as are many books today. Rather, because the New Testament is open to a broader range of reality it implies that the starting point for a theology of death and of resurrection is moral outrage against the world in which there appears to be no justice on which the weak can count, a world in which sucklings are bombed and rabbis gassed. The central issue is not whether man has an essence that survives death but whether the God in whom he believes, however falteringly, has enough moral integrity to "make good" with the life he himself called into existence. In the last analysis, the central theological issue in the death of man is the character of God. In its own diverse ways the New Testament has always been saying this. It can still hold our feet to the right fire.

Milton McC. Gatch received his Ph.D. in Church History at Yale and now teaches English at the University of Missouri. He depicts church theologians from the Greek Fathers through the Reformation as unwilling to endure unanswered questions. Concern for the plight of the soul after death and fear for its ultimate destiny came to dominate reflection on death. Thus, resurrection gave way to immortality, and corporate salvation —God's restoration of a people—gave way to a preoccupation with individual salvation.

III

Some Theological Reflections on Death from the Early Church Through the Reformation[1]

Milton McC. Gatch

What, in the view of Christian theologians, happens to man when he dies? That, in a word, is the issue to be faced in this chapter. Christian teachings about afterlife and the doctrine of purgatory will be given primary attention because they are the loci of teachings concerning active existence for man (man's soul) in the interim between his death and the Day of Judgment. "Purgatory" can be defined as a state in which man is punished for (or purged of) his sins. Since in such a state man is more obviously acting or being acted upon than in a state of "rest" or "bliss," I suggest that we will find by looking into this

[1] The following abbreviations (in the order of their appearance) are used in the notes: *ANF: Ante-Nicene Fathers* (Grand Rapids: Eerdmans, 1957); *NPNF: Nicene and Post-Nicene Fathers* (Grand Rapids: Eerdmans, n.d.); *PG:* J.-P. Migne, ed., *Patrologia Graeca; LCC: Library of Christian Classics* (Philadelphia: Westminster Press, 1953 sqq.); *FC: Fathers of the Church* (New York: Fathers of the Church, var. dates); *PL:* J.-P Migne, ed., *Patroligia Latina; SCG:* Thomas Aquinas, *Summa Contra Gentiles; Inst.:* J. Calvin, *Institutes of the Christian Religion; Dial:* Gregory, *Dialogues.*

teaching an exceptionally important index of the views of the theologians in question as to the state of man after his death. "Afterlife" indicates, in a more general sense, a continued existence for the souls of the dead before Doomsday. By examining attitudes towards these concepts at several crucial historical moments by means of analysis of significant theological documents, we can hope for some understanding of the intellectual formulations which have undergirded the church's pastoral approach to the dying.

The Early Church: Gregory of Nyssa

The Fathers of the church were faced with the unique problem of coming to terms with the very basic Greek notion of the immortality of the soul.[2] The New Testament writers had no such doctrine. Paul, for example, speaks of death as "sleep." He and other New Testament writers hold that, after sleeping, "the dead will be raised imperishable" (I Cor. 15:52 RSV) on the day of resurrection. There is, thus, an interim between death and resurrection about which the New Testament is essentially silent. True, the New Testament writers seem to have believed, as Oscar Cullmann puts it, "that the inner man, who has already been transformed by the Spirit (Rom. 6:3 ff.), and consequently made alive, continues to live with Christ in this transformed state, in the condition of sleep."[3] But the earliest Christian writers were unwilling to describe the waiting or sleeping condition, and

[2] For the Greek doctrine and its relation to the Fathers, see Werner Jaeger, "The Greek Ideas of Immortality" (Ingersoll Lecture, 1958) in Krister Stendahl, ed., *Immortality and Resurrection* (New York: Macmillan Paperbacks ed., 1967), pp. 97-114. A different view is expressed by Harry A. Wolfson, "Immortality and Resurrection in the Philosophy of the Church Fathers" (Ingersoll Lecture, 1956) in the same volume, pp. 54-96.

[3] Oscar Cullmann, "Immortality of the Soul or Resurrection of the Dead?" (Ingersoll Lecture, 1955), *Immortality and Resurrection,* p.44.

they certainly did not talk about the immortality of the soul.

The history of the development of Christian thought in the Early Church is, to a large extent, the story of the accommodation of this primitive Christian position to the concepts of Greek philosophy. To make sense of their faith in the Hellenistic world, Christians had to explain it in terms of Hellenistic philosophical language which to an unparalleled extent, had molded the very thought patterns of the Graeco-Roman world. In this process the introduction of the notion of the immortality of the soul played—with the inseparable philosophic picture of the nature of the cosmos—the most significant role. Perhaps one indication of the importance of the adoption of the doctrine of immortality by Christian theologians is the almost universal tendency to describe death as "the separation of the body and the soul." "This description of death as the separation of body and soul," remarks a liberal twentieth-century Catholic theologian, "is . . . used in such a matter-of-fact way, from the earliest Fathers up to the catechism of Cardinal Gasparri, that we must consider and accept it as the classical theological description of death." [4]

Yet the adoption of Hellenistic language and of the notion of immortality by the Early Church did not necessarily result in a capitulation of Jerusalem to Athens. Early Christian writers saw no choice but to adopt the idea of an immortal soul, but they were equally insistent upon the fact that there remains an interim between death and the resurrection of the body during which, while one must not say that the soul is dead, one cannot say where it is or what it is doing. Thus in the second century Irenaeus[5] held that the soul is immortal; it does

[4] Karl Rahner, *On the Theology of Death,* trans. C. H. Henkey ("Questiones Disputatae"; New York: Herder & Herder, 1961), p. 24.

[5] *Against Heresies* V. 31 (*ANF,* I, 560).

not die with the body but is waiting for the resurrection from the time of death. It waits in an "invisible place" which the theologian does not want to describe. It waits during an interim in which it is apparently inactive.

When Irenaeus wrote, it was understandable that theologians would be careful, if only by reason of proximity, to retain the New Testament notion of death, even though clothing it in the philosophical language of the Greeks. Our point is not made, therefore, unless it can be substantiated by reference to later Greek Fathers. To this end it will be helpful to look rather extensively into the work of Gregory of Nyssa, youngest of the great triad of Cappadocian Fathers. Heir to the platonizing tradition of Origen, Gregory is generally considered the last of the truly creative Greek Fathers.

Gregory's most extensive treatise on the subject of man's ultimate destiny is his dialogue *On the Soul and the Resurrection,*[6] which was written about A.D. 380. It is cast in the form of a last conversation between the bishop of Nyssa and his dying sister Macrina. Gregory has gone to her, deeply troubled by the death of their brother St. Basil the Great; and in the presence of Macrina's friends they discuss the matters of death and human destiny at great length, the sister assuming the role of "teacher."

On the Soul and the Resurrection was probably written as a footnote to another work (itself intended to complete an unfinished task of his elder brother Basil) and actually represents a change on Gregory's part "in a more spiritual direction."[7] Yet the extent to which Gregory guards the biblical doctrine from the encroachments of Greek notions of afterlife is remarkable. Gregory has come to

[6] *NPNF,* 2nd Ser., V, 430-68 (subsequent citations to page and column of this version). Original text in *PG,* XLVI, 11-160.

[7] L. G. Patterson, "The Conversion of Diastema in the Patristic View of Time," in R. A. Norris, Jr., ed., *Lux in Lumine: Essays to Honor W. Norman Pittenger* (New York: Seabury Press, 1966), p. 105.

Macrina for consolation. He opens their discussion by posing questions concerning the existence and destiny of the soul. The soul, declares his sister, "is an essence created, and living, and intellectual, transmitting from itself to an organized and sentient body the power of living and of grasping objects of sense, as long as a natural constitution capable of this holds together." [8] It has "a rare and peculiar nature of its own" and is independent "of the body with its gross texture." [9] Inasmuch as man is a microcosm, "a little world in himself [containing] all the elements which go to complete the universe,"[10] the soul is the divine element in man and must be immortal. Furthermore, the soul is the vivifying force, and, even after death and the decay of the body, "that bond of a vivifying influence" does not vanish.[11] So the soul, which is immortal, yet "exists in the actual atoms which she once animated, and there is no force to tear her away from her cohesion with them." [12] That is a truly remarkable doctrine, and one which would surely have confounded the Greek philosophers more than the New Testament writers. Man is given life by an immortal soul; but the soul is inseparably bound to the body.

There follows, to continue summarizing the document, an excursus on the relation of the soul to the emotions or passions in which it is concluded that emotion is related to sensation and therefore to "brute creation" and that the value of emotion depends on the use to which it is put by the human will.[13] Next Gregory asks about Hades and is told by Macrina that Hades is a "word for a place in which souls are said to be [and] means nothing else but a transition to that Unseen world of

[8] *On the Soul . . .*, p. 433b.

[9] *Ibid.*

[10] *Ibid.*, p. 433a.

[11] *Ibid.*, p. 437a-b.

[12] *Ibid.*, p. 438b.

[13] *Ibid.*, p. 442a.

which we have no glimpse."[14] Since the soul is immaterial, there is no way to localize its existence after death, and speculation about the locus of its existence is futile.[15] There are points in this part of the work where Gregory sounds very much like a demythologizer.

Gregory then draws Macrina back to the mainstream of their discussion, asking how the soul will "follow along" with the destroyed body. The soul, Macrina replies, has the unique "power of recognition" which, for example, an artist has for that which he has created; and therefore it cannot fail to recognize its body either when it is decayed or at the resurrection.[16] To those who would object by citing the parable of Dives and Lazarus she adds, it must be argued that the physical details of that story must be translated to "an equivalent in the world of ideas." The Gospel parable says simply that the living must keep free of obsessive "attachments" to the fleshly lest, even in the disembodied state, they be subject to the same distractions.[17] Thus there is a sense in which it may be said that the soul during the interim after death is still being drawn from evil to good. The good soul tends always toward the Godhead, as though it were light and drawn upward; but that which has been overly distracted by the life of the flesh tends toward the fleshly, as though it were heavy and pulled down.[18] In the light of the exegesis of the Lazarus parable, however, the physical imagery of this passage must be understood metaphorically.

Finally, Gregory turns to the problem of resurrection, establishing the logical possibility of rejoining the soul and the body, treating the problem of evil and establishing the notion that the resurrection will occur when the per-

[14] *Ibid.*, p. 443b.
[15] *Ibid.*, p. 444a.
[16] *Ibid.*, pp. 445-46.
[17] *Ibid.*, pp. 446-48.
[18] *Ibid.*, pp. 448-53.

fect number of human souls has been attained.[19] Answering her brother's last objections, Macrina discusses the manner in which man is purged so that he can appear at Judgment in a state of incorruption.[20]

It ought to be clear even from this summary of *On the Soul and the Resurrection* that Gregory of Nyssa, standing in the Platonic tradition of philosophy and at the end of the Greek patristic tradition, has steadfastly refused to speculate about the status of the soul between death and resurrection. Body and soul are in a strange but real way inseparable. The immortality of the soul is a premise, but it is radically interpreted in the light of the resurrection. Immortality is a source of consolation for the living as they contemplate death, but hope is primarily aimed at the age beyond temporality when the perfect number of souls will have been created and, purged of all evil, incorrupt man will dwell eternally in body and soul with God.

It has frequently been remarked that the situation depicted in Gregory's dialogue closely resembles that of the *Phaedo* of Plato,[21] in which the condemned Socrates comforts his friends by discoursing on death and immortality just before taking the fatal draught of hemlock. Nyssa has chosen to model his work on the most famous and most important classical work dealing with immortality. Thus he sets the Christian doctrine in bold contrast with the philosophical. Most explicitly, he rejects Plato's notions of reincarnation, immediate judgment after death, and the ultimate separability of soul and body. These notions were, of course, treated mythologically by Plato;[22] but

[19] *Ibid.*, pp. 453b-59.

[20] *Ibid.*, pp. 460-68.

[21] See Hans von Campenhausen, *The Fathers of the Greek Church,* trans. Stanley Godman (New York: Pantheon Books, 1959), p. 109.

[22] *Phaedo,* 114b. See also Paul Friedlander's treatment of Plato's eschatology in Chap. IX of *Plato: An Introduction,* trans. Hans Meyerhoff ("Bollingen Library"; Torchbooks; New York: Harper & Row, 1964).

even so they were fundamentally incompatible with the Christian position and had to be answered. Indeed, it may be that the implied contradiction of the Platonic tradition in *On the Soul and the Resurrection* is as significant as the more immediate criticism of Origen and other earlier theologians who had tended to overemphasize the importance of the separability of the soul from the body.[23] At any rate the pattern of Gregory's eschatology is clearly biblical rather than Platonic. One might more easily find a doctrine of purgatory in Plato than in Nyssa; and, I would suggest, the same might be said on the whole of the tradition of the Fathers of the Greek Church.

At the end of the great age of Greek theology Christian thought had accepted the doctrine of the immortality of the soul but had refused to postulate for the soul an active and independent posthumous existence or purgation. As in the New Testament view man slept until the final judgment, so in the patristic view he waited in the "realm of the Unseen" for the resurrection. In the classical age Christian eschatology refused to succumb to pagan eschatological mythology.

The Age of Transition: Gregory the Great

Interesting though the works of the Latin Fathers are on the subject of afterlife, they represent a situation which (with allowances for the peculiar tone of Latin Christianity) is parallel to that of the Greek-speaking theogians. There are hints in the works of Augustine and others of a tendency to push purgation of sins back from the events expected to accompany the resurrection to the

[23] On Gregory's teaching as a refutation of Origen, see Jean Daniélou, "La Résurrection des Corps chez Gregoire de Nysse," *Vigiliae Christianae,* VII (1953), pp. 154-55.

interim after death,[24] but even this movement was very carefully limited and more closely connected with piety and penitential practices than with doctrinal and philosophical issues.[25]

Martin Luther and others since have laid the blame for the introduction of an explicit postmortem purgatorial state at the feet of a pope who ruled from 590 to 604 and who "being in the night-time deceived by a vision, taught something of purgatory."[26] That pope, Gregory the Great, is in many ways a transitional figure between the classical and medieval worlds; so we must look closely at the fourth book of his *Dialogues,* the work to which Luther was probably alluding, and determine whether there is justice in the charge that Gregory is the originator of purgatory.

The *Dialogues* of Gregory the Great[27] form a curious volume, the unity and purposes of which have not always been appreciated. The first book opens with a typical Gregorian lamentation of the fact that he has been forced to leave the peace and security of contemplative monastic life for the stormy sea of worldly life and is thus tossed like a ship on the tempestuous sea, longing all the while for the shore. He compares his lot unfavorably with that of the many who are able to spend their lives "in seclusion" and "free from worldly occupations." Peter, a deacon of the Roman church who has found him thus dejected, remarks that he knows of no Italians of marked virtue, of

[24] I find *City of God* XXI. 13 the most explicit passage in this connection. See also *Enchiridion* 67-69, 109 (LCC, VII).

[25] See Frederik van der Meer, *Augustine the Bishop,* trans. Brian Battershaw and G. R. Lamb (New York: Sheed & Ward, 1961), pp. 471-74.

[26] *Table-Talk* #DXV in H. T. Kerr, Jr., ed., *A Compend of Luther's Theology* (Philadelphia: Westminster Press, 1943), p. 243.

[27] Trans. O. J. Zimmerman (*FC,* XXXIX). This trans. cited by book and chapter herein; it has been checked against the Latin text in *PL,* LXXVII, cols. 194-430 (*Dial.* II is omitted there but printed in *PL,* LXVI with other materials relating to Western monasticism). Zimmerman follows the chapter division of the edition of U. Morrica (1924).

no men who have performed "miracles" or signs. So the pope proceeds to edify the deacon in four conversations based on authoritative reports of Italian saints and wonder workers.[28]

The first book is devoted to figures of the fairly remote past. The second is devoted entirely to St. Benedict of Nursia and, as the only source for the life of Benedict, has been the most widely read (and, recently, the most controversial) portion of the work. *Dialogues* III is an account of the wonders wrought by more recent Italian saints. It concludes with the observation that, since the coming of the Lombards, "in this land of ours the world is not merely announcing its end, it is pointing directly to it." Thus it is especially urgent that men seek "after the things of heaven." This remark leads Peter to ask for proofs of "the existence of the soul after death." [29] In his development of this theme in the final book Gregory appears to draw more largely than before on examples from his own times; indeed, a striking number of illustrations is based on events which occurred in the monastic household Gregory had established in his family's home in Rome. In other words, although in certain ways books II and IV seem to be topical, the material of the *Dialogues* as a whole is also arranged chronologically; and the topical theme of the final portion emerges at least in part because of Gregory's preoccupation with the eschatological urgency of his own times. The eschatological schema of Book IV leads almost inevitably to the conclusion that one must lead an absolutely righteous life. Gregory ends on a homiletical note:

> So, while we are enjoying days of grace, while our Judge holds off the sentence, and the Examiner of our sins awaits our conversion, let us soften our hardened hearts with tears

[28] *Dial.* I. Prologue.
[29] *Dial.* III. 38.

and practice charity and kindness toward our neighbor. Then we can be sure that, if we offered ourselves during life as victims to God, we will not need to have the saving Victim offered for us after death.[30]

The work thus travels full circle and returns to the theme with which it began: the difficulty and necessity of eschewing worldliness and, at the same time, dealing with the issues of life in the world.

As the *Dialogues* deal with the acts of saints, notably their miracles and their visions, it should be evident at the outset that it belongs not so much to the philosophical and theological traditions which have thus far occupied our attention as to the tradition of the *Vitae Patrum* which glorifies the heroic conquest of temptation and evil by the ascetics. While the book has its classical heritage—its dialogical form, its allusion to the doctrines of the theological tradition, its concern in the final book with the problem of immortality—it is designed to convince not by logic but by appeal to example: Men are in exile in this life and, "being carnal men without any experimental knowledge of the invisible, we wonder about the existence of anything we cannot see with our bodily eyes." [31] Thus, so long as Gregory can present examples of "experimental knowledge" based on second- or third-hand accounts, he is convinced that his arguments are as compelling as those of the Evangelists Mark and Luke who also relied "on the word of others." [32] This new method not only strains our credulity but also raises questions of interpretation which are, as what follows should show, remarkably difficult.

Book IV of the *Dialogues* seems, when it is examined

[30] *Dial.* IV. 62.

[31] *Dial.* IV. ("Sed carnales quique, quia illa invisibilia scire non valent per experimentum, dubitant utrumne sit quod corporalibus oculis non vident.")

[32] *Dial.* I. Prologue.

closely, to betray some principles of organization. Chapters 1-5 are an introductory statement, laced with biblical allusions, on the survival of the soul, a doctrine which Gregory accepts as a first postulate of Christian belief. In the following section (Chapters 6-25), evidence is presented from visions of the passage of the soul at death to an incorporeal existence. The major portion of the book (Chapters 26-56) is concerned with the nature of that existence. The perfect go straight to heaven. The souls of the dying may have prophetic insight of worldly events or of their own future condition. Souls know and consort with each other. The dead are occasionally revived, either to warn others or to be given a second chance. For the same reasons living men are sometimes given a glimpse of their own destinies. From the evidence of these kinds of authorities we are to believe that the soul must endure a postmortem purgation. Finally, hell is described as an eternal death for the immortal souls of the wicked. Something is said about the importance of dreams and of the danger of burying evil men in the church. In the concluding chapters (57-62) Gregory speaks of the benefits wrought by the Mass for men, living and dead, whose sins require expiation.

Gregory clearly postulates for the soul, good or evil, an existence following death which is related to the quality of its life in the world. That in itself is a departure from Gregory of Nyssa's view and even something of an advance on Augustine's limited notion of "a secret shelter . . . as each is worthy of rest or affliction." [33]

The crucial question is that of purgatory: "I should like to know," as Peter poses it, "if we have to believe in a cleansing fire after death." [34] Gregory's reply begins with the assertion that "each one will be presented to the

[33] *Enchiridion* 109.
[34] *Dial.* IV. 40 ("Doceri vellem si post mortem purgatorius ignis esse credendus est.").

Judge exactly as he was when he departed this life." But "there must be a cleansing fire . . . because of some minor faults that may remain to be purged away." [35] In other words, since the soul is going to be granted a postmortem existence more active than that allowed by the biblical and Greek traditions, it may be necessary to move the cleansing fire from the events of the Last Day to the day of death. But the language of this passage is evasive: It need not refer to a purgation which occurs immediately.

Gregory passes to an example of Paschasius, a Roman deacon, who was on the wrong side in a disputed papal election. When Paschasius died, a "possessed person" was healed by touching the dalmatic on his bier. But much later the bishop of Capua saw the deceased deacon at the public baths and was told that he served there because of his sin in supporting the wrong candidate for the papacy. The bishop prayed for Paschasius and obtained his release. The point Gregory wants to make is that, though on the whole meritorious, a man may still have to make satisfaction for his lesser sins.[36]

At this point, Peter shifts the subject and inquires why it is that in recent times "the spiritual world is moving closer to us manifesting itself through visions and revelations." Because, he is told, the end is nigh. The shadows are fading as the new day dawns.[37] The conversation returns briefly to Paschasius and then proceeds to a new topic: hell, its location and nature.[38]

The conclusion to be drawn about this sequence is, I should think, that it cannot be regarded as the conscious and explicit introduction of a doctrine that there is a place in which the souls of the dead are purged until they are utterly cleansed. It is, rather, a statement in

[35] *Dial.* IV. 41.
[36] *Dial.* IV. 42.
[37] *Dial.* IV. 43.
[38] *Dial.* IV. 44 sqq.

visionary terms that even the elect must, in the economy of God's justice, do satisfaction for their errors. Gregory's teaching may lay the groundwork for the future development of a notion of purgatory, but it would be unfair and anachronistic to translate a metaphorical statement into an exposition of doctrine.

This impression is, incidentally, strongly reinforced by a reading of Gregory's other works. In the one letter in which he mentions *Dialogues,* he states that he has been persuaded to write a book about the miracles of the Fathers by the importunity of members of the papal household.[39] Thus, it seems, the author himself thought the work peripheral to his primary purposes. While the homilies occasionally use the same kinds of materials as the *Dialogues*—indeed Gregory acknowledges that at least six examples in *Dialogues* IV are from the *Homilies on the Gospels*[40]—it is evident in the Epistles and elsewhere that his primary concern is not with the immediate fate of the soul but with the historical crisis presented by plague, barbarian invasion, and the disintegration of civil order. His concern is to convince men of their duty to do justice in history and, thus, to appear blameless at the impending judgment. It would be unfair then to force the interpretation of the *Dialogues* beyond its ambiguities to a developed notion of purgatory. Gregory is obsessed with divine judgment which is both meted out in present history and at the end of history. Salvation is only perfected by the Last Judgment, and so what happens before that event is not an integral feature of atonement.

The *Dialogues,* then, belong to a tradition other than

[39] "Fratres mei . . . omni modo me compellunt, aliqua de miraculis patrum, . . . sub brevitaie scribere" (*Epistle* III. 50; *Monumenta Germaniae Historica,* Epistolarum I, pp. 206-7; trans. as III. 51 in *NPNF,* 2nd Ser., XII, p. 135).

[40] See *Dial.* IV. 15, 16, 17, 20, 28, 40.

that of theology and philosophy strictly defined. They form a book whose intent is pastoral and speak in terms of visions and wonders. Unconcerned with the niceties of the problem of immortality, they tend to push events and processes which in biblical eschatology and apocalyptic were reserved for the denouement of sacred history into the interim after the death of the individual. Gregory believes that the soul is immortal and has an active afterlife. But it is not at all clear that it was his intention to teach that the soul actively and literally undergoes punishment immediately upon the death of the body. Profoundly classical, distinctly pastoral, obviously caught in a transitional moment when the forms of expression are breaking down and new forms have not yet been perfected, Gregory raises more questions than he answers. But there is reason to believe that Luther's accusation was at least anachronistic, that the Reformer was blinded by the success of his own medieval predecessors when he pointed to Gregory as the originator of purgatory.

The Early Middle Ages: Aelfric of Eynsham

It is too often the custom in treating Christian intellectual history to leap from Augustine of Hippo to Anselm of Canterbury. That ought never to be done, and it certainly cannot be done in this discussion of the emergence of a doctrine of purgatory and developing emphasis on afterlife. For it is in the theological tradition of the early Middle Ages that one's suspicions about the incidental nature of Gregory's teaching on purgatory are confirmed. And it is in the same period that one begins to discern that the enunciation of such a doctrine in a later period is inevitable.

Two marks characterize the theology of the seventh through the tenth centuries. The first is a passion to collect, preserve, and transmit the teachings of the Fathers.

However much one admires the achievements—and even the innovations—of the scholars of this age, he must recognize the conservative temper of the monks who were its chief professional learned persons. The task of the scholar was seen as that of assembling the authoritative statements of the past on the subjects in which he was interested and of passing them on to future generations. Often his ability to assess the value of his sources was primitive (which is to say that his credulity was astounding) but the only measure he knew for determining orthodoxy was authority: the authority of antiquity or the authority vouched by the sanctity of an author or supposed author.[41]

The second mark of the theological atmosphere of the early Middle Ages is what has been characterized as the heroic outlook. In this remarkably unsettled period of history high value was placed on personal ties of loyalty and on the ability of the strong lord to provide his retainers with security and the necessities of life in return for their own service and loyalty. So, by analogy, Christ was regarded as the lord and hero par excellence, unremitting in his demand of obedience, who overcame Satan's power and his claims over the loyal Christian retainer. He had triumphed over death and one day would preside, as did the earthly lord in his hall, over the eternal and blissful banquet of his chosen and faithful followers.[42] Both of these characteristics must be kept in mind as one examines the Old English homiletic literature.

Of the theologians of the early Middle Ages, Aelfric of Eynsham, who flourished in the late tenth century, can be taken as an example. His work is unusual on two

[41] See Jean Leclercq, *The Love of Learning and the Desire for God: A Study of Monastic Culture,* trans. Catharine Misrahi (Mentor-Omega Books; New York: New American Library, 1962), Part II, *passim.*

[42] See R. W. Southern, *The Making of the Middle Ages* (London: Hutchinson, 1953), pp. 234-35.

counts. First, Aelfric wrote in English, his native tongue —something no continental theologian whose work has survived had essayed. He was, in the second place, more critical of his sources than many other homilists of the same period; and he wanted to set into English a series of sermons—almost a homiletic *summa theologiae*—of more certain orthodoxy than those of his predecessors. But his aim was a typical one: to edify the laity by providing the clergy with materials for preaching based on the best of the sermon collections made in Latin by the Carolingian theologians and on the Fathers themselves. As a prose stylist and judge of his sources, Aelfric is one of the most significant (and neglected) literary figures of the early Middle Ages.

Aelfric's longest and most complete treatment of the whole problem of eschatology is the *Sermo ad Populum in Octavis Pentecosten Dicendus.*[43] This sermon is drawn from materials collected and expounded in the late seventh century by Julian of Toledo in a treatise entitled *Prognosticon futuri seaculi.*[44] Aelfric himself had written a Latin epitome of Julian's work very early in his career, but he did not produce his English homiletic version until about 1005, well after most of his homiletic corpus had been completed.[45] Thus the views he expressed in the sermon for Pentecost may be regarded as those that he held throughout his career.

After an introduction dealing with the liturgical drama of salvation which concludes at the season for which the

[43] John C. Pope, ed., *Homilies of Aelfric, a Supplementary Collection* (Early English Text Society, No. 259; London: Oxford University Press, 1967), pp. 415-47. Citations are to the lines of the text, which is written in Aelfric's mature, alliterative prose style and printed in lines. Translations mine.

[44] *PL, XCVI,* 461-524.

[45] For the place of the epitome in Aelfric's corpus see my "Ms. Boulogne-Sur-Mer 63 and Aelfric's First Series of Catholic Homilies," *Journal of English and Germanic Philology,* LXV (1966), 482-90.

sermon was prepared, Aelfric treats of eschatology under three headings: death and the value of intercession (lines 94-215), the condition of the soul after death (lines 216-272) and the Day of Judgment (lines 273-574).

The material of the first section displays, if not an awareness of the philosophical issues, dependence on sources which considered the problem of eschatology in the light of the Graeco-Roman philosophical tradition. The death of the mortal body is unimportant in comparison with the destiny of the soul. For there are two deaths, that of the body, which all men must suffer, and that of the soul, which only the wicked endure and which is only metaphorically a death since it is more accurately described as the endurance of eternal punishment. To avoid this fate it behooves us to lead a life acceptable to God and earn a place in heaven where a multitude of the saints already waits for us. If we are to win this goal, we need the prayers of the saints and the church. At the hour of death God's angels come to judge the soul and lead it to heaven, to hell, or to a condition in which it will be purged of its minor sins until released by expiation or by intercession. Sometimes, for those in the latter condition, a painful death serves the purpose of purgation.

Aelfric's treatment of the destiny of the soul between death and judgment is based on the notion that the soul has "the likeness of the body in all its members" (line 217) and can therefore experience "comfort or pain" (line 218) according to the merits of its life in the body. Those who can be saved but need purgation suffer as long as is necessary. The saints "dwell in heaven" (line 236), interceding for the living and those undergoing purgation, just as we on earth can profitably pray and offer masses for those being punished. The blessed, though their bliss is eternal and though they see the splendor of

God, yearn for the coming of the judgment so that their joy may be complete. The damned, for whom prayer is of no avail, are also solicitous for the living.

It would be beyond the scope of this paper to summarize the third, and longest, portion of Aelfric's sermon, in which he outlines the events of the final drama of salvation. But it should be noted that it comprises well over half of the entire work and that it inspires Aelfric to a generally higher level of eloquence and rhetorical display than do the earlier portions of the piece. One has the impression that he includes the first sections because their materials are covered in his sources and, thus, must be put in for the sake of completeness.

There is no escaping the fact that Aelfric, more clearly than any of the other theologians discussed above, teaches that in the interim after death there is an active existence for the soul in which it suffers eternal or temporal punishment or enjoys eternal bliss until the fullness of time when "there are as many [just souls] as God ordained originally when he first created the whole world" (lines 259-260). Like Augustine's and Pope Gregory's, Aelfric's teaching is closely tied to the practices of penance and of prayer for the dead. Unlike Gregory, the Abbot of Eynsham does not rely on visionary materials to establish his case.[46] In part, the development reflected in the *Sermo ad Populum* is a by-product of the failure of the intellectuals of the early Middle Ages to keep alive the philosophical tradition. Aelfric (like his contemporaries) was unaware of the non-Christian sources of the doctrine of immortality and therefore unconcerned with the difficulties raised by an uncritical adoption of immortality and of the notion of an active afterlife. Immortality was

[46] There is one exemplum, lines 168-76, which is similar to Gregory's wonder tales. It was added by Aelfric to his source material but does not significantly alter the course of the argument.

unquestioned, but the issues of immortality were unknown.

But Aelfric was also prevented from devoloping the picture of afterlife by the very characteristics of theological method and the temperament of his age. The method of the age was encyclopedic: theologians gathered the wisdom of the giants of the intellectual heritage of the church. Finding little about the postmortem condition of the soul in the authorities of the tradition, they had no tools with which to develop a new doctrine. Again and again Aelfric cites old books as his sources; and as often he makes it clear that he has no intention of saying anything not vouched for by sound authority. Thus, had he wanted to, he could not have elaborated a doctrine of purgatory because to do so was beyond the very limited task set forth in the unquestioned understanding of the nature of theological method. Within a century after Aelfric's death a new generation of scholars instigated a "cultural revolution" [47] by restoring logical studies to the curriculum. When logical questions were asked of the materials of theology and when some awareness of other philosophical issues was manifested, the doctrine of immortality could be restated, and a doctrine of purgatory might more easily be made an integral part of the theological system.

But it is equally important that the mentality or temperament of the times left theologians such as Aelfric disinclined to move towards a developed notion of purgatory or of the afterlife in general. For the heroic view of life was concerned with the individual as he took his place and played his role in the host of his lord, be that lord temporal or eternal. In the heroic age the tragic figure was the man without a lord or companions: the

[47] David Knowles, *The Evolution of Medieval Thought* (London: Longmans, Green & Co., 1962), p. 75.

destitute figures, say, of two very moving Old English poems, *The Wanderer* and *The Seafarer*,[48] who realize when bereft of earthly solace that the only hope lies in being loyal retainers and companions of God. Thus it was not the lot of the soul that preoccupied early medieval man but the destiny of the whole man: at the end would he be at the table of the great Lord at his eternal banquet; or would he remain subject to Satan, the lord of darkness who, but for the triumph of Christ, laid claim on all men? Given the doctrine of atonement implied by this set of values and attitudes, the doctrines of purgatory and of afterlife in the interim could never supplant the vivid picture of the heroic apocalypse in the imagination of theologian and layman alike.

Early medieval theology had all the materials for a doctrine of purgatory and of an active spiritual afterlife. But the methodology and the mentality of the period prevented theologians from seeing this fact and developing the doctrines fully and logically. The doctrines remained peripheral and unarticulated. In a sense, the period is one in which one must report no development, because the theological role was to conserve rather than to innovate. In another sense, however, there is a development inherent in the very act of collecting materials, for the emphases of compendia often differ from those of sources. Furthermore, these long centuries during which immortality went unquestioned as an integral Christian postulate made it easier, when the texts of the ancient philosophers had been recovered, to regard their teachings about the soul and its destiny as amplifications of the gospel.

[48] Both in *Poems from the Old English*, trans. Burton Raffel (Bison Book; Lincoln: University of Nebraska Press, 1960), pp. 41-44 and 13-16, respectively.

The High Middle Ages: Thomas Aquinas

When one leaps from the early eleventh to the mid-thirteenth century, he discovers himself in an utterly different theological milieu. More will be said below about the reasons for this phenomenon. For the present, however, it is advisable to examine our document, the *Summa Contra Gentiles* of Thomas Aquinas.[49]

Written between 1258 and 1263, this treatise was intended to assist Christians as they faced Islam both as a missionary challenge in Spain and, through the Islamic commentators on Aristotle, an intellectual challenge at Paris and other universities.[50] Thomas' better known *Summa Theologiae* was incomplete at his death, and its eschatological articles were provided later by disciples, so *Contra Gentiles* is the most complete treatment of our subject available.

The first characteristic which distinguishes Thomas' work from that of the early medieval theologians is its profound interest in the doctrine of the soul as a metaphysical problem. Indeed, the problem of the soul was one of the chief topics of debate in the thirteenth century. Thomas, working on the Aristotelian base, developed a doctrine

> that the soul, as pure form, actualizes the body as its matter, and that the intellective soul contains in itself in an eminent degree all the perfections of the sensitive and vegetative souls, which it supplants in the embryo of the human being at the moment of its creation.[51]

[49] *On the Truth of the Catholic Faith: Summa Contra Gentiles,* trans. Anton C. Pegis (Bk. I), James F. Anderson (Bk. II), V. J. Bourke (Bk. III), and Charles J. O'Neil (Bk. IV) (Image Books; Garden City, N. Y.: Doubleday & Co., 1955-57).

[50] M. D. Chenu, *Toward Understanding Saint Thomas,* trans. with authorized corrections and bibliographical additions by A. M. Landry and D. Hughes (Chicago: Henry Regnery, 1964), pp. 289-92.

[51] Knowles, *Evolution of Medieval Thought,* p. 295; see also pp. 291-96.

In a metaphysical context similar to that of his doctrine of transubstantiation, Aquinas considered at length the issues of the relation of soul and body after death and of the interim between death and resurrection. He accepted immortality as a fundamental Christian tenet; but, unlike the early medieval theologians, he was aware of the philosophical issues raised, and treated them sensitively and extensively.

But, as is evident from the treatment of the problem of the soul's destiny after death in *Contra Gentiles,* theological issues were also profoundly involved. The subject of eschatology is treated in Book IV, which deals with salvation. Thomas believed that salvation is by grace alone. Thus he treats the doctrines of Christ, the Holy Spirit, and the Trinity as loci of teaching about God's gracious or saving activity among men and turns to the sacraments which he regards as "instruments . . . of a God who was made flesh and suffered," as "visible things" which "work out a spiritual salvation." [52] At the end, he discusses the Last Things, the consummation of the work of salvation.[53]

The organization of these final chapters is, at first glance, curious; for Aquinas deals immediately with the resurrection of the dead—that great stumbling block to the "Gentiles"—with objections to it and with the nature of the body which is to be raised. As Christ died for "the remission of sin . . . the sacraments work in the power of Christ." Similarly, as Christ was raised to effect "our liberation from death" mankind will be raised at the end of history.[54] This resurrection, metaphysically conceived, is necessary since the soul "is the form of the body" and "it is . . . contrary to the nature of the soul to be without a body." [55] Resurrection is also necessary

[52] *SCG* IV. 56. 7.

[53] *SCG* IV. 79-97.

[54] *SCG* IV. 79. 3-4.

[55] *SCG* IV. 79. 10. These assertions are explicitly related to the philosophical proof of immortality in *SCG* III.

in the light of "the natural desire of man to tend to happiness." Since perfect happiness is impossible in this world and impossible as well for the disembodied soul (for in that state it is imperfect), perfect happiness must await a future state in which body and soul will be reunited.[56] The same can be said in the light of the necessity that men be punished for their sins: ultimate punishment, like ultimate reward, demands reunion of soul and body.[57] In his risen and glorified or in his damned state, man will be immortal, animal, and incorruptible.[58] The effect of Thomas' treatment of resurrection is to make it absolutely clear that he takes very seriously the biblical texts upon which it is based and is intent upon interpreting those texts in a clear and logical metaphysical context. He is also concerned to fortify the biblical notions that Christ's sacrifice is an act of God's justice and that, without grace, man cannot be saved.

These latter considerations also motivate the treatment of the fate of the soul between death and resurrection. Punishment and reward are of the essence of God's justice:

> Therefore, both reward and punishment flow suitably from the soul to the body, but it does not belong to the soul by reason of the body. There is, therefore, no reason in the infliction of punishment or bestowal of reward why the souls should wait for the resumption of their bodies; rather, it seems more fitting that, since the souls had priority in the fault or merit, they have priority also in being punished or rewarded.[59]

One further element necessitates this conclusion: The soul as the rational element in man can have a vision of

[56] *SCG* IV. 79. 11.
[57] *SCG* IV. 79. 12.
[58] *SCG* IV. 82, 84-85.
[59] *SCG* IV. 91. 4.

the divine once it is separated from the corruptible body; and, since that vision is "man's ultimate beatitude, which is the 'reward of virtue'," punishment or reward is ineluctably the lot of the soul immediately after it is separated from the body.[60]

But the soul which is ultimately to be rewarded must be "entirely purified":

> to be sure, the soul is purified from this uncleanness in this life by penance, and the other sacraments, . . . but it does at times happen that such purification is not entirely perfected in this life; one remains a debtor for the punishment, whether by reason of some negligence, or business, or even because a man is overtaken by death. Nevertheless, he is not entirely cut off from his reward, because such things can happen without mortal sin, which alone takes away the charity to which the reward of eternal life is due. . . . They must then be purged after this life before they receive the final reward.[61]

Purgatory, in other words, is made necessary in the Thomistic system by the sacramental understanding of penance. In the sacrament of penance the minister acts for Christ as judge of the sinner who is contrite for sins he has committed after baptism; and as judge imposes upon the penitent an obligation or "satisfaction." "By this a man is entirely freed from the guilt of punishment when he pays the penalty which he owed." [62] As further justification for the doctrine of penance, Aquinas cites the church's custom of praying for the dead,[63] but one has the impression that this argument is traditional and not in the least essential to his position.

[60] *SCG* IV. 91. 2. See also III. 51.
[61] *SCG* IV. 91. 6.
[62] *SCG* IV. 72. 14.
[63] *SCG* IV. 91. 7.

After a passage in which he heightens interest in the state of the soul by arguing that the wills of souls separated from the body are immutable,[64] Aquinas finally considers the Last Judgment. There is, he declares, "a two-fold retribution for what a man does in life": One occurs for the soul immediately it is separated from the body, and the other will take place when the soul is reunited with its body. There is individual judgment at death, and there is general judgment at the end.[65] Metaphysically, since the soul is the form of the body and incomplete without the body, the Last Judgment is necessary. Practically speaking, the apocalypse is only the ratification of the judgment of the soul at the hour of death.[66]

Thus, Thomas Aquinas takes the biblical doctrine of the resurrection of the dead very seriously and, at the same time, integrates that element of the church's teaching with the immortality of the soul in a metaphysically more satisfactory manner than even the great Greek Fathers. But this very success is one of the signs of a profound alteration of theological emphasis. For Thomas and his contemporaries were unwilling to leave unanswered or as a matter of mystery the question of the soul's fate between death and the resurrection. They were impelled to ask what immortality means in the Christian scheme. Their answer was that the soul is judged at the hour of its separation from the body and enters immediately into its reward or punishment. The answer was not exactly a new one; it had been implied by the Fathers and stated by early medieval theologians. But it was pursued to its logical ends and given a new force in the high Middle Ages. The Last Judgment becomes a ratification of individual judgment. It represents the consummation of

[64] *SCG* IV. 92-95.

[65] *SCG* IV. 96. 1.

[66] Thomas' disciples who completed *Summa Theologiae* (III. a Suppl. Q. 88.2) come closer to this position than Thomas himself.

salvation and the goal of history, but it has lost its force as the focus of eschatological concern.

The very organization of Thomas' treatment at the end of the *Summa Contra Gentiles* demonstrates this phenomenon. The convincing and extended metaphysical case for the necessity of resurrection based on the notion that the soul is the form of the body is followed by a discussion of the soul's destiny before the Resurrection. The reader's interest in this subject has been whetted by the important role played by the doctrines of the soul and immortality in the earlier books of this *Summa* (particularly in Book III on "Providence") and in the entire Thomistic corpus. Thomas' concern for this aspect of the history of the individual thus undercuts his concern with the denouement of the history of mankind. And the two brief concluding chapters on the Last Judgment do not serve to restore the reader's interest in that event. It is, indeed, the consummation; but somehow, since the souls of those saved by the grace of God have already achieved the beatific vision, the coming of the end has lost its urgency and its place as the event for which the whole creation yearns.

The increased importance of purgatory in this whole scheme only intensifies this development. If salvation is by grace, and if the sacraments are the chief vehicles of grace, then satisfaction or punishment imposed after priestly judgment and absolution becomes a vital element. Those who have not been purged while living must not be consigned to eternal punishment but must, in their disembodied state, be allowed to complete their satisfaction. At the time Aelfric wrote, the sacrament of penance, while certainly emerging, had not reached its fully articulated form[67] By the thirteenth century penance was a

[67] See John T. McNeill, *A History of the Cure of Souls* (Torchbooks; New York: Harper & Row, 1965), Chap. VI, *passim.*

vital element in the understanding of the justice and mercy of God. Thus purgatory, as the state in which God graciously allowed one to complete his purgation, became increasingly important, and the tendency to view the existence of the soul in the interim after death as an active one was enhanced. Sacramentalism and the new interest in philosophical issues concerning the soul gave rise to an entirely new configuration of eschatological expectations.

Two further elements in the intellectual atmosphere of the high Middle Ages ought also to be cited.[68] First, the explanation of the atonement had been utterly revised. In the patristic and heroic theologies Christ was understood to have rescued man from bondage to Satan. The heroic age had emphasized the descent into hell as the event in which Christ overcame Satan in a titanic cosmic struggle and thereby enabled his followers to elect a new allegiance to himself. But, more logically oriented, the later theologians had found the notion that fallen man belongs by right to Satan distinctly unpalatable. Anselm, in *Cur Deus Homo,* overthrew this notion and substituted for it the explanation that God's justice demanded of man a satisfaction for sin so great that man was utterly unable to pay. Thus God himself had become man to satisfy the demands of his own justice. As a satisfaction of God's demand for justice after the gift of baptism, purgatory assumed a natural place in systems which followed this legalistic view of the atonement.

Second, and concurrent with this development, was the emergence of a new outlook on life—an outlook which placed a far greater emphasis than did the heroic on the individual and the character of his life. The tone of Christian piety was transformed. There was a new introspectiveness and a new desire for knowledge of self. The worth-

[68] See Southern, *Making of the Middle Ages,* Chap. V., *passim.*

iness of the individual to receive salvation and, thus, his scrupulous satisfaction of the demands of God's justice influenced a shift in emphasis from cosmic to individual salvation. The cosmic goal remained, but the judgment of the individual was set at the hour of his death.

The doctrine of purgatory, then, and a new kind of concern for the fate of the individual's soul from death to Doomsday are developments of the high Middle Ages. Until that era, Christians were on the whole satisfied to leave the riddle of the interim unanswered, to focus their hopes on the Last Judgment. The interim had been an open question. But new formulations and new questions led them to close the gap and portray in greater detail the joy, the agony, or the temporary suffering of man's soul after death.

The Reformation: John Calvin

The fourteenth and fifteenth centuries have often been viewed by Protestants as the age during which the abuses inherent in the thirteenth-century social, intellectual, and theological "syntheses" ran rampart. It is true that feudalism was giving way to nationalism. It is apparently true that abuse was rife among some popular preachers and that superstition increased among the unlettered. It is true that the hierarchy tended to fix its views on indulgences as related to purgatory and that, among other things, at the Council of Florence the papacy tried to impose the Western understanding of purgatory and afterlife upon the Greeks.[69] But it is also becoming clear that this view of the character of the period is simplistic. It is unfair to speak of a triumphant synthesis in the thirteenth century; and it is being recognized that lively

[69] Florence, Session VI in Centro di Documentazione-Bologna, ed., *Conciliorum Oecumenicorum Decreta* (Freiburg: Herder & Herder, 1962), pp. 503 line 30 to 504 line 14.

theological debate, which was necessary preparation for the Reformation debate, took place throughout the intervening period. The age was one of violent disagreement —even revolution—within Christendom. As for superstition, it must not be confused with the long tradition of apocryphal, visionary, apocalyptic literature which from earliest times had been popular and had produced some of the greatest Christian imaginative literature: we have seen that tradition in Pope Gregory I; it had its most sublime expression in the *Divine Comedy* of Dante.

Professor Heiko Oberman[70] and others have recently been pointing to a new conclusion about the nature of late medieval theology and showing that it was marked by ongoing debates concerning the doctrines of justification, authority, and the church. It begins to appear that future generations will understand the sixteenth century as the last phase of medieval intellectual history and the seventeenth as the beginning of a new era. It is, at any rate, in this light that I believe we must regard the Reformers' attitude on the problems of purgatory and immortality; and, to establish my point, I should like to look to Calvin in whose writings it is most easily discerned.

John Calvin set out, like Thomas, to write a system or *summa* of Reformed theology in which, dealing with an astounding range of patristic and scholastic literature, he preserved the tradition of dialectic which primarily characterizes medieval theology. The *Institutes of the Christian Religion*[71] is a debate with the tradition, and

[70] *The Harvest of Medieval Theology: Gabriel Biel and Late Medieval Nominalism* (Cambridge: Harvard University Press, 1963) and *Forerunners of the Reformation* (New York: Holt, Rinehart & Winston, 1966).

[71] Ed. J. T. McNeill; trans. F. L. Battles; *LCC*, XX-XXI. See also Heinrich Quistorp, *Calvin's Doctrine of the Last Things*, trans. Harold Knight (London: Lutterworth Press, 1955), for a reliable secondary survey.

especially with the medieval tradition; and therefore it stands as much within the heritage as over against it. Indeed, the elaborations the work underwent as it grew from a comparatively small volume in its first edition of 1536 to its final, massive form in 1559 serve mainly to increase the scope of Calvin's dialogue with his predecessors and contemporaries. The fact that Augustine, after Paul, is Calvin's most compatible theological colleague only ties him to one of the two chief strands of medieval theological thought.

Calvin's treatment of the last things is integrated into Book III of the *Institutes,* rather as Aquinas' is concentrated in Book IV of *Summa Contra Gentiles.* Indeed except for the fact that Calvin relegates his discussion of the Sacraments to Book IV as a subdivision of ecclesiastical polity, there are striking similarities in their treatments. Both consider eschatology under the heading of salvation; having treated the problem of the knowledge of God, they turn to his saving work.

Calvin, after a consideration of the nature of faith, explains that repentance is the manner in which faith works to reorient man's life to God. Repentance is "regeneration, whose sole end is to restore in us the image of God that had been disfigured and all but obliterated through Adam's transgressions." [72] Thus understood, the mortifying and vivifying work of repentance must not be allowed to become an outward work, a chief end of Christian life.[73] For this reason, the whole rationale of sacramental penance is to be attacked. The penitential system serves only to drive man to desperation, because it does not "teach [man] in his humility to give glory to God." [74] This is not to say that confession is not a vital element

[72] *Inst.* III. iii. 8.
[73] *Inst.* III. iii. 17.
[74] *Inst.* III. iv. 3.

of Christian life and ecclesiastical discipline,[75] but that scriptural and primitive practices have been perverted. It is the element of satisfaction in medieval theory which most distresses Calvin, for it is Christ who is the propitiation for the sins of the world.[76]

Thus, the whole system of indulgences and the doctrine of purgatory must be wiped out if the church is to return to a proper understanding of repentance. The notion of a treasury of merits, on which indulgences rest, is blasphemous, for it leaves "Christ only a name [and makes] him another common saintlet who can scarcely be distinguished in the throng." [77] Purgatory falls with indulgences and with the doctrine of satisfaction: "If it is perfectly clear . . . that the blood of Christ is the sole satisfaction for the sins of believers, the sole expiation, the sole purgation, what remains but to say that purgatory is simply a dreadful blasphemy against Christ?" [78] The standard biblical proof texts are shown to refer to the fact that man undergoes tests in life, that he bears the cross.[79] The appeal to the custom of praying for the dead fails, for the "ancients" prayed "in memory of the dead" and "were in doubt concerning the state of the dead." [80]

Thus for Calvin the medieval doctrine of purgatory falls not because of its connection with notions of immortality or of afterlife, but because it is a perversion of the tradition. It rests on a false, sacramentalized understanding of repentance and on the custom of prayers in memory of the dead. It is an abomination because it undercuts the sole ground of salvation: the sacrifice of

[75] *Inst.* III. iv. *passim.* and IV. xii. See also McNeill, *Cure of Souls,* pp. 197-200.

[76] *Inst.* III. iv. 25-27.

[77] *Inst.* III. v. 3.

[78] *Inst.* III. v. 6.

[79] *Inst.* III. v. 7-9.

[80] *Inst.* III. v. 10.

Christ by whose merit alone the elect are redeemed. It is unnecessary and unthinkable.

What, then, of the problem of afterlife before the resurrection of the dead? In the first book of the *Institutes* in its final form there is a lengthy discussion of the immortality of the soul which is presented in connection with the doctrine of creation. It is, for Calvin, "beyond controversy" that "man consists of a soul and a body," that soul (or spirit) is immortal,[81] and that the soul is in man "the proper seat" of the image of God.[82] While scripture teaches the immortality of the soul, the proper realm for discussion of the "faculties" of the soul is philosophy; and, among the philosophers, Plato is commended as a good teacher in this area of learning that is "not only enjoyable, but also profitable." [83] These views are implicit when—after disposing of false views of repentance and of purgatory—Calvin discusses the nature of Christian life in the world. A strong element of what Max Weber called the "worldly asceticism" of Calvin is "meditation on the future life," which is resignation to the fact that life in the world is "nothing but struggle" and concentration on the only hope: "heavenly immortal ity." [84] If there is a purgation, it is this present life. Thus, Calvin concludes, in terms which recall the stoicism of Cicero, the Latin literature of consolation, and the asceticism of the monks, "in comparison with the immortality to come, let us despise this life and long to renounce it." [85] Although there are allusions in this passage to the Last Judgment, the major thrust—reinforced by commendation of the "contempt of death" of the pagan philosophers—

[81] *Inst.* I. xv. 2.
[82] *Inst.* I. xv. 3.
[83] *Inst.* I. xv. 6.
[84] *Inst.* III. ix. 1.
[85] *Inst.* III. ix. 4.

is to emphasize an immediately enjoyed immortality of the soul.[86]

Finally, after outlining his crucial doctrines of justification and election,[87] Calvin treats the resurrection. Bereft of a purgatory and of metaphysics, his analysis is yet very like that of Thomas. It begins with an assertion of the vital importance of the biblical doctrine and an analysis of the nature of the body to be raised; there is a refutation of false speculations about the nature of the glorified body.[88] At this juncture Calvin inserts a passage on the interim existence of the soul in which he attacks those who have taught either that the soul sleeps with the body or takes a new body.[89] It is not proper to "inquire too curiously concerning our souls' intermediate state"—"Abraham's bosom" [Luke 16:22] is designation enough for the faithful—but this much is clear:

> namely, that the souls of the pious, having ended the toil of their warfare, enter into blessed rest, where in glad expectation they await the enjoyment of the promised glory, and so all things are held in suspense until Christ the Redeemer appears. The lot of the reprobate is doubtless the same as that which Jude assigns to the devils: to be held in chains until they are dragged to the punishment appointed for them.[90]

Finally, Calvin describes the resurrection itself, the acceptance of the elect, and the alienation of the reprobate.[91]

In the consideration above of the comparable portion of the *Summa Contra Gentiles,* it was maintained that

[86] *Inst.* III. ix. 5-6.
[87] *Inst.* III. xi-xxiv.
[88] *Inst.* III. xxv. 1-5.
[89] *Inst.* III. xxv. 6, and notes 12-13.
[90] *Inst.* III. xxv. 6.
[91] *Inst.* III. xxv. 7-12.

Thomas leaves the impression of being primarily interested in the interim destiny of the soul, of its individual judgment of which the general judgment is but a reaffirmation. I would argue that, although many mythological details (like the judgment of the separated soul) are missing in Calvin, he, too, betrays a greater concern with immortality than with the resurrection. For both theologians the last state of man only perfects the condition of the elect and reprobate in the interim after death. Combined with the interest elsewhere in the *Institutes* in immortality and with the commendation of the teachings of Plato and other "philosophers" on this score, Calvin's treatment of eschatology betrays a greater concern for the interim blessedness or punishment of the soul than for its reunion with the body at the end of the age.

The Reformer, then, attacked purgatory as a teaching inseparably connected with what he regarded as the most corrupt part of the medieval ecclesiastical system, the sacrament of penance. It was false to say that the temporal church can impose works of satisfaction which would continue after death. And it was dubious to argue by pointing to the ancient custom of praying for the dead that the souls of the dead suffered purgation from which the church might release them by prayer. But, unlike at least some of the Greek Fathers, the Reformer did not see that the concept of the immortality of the soul was not biblical but Greek. Thus his claim to have reverted to the pure teaching of the Bible must be challenged. He stood directly in the tradition of the medieval churchmen who felt that an active interim existence for the soul was part and parcel of the basic Christian eschatology. Although Calvin left the details of the interim vague, as had the Fathers, the tone and emphasis are not those of the patristic period. The emphasis of teaching about eschatology remained in the sixteenth century, as in the Middle Ages, on the interim after death and not on the Last Judgment.

Conclusions

This essay has attempted too much in too little space. The reader will have recognized how much is missing. Each of the authors discussed deserves more attention; others who should have been included have been passed over; had other authors been mentioned, lines of influence could have been more clearly delineated. Whole areas of inquiry have not been touched: Artistic and archaeological remains and the liturgy say, in some ways, more than the theologians. Nevertheless, the author believes this paper is a valid interpretation of the history of a group of seminal ideas. It remains only to summarize our findings.

Primitive or biblical Christianity had no doctrine of the soul or immortality but a vision of an apocalypse in which, the dead having been raised and the living transformed, the eternal reign of God would be inaugurated. As Christianity moved out of its Palestinian and Judaic orbit, however, and as the expectation of the denouement gradually receded, Christian apologists had to come to terms with the Hellenistic world view which accepted immortality of the soul as axiomatic. Thus the issue arose: How would the biblical expectation of a resurrection of the body be reconciled with the Greeks' expectation of an active, disembodied, and purified existence for the soul as soon as it is released from its corporeal prison?

In the Greek Fathers the problem was crucial and its development was turbulent. Yet at the end of the period, Gregory of Nyssa remained aware of the original issues. He accepted immortality: The soul lives after death. But he was cautious about the nature of its existence and careful to tie its destiny to that of the body, with which the soul would be raised at the end of the age. Thus the configuration of the biblical expectations was preserved. Any indication that there was to be a postmortem purgation of sins was carefully reserved by Gregory for a period between the resurrection of the dead and the Last Judgment.

Gregory the Great, a transitional figure at the end of Latin antiquity, tended to give way on this point. In his *Dialogues,* on the evidence of miracles, he posited an active postmortem existence that might include temporary punishments. He was not concerned with the niceties of the philosophical problem of immortality, however; and, since he seems in other writings to have been more concerned with an expectation of the Last Day than with the problem of the interim after death, it is unfair to push too far the implications of the visionary arguments of the *Dialogues.*

In the early Middle Ages there was even less concern with immortality as a philosophical problem, and, although the materials for a doctrine of purgatory were available, the theologians did not have the tools to develop the notion. Not only did methodology stand in their way, however. The heroic mentality, of which Aelfric of Eynsham is exemplary, was more entranced by the New Testament's apocalyptic vision of the denouement of history and the victory of the Lord of lords than concerned with the destiny of the individual soul.

It remained for the theologian of the high Middle Ages to refine the notion of an immortal afterlife, and two elements can be seen as accounting for this phenomenon. First, revived interest in philosophy raised the question of the soul and its immortality, although the conflict of this philosophical tradition with the biblical was no longer apparent. Thus, although such theologians as Aquinas strove to maintain the biblical pattern, a subtle shift of emphasis from the end of the age to the interim before the end can be observed. Second, the doctrine of atonement commonly taught, combined with the development of sacramental penance with its demand of works of satisfaction, required a purgational state and reinforced the tendency to stress the fate of the soul.

The Reformers attacked, and successfully so, the purgatorial teachings of their forbears, but only as a part of their attack on the notions of satisfaction. In Calvin, at least, the immortal soul of the philosophic tradition remained an important concept and, structurally if not ideologically, retained the centrality it had achieved in medieval *summae theologiae.* For all the emphasis they put on the priority of scripture the Reformers followed the Schoolmen in their eschatological emphasis. Thus immortality triumphed over resurrection and became an integral tenet of the two chief branches of Western Christendom.

John Killinger, Associate Professor of Preaching at Vanderbilt Divinity School, maintains that death seen from the perspective of contemporary literature shows the decline of traditional religious concerns. Death is the end; any notion of transcendence or immortality or resurrection is missing. The Enlightenment-inspired optimism over man's goodness and potential happiness gave way, first, to the skepticism of naturalism, then to the pessimism of the existentialists, and finally to the despair of the theater of the absurd.

To counteract this sense of hopelessness, Mr. Killinger maintains that a man must by his commitments fashion a sphere of limited belief. Thereby man is able to arrange the particles of his experience into a meaningful whole.

IV

Death and Transcendence in Contemporary Literature

John Killinger

In Willa Cather's quiet and gracious novel of 1931, *Shadows on the Rock,* the Count de Frontenac, Governor of Canada, lay dying in his château on the high rock of Quebec, with the waters of the St. Lawrence flowing down below his window. We are told that he was ready to die, that indeed he would be glad to die here alone without a troop of expectant relatives around the bed, such as would have been present had he been dying in his homeland and not in Canada.

He would die here, in this room, and his spirit would go before God to be judged. He believed this, because he had been taught it in childhood, and because he knew there was something in himself and in other men that this world did not explain. Even the Indians had to make a story to account for something in their lives that did not come out of their appetites: conceptions of courage, duty, honour. The Indians had these, in their own fashion. These ideas came from some unknown source, and they were not the least part of life.[1]

The spirit of these words now strikes us as being somehow quaint and old-fashioned. To readers accustomed to the coming of death in the novels of Hemingway or Camus or Malamud, there is something idyllic and unreal about such a scene: Men today do not ordinarily die with such classic confidence in religion. Modern protagonists do not necessarily fear death; but neither do they approach it with belief in judgment and the afterlife. Many of them are in fact prepared for annihilation and do not expect to survive the first wave of unconsciousness crossing the seawall of life.

The nineteenth century had of course already faced the fact that the Renaissance left dramatic erosions in the medieval notions of death and the life after death. Schopenhauer's widely read *Die Welt als Wille und Vorstellung,* published in 1819, spoke of death as a kind of Nirvana or void into which life empties itself at the end, releasing the individual from the pain and suffering of human consciousness. The world we experience, said Schopenhauer, is not really objectively the world "out there," but a combination of stimuli out there and our ways of receiving and reacting to the stimuli; and, because the will which shapes the ideas we have of the world is essentially blind, we are forever struggling without accomplishing anything truly ultimate. Death, as the dissolution of the will, means the end of the struggle.

This kind of reasoning permeated the writings of the last century, and may be seen, in various forms, in the works of such well-known authors as Shelley, Matthew Arnold, the Rossettis, Balzac, Zola, Hauptmann, Ibsen,

[1] (New York: Alfred A. Knopf, 1931), p. 247.

Meredith, George Eliot, and Thomas Hardy. Hardy, who was admittedly influenced by Schopenhauer, turned his heavily contrived but beautifully somber novels into maelstroms of chance and desire that chewed up and spat out in broken form the good people who attempted to live by heaven's law but were seldom protected by any beneficent Caretaker. In a more whimsical mood, he wrote the poem "Ah, Are You Digging on My Grave?" in which a woman who has only recently been buried becomes aware of stirrings on her grave and wonders who is there. Is it her lover? No, for he has already married another woman. Is it her nearest of kin? No, for her relatives are practical people, who see no use in planting flowers for those already dead. Is it her enemy? No, for she has decided that the dead woman was not worth her hating. Then who, pray tell, could it be? It is her little dog. Ah, there is nowhere a fidelity to equal that of one's dog. But the pet apologizes for having disturbed the woman:

> "Mistress, I dug upon your grave
> To bury a bone, in case
> I should be hungry near this spot
> When passing on my daily trot.
> I am sorry, but I quite forgot
> It was your resting-place." [2]

Nothing at all survives the final dissolution—not even love. Death sheers off all relationships and imposes an implacable ultimacy on everything.

It would be untrue to say that there is not a large corpus of modern letters in which a more or less traditional religious understanding of life prevails, and in which the Christian in particular is represented as having

[2] From *Collected Poems,* copyright 1925 by The Macmillan Company. Reprinted by permission of his Estate; The Macmillan Company; Macmillan & Co. Ltd., London; and The Macmillan Company of Canada Limited.

an appeal beyond death. The names of Eliot, Auden, Claudel, Mauriac, Silone, Bernanos, Paton, Greene, and Powers, for example, remind us quite forcefully of the continuity of a fairly well-defined religious view of death and the life after death. We would not be true to the facts if we were to suggest that Schopenhauer's ideas have become the modern rule.

But several extremely significant currents of writing in this century have broken with the church's teachings about mortality and afterlife, and have treated man as a mere organism, albeit a highly complicated one, whose life is strictly confined to the limits of his earthly strength and power. The authors within these currents have not, in most cases, abandoned humanistic values, but they have rather strictly disavowed theological ones. For one reason or another they have preferred not to commit themselves to systems of belief predicated upon revelation or traditional understanding.

While it is possible to define several schools of contemporary secular thought about death, there are three which appear at this point to be particularly representative of such thought in the world of twentieth-century letters. The first is that of literary naturalism, which was generally preoccupied with the sheer "physicality" of death, and which formed a convenient bridge from the nineteenth century for a kind of quasi-scientific approach to the fact of human mortality. The second school is that of existential philosophy, whose growth was favored by the conditions of war and postwar life in Europe between 1914 and the middle of the century. And the third school, somewhat less clearly defined, is that of the post-existentialist writers, represented by such figures as Robbe-Grillet and Sarraute and the dramatists of the absurd. An examination of these schools or currents in modern writing will help us to identify and understand what we are speaking of when we talk of contemporary secular attitudes toward death.

Naturalism and Death

No reader of Zola ever forgets the gruesome scenes of the dead and the dying in his novels. With fanatic respect for the cumulative power of small details, Zola turned a camera lens on his subjects and recorded every item about them, however remote or minute. The analogy of the photographer's art is really inadequate to describe his work, for the element of perspective always present in photography is often missing in the naturalistic novel. Details frequently loom into view completely out of proportion to their ordinary significance in relation to the whole. One cannot peremptorily quarrel with the novelist on this account, as it often happens that life is perceived in the mind of the beholder as being much more disorderly and illogical than it is made to appear in popular art or philosophy. Some fragments of experience assume an aspect of horror or reality far greater than that ordinarily attributed to them. This is especially true of experiences related to the approach and presence of death; familiar objects and moments seem without any rational basis to fix the mind's attention with sudden demonic power, inflated with importance far beyond their normal boundaries. Zola and the naturalistic writers who were greatly influenced by him at the *fin de siècle* understood the macabre attraction of the minutiae of death, and exploited this very natural phenomenon in nearly every conceivable way. Ambrose Bierce, an American follower of Zola, wrote a volume of short stories entitled *In the Midst of Life,* every tale of which focused in one way or another on the problem of death, often with a bizarre effect. His treatment of the subject, shocking in its day, frequently made illegitimate use of the Zolaesque technique but it represents the revolt of the naturalistic school against the reserve and reticence of traditional writers in dealing with the topic of death. Under the pen of the naturalist, death became more studiedly realistic; once heroic or melodramatic, it became shriven of any beauty and grandeur it might have possessed; at times it even tended toward the grotesque and the obscene.

In terms of the historical battle between religion and Darwinism in the late nineteenth and early twentieth centuries, naturalism represented a victory for Darwinism. While it could hardly pretend to be scientific in any experimental sense, it was at least methodologically scientific, basing its descriptions of men and events on actual observation and not on feeling or mere conjecture. Flaubert's description of death by poison in *Madame Bovary,* for example, reads almost verbatim like the account of death by the same poison in the *Encyclopaedia Britannica.* The meaning of religious belief in the crises of life is rarely considered, and, if it is noted at all, it is only in terms of the overt reactions of the religious person or persons to the crises.

One of the most outstanding representatives of the naturalistic point of view in this country was Theodore Dreiser, whose publications spanned nearly the entire first half of the century. Grant C. Knight once observed in a conversation that if he had been asked to name the author who had achieved the most panoramic vision of the American scene, he would have replied with Dreiser's name. Dreiser read and enjoyed Balzac, and later discovered and became enamored of Zola, but his own naturalistic style actually derived from his experience as a news reporter and from his avid study of science and scientific philosophy. In his autobiography he recalled with particular vividness the impression which Herbert

Spencer's *Synthetic Philosophy* and Thomas Huxley's *Science and Christian Tradition* had made on him:

> Up to this time, there had been in me a blazing and unchecked desire to get on and the feeling that in doing so we did get somewhere; now in its place was the definite conviction that spiritually one got nowhere, that there was no hereafter, that one lived and had his being because one had to, and that it was of no importance. Of one's ideals, struggles, deprivations, sorrows and joys, it could only be said that they were chemical compulsions, something which for some inexplicable but unimportant reason responded to and resulted from the hope of pleasure and the fear of pain. Man was a mechanism, undevised and uncreated, and a badly and carelessly driven one at that.[3]

Few writers dramatized the concept of "the survival of the fittest" so relentlessly as Dreiser. Over and over again, in nearly every major novel he wrote and in many of the plays and short stories, he hammered away at his point that man is only a poorly devised and carelessly driven mechanism, whose only dimension in a reality transcending earth and time is the one in his own imagination.

The symbol of the struggle for survival was pictured with utmost clarity in *The Financier,* the first volume in his trilogy of novels based on the life and career of the international business tycoon Charles T. Yerkes. Young Frank Cowperwood, the fictional Yerkes, visits a fish market every day to watch a contest to the death between a squid and a lobster in the tank outside the store. Actually it is not much of a contest. The squid has nothing but defensive maneuvers in its favor. The lobster has only to harass his opponent, and wait and watch, until the squid becomes too enervated and undernourished to

[3] Theodore Dreiser, *A Book About Myself* (New York: Premier Books, 1965), p. 380.

resist any longer. When the moment of the lobster's victory finally comes, Frank is ecstatic. He goes home thinking that he has learned life's ultimate lesson. And his subsequent meteoric career as a businessman is based solely on that lesson. Man succeeds in the world in proportion to the degree to which he is realistic and is willing to regard life as a contest.

Dreiser's vision of things was an obvious reaction to his own struggle for existence. As the son of an immigrant textile weaver and peddler, he had an impoverished childhood. His education was ill sustained, and he got on in the world by dint of sheer determination. Somehow he interpreted his father's failure as owing in part to the father's religion and desire for a pious life. The father had to be wrong. The misery of his family was proof enough of that.

As an author Dreiser therefore stood in the vanguard of those demanding for American letters a new secular freedom from the oppression of religious censorship. There were hundreds of thousands of young men in America, he thought, who were like Clyde Griffiths in *An American Tragedy*. They felt violently the contradictions between the evangelical persuasions of their parents and the materialistic culture being spawned by the world's leading industrial society. The only solution for them was to adapt to the new situation in American life and identify religion with the kind of sentimentality so hazardous to the contestant in any struggle.

The greatest factor in religious belief of any kind, said Dreiser, is the fear of death or annihilation.

> For here, now, is one walking with you. He is tense, alert, strong, charming, alive. Then for a very little while, maybe, he is gone from your presence. And then of a sudden that ever appalling word—dead. He is dead. He or she was alive and now is no more. The look, the feel, the voice, the tem-

perament, the dreams, the plans—all gone. No word, no sound. No trace. The effective and valuable and always amazing body that you knew—dissolved. You stand—astounded—but without answer.[4]

Therefore, according to Dreiser, men posited a God with power over mortality—a God who could answer the silence and the coldness and the dissolution.

"As for myself," wrote Dreiser,

I really view myself as an atom in a greater machine, just as is the cell in the greater body of which it finds itself a part. But as for myself being a free and independent mechanism with a separate "spirit" of its own?—Nonsense! Science knows nothing of a soul or spirit. And I personally have never been able to find any trace of one, in me or any other. When I am dead, as I see it, I shall be dissolved into my lesser constituents; I shall then be, if anything, a part of universal force, but merged and gone forever.[5]

It is interesting to note that Dreiser had an experience of religious conversion, albeit a rather mild one, in his last years, and that his final novel *The Bulwark* is a testimony to the glory and inscrutable workings of a Divine Mystery behind the veil of creation. Solon Barnes, the Quaker hero of that novel, takes great consolation on his deathbed from hearing passages from John Woolman's *Journal,* especially passages related to Christ's victory over death for the sinner. There is no sudden turning to professions of belief in life after death, but there is an obvious mood of serenity and trust in the face of what is coming. When Solon's daughter Etta is reproached for weeping after his interment, she replies, "Oh, I am not crying for myself, or for Father—I am crying for *life.*"[6]

[4] Dreiser, "What I Believe," *Forum,* Nov., 1929, pp. 281, 317.
[5] *Ibid.,* p. 320.
[6] Dreiser; *The Bulwark* (Garden City, N. Y.: Doubleday, 1946), p. 337.

This is the new quality which appeared in Dreiser's writing at the end of half a century of being an author.

Naturalism cannot be said to have prevailed as a force in contemporary literature. It is too preoccupied with the obvious, too crude, too relentlessly mechanistic or deterministic for the tastes of most modern readers. The scientism which provided its tone and program has itself been replaced with a more modest and palatable kind of scientific view. But naturalism did make its point about the importance of environment and of the way a person or thing is constituted in nature. And as far as death is concerned there is a natural process of decay and deterioration at work in us that is inadequately answered by glib creedalisms about immortality and the everlastingness of the soul. It was impossible, after the first quarter of this century, to ignore the very serious test put to religious faith by the simple fact that one dies physically —especially after so many died in the trenches of Western Europe during World War I.

Existentialism and Death

Camus once noted that in the years between 1914 and 1945 over 35,000,000 persons were uprooted, displaced, or killed by war. The enormity of the fact overwhelmed him. How did one comprehend it? What did it do to one's way of thinking about life? For one thing, it raised scandalous questions about the nature and existence of God. For another, it dramatized the foolishness of an earlier optimism about the nature and destiny of man. The world had assumed a new and, at times, it seemed, almost total dimension of absurdity.

It was under the pressure of this absurdity wrought upon life by the omnipresent fact of mortality that the existentialist writers, most of them taking their key from

Martin Heidegger's proposition that man is the being who lives facing his own death (*das Sein zum Tode*), developed a philosophy of life literally grounded in the consciousness of death and annihilation.

But it is getting ahead of the story a bit to begin talking immediately of Sartre and Beauvoir and Camus and the other authors who made existentialism almost a household word by the middle of the century. Although theirs was the classic formulation of many of the doctrines of existential philosophy, evidences of existential thinking began to appear in other sources even before them. One writer who is especially useful for illustrative purposes in this regard is Ernest Hemingway, whose writings show an obvious transition from a position influenced by the naturalists to one generally identical with that of the existentialists.

Hemingway's early sketches and short stories, many of which were collected in his first important volume *In Our Time,* demonstrate his affinity for Ambrose Bierce and other sensationalists of death. There are pictures of the dead and the dying all the way through the collection. The world of this fiction was a violent world, a place of grotesqueries and absurdities capable of terminating any man's sanity. In Hemingway's first novel, *The Sun Also Rises,* however, the craziness of war provides only a muted background for the emergence of the Hemingway protagonist, the hero who sees life with a special kind of vision because he has also beheld death at close range. The protagonist is a wounded man—as indeed he will be throughout the remainder of Hemingway's fiction. His wound is part of his essence. He would not be himself without it. As Philip Young says, it is as psychical as it is physical.[7] It tells him what life and the world are about.

[7] *Ernest Hemingway* (New York: Rinehart, 1952).

It says to him in the first place that God is no longer a possibility for man; reluctantly, the hero admits that he cannot pray in the old cathedrals of Europe, that faith does not make a difference in life, that God, if he ever did exist, cannot exist now where atrocities and murder are still fresh in the mind. It reminds the hero, in the second place, of his own mortality; it is the symbol of the death he almost had and of the one that will overtake him someday, perhaps when he least expects it; and because he can never leave his wound behind, he can never get away from the awareness of his own death. Finally, the wound as a *momento mori* becomes a formative principle in the esthetics of life itself; the man faithfully bearing his own death behaves with "grace under pressure" and bestows a kind of artistic form on all his acts.

The notion of the traumatic, reordering force of the death experience was not new with Hemingway, of course. There are analogues for it all through history. Tolstoy's *The Death of Ivan Ilyitch* and Dostoevsky's account of his own near death before a firing squad in *The Idiot* are memorable appearances of this motif in the nineteenth century. But Hemingway made the facing of death his one theme; in one way or another, it polarizes every important story he wrote. When there was no war for him to go to, he went to the bullfights, where for a nominal fee one could sit in the barrera seats and see death every afternoon; or he went hunting in Africa, where the gamesman is both hunter and hunted, risking death while seeking to give it cleanly and fairly. The bullring in his fiction became a sort of theater of death, with the matador as a kind of high priest performing the sacrament for all of the *aficionados* in the stands. Once, in the serialized publication *The Dangerous Summer,* he described a very good bullfighter as moving "as though he were serving Mass in a dream."

This is the sort of thing Amos Wilder is talking about when he speaks of "secular revelation" or "secular transcendence."[8] The old forms of transcendence are gone: Hemingway's characters disavow the possibility of having God any longer, and man is on his own, so to speak. But something happens to man in the presence of death: If he is any good, he is galvanized into something a little more than the sum of his parts; he reacts with courage and dignity in the face of annihilation and nothingness; he becomes the hero.

Both motifs, the disappearance of the old religious transcendence and the appearance of a new, human sort of transcendence, are seen in the frequently anthologized short story "A Clean, Well-Lighted Place." In this story, an old man comes every night to drink at a certain bar. The waiters stand a little in awe of him. He sits alone and drinks without spilling, until finally they must send him out and close the bar. Every night it is the same. He is a lonely old man. The night is a mist waiting to swallow him up out there. One night he will just cease to exist. Emptiness and nothingness are the atmosphere of the story. The ceremonial undertone, emphasizing the old man's holding out almost ritualistically against his final annihilation, is enforced by the parodying of the Hail Mary as "Hail nada, full of nada," and of the Our Father as "Our nada which art in nada, nada be thy name"—nada of course being the Spanish word for nothing. There is no God, and no life after death—but while there is man, there is dignity, and a kind of modified transcendence.

Frederick J. Hoffman characterizes what has happened in modern literature as a transference of eternity from

[8] "Mortality and Contemporary Literature," *The Harvard Theological Review,* LVIII, No. 1 (January, 1965).

a *linear* to a *spatial* state.[9] A similar transference has of course occurred in contemporary theology: It began to be seen in Rudolf Bultmann's existentialist approach to faith and in C. H. Dodd's description of "realized eschatology" in the Fourth Gospel, and is conspicuously evident in the so-called "secular theology" stemming from Bonhoeffer's prison writings and the more recent God-is-dead theologians. Eternal life has become a matter of *quality* and not of quantity. The question is "What kind of life do I have?", not "How long shall I have it?" In this regard Wilder has called our attention to Marianne Moore's poem "What Are Years?", which says that the man who "sees deep and is glad," who "accedes to mortality," is like a tide striking a chasm in the sea so that it rises up on itself and continues its being in the very act of surrender. The poem concludes with the paradoxical statement that "This is mortality,/This is eternity."[10] The linguistic analyst would dispute such a play upon words, but the idea has found resonance in many works of literature in this century. Death becomes the act of compression, packing life with sensibility and meaning.

The German poet Rilke provides another example of this kind of thinking. He was keenly aware of the presence of death in life, growing, as he put it once, like a kernel in fruit.[11] He saw a melancholy beauty in pregnant women, where birth and death are always developing simultaneously beneath folded hands.[12] He knew that men fear death because "it is so utterly inconceivable,

[9] "Grace, Violence, and Self: Death and Modern Literature," *Virginia Quarterly Review,* XXXIV (Summer, 1958), 440; reprinted as first segment of *The Mortal No: Death and the Modern Imagination* (Princeton: Princeton University Press, 1964).

[10] "What Are Years?", from *What Are Years* (New York: The Macmillan Co., 1941), p. 1.

[11] Rainer Maria Rilke, *The Notebooks of Malte Laurids Brigge,* trans. M. D. H. Norton (New York: Capricorn Books, 1958), p. 18.

[12] *Ibid.,* p. 23.

so totally opposed to us, that our brain disintegrates at the point where we strain ourselves to think it."[13] But Rilke was unwilling to regard death as strictly an enemy, as the Grim Reaper of the medieval imagination, for the contemplation of death has too vast and sweet a significance for life itself to leave the matter there. As Siegfried Mandel has seen it, Rilke refigured traditional Christian belief and replaced the God-within (*entheos*) with the death-within (*enmori*).[14] Thus human experience became for him, in a measure, a kind of eternity. We hear something of this sort in *The Notebooks of Malte Laurids Brigge* when Brigge says, "We sense that God is too difficult for us, that we must defer him, in order slowly to do the long work that separates us from him."[15] And we hear it even more explicitly in a letter from Rilke to Franz Xaver Kappus, urging him:

> You are so young, so before all beginning, and I want to beg you, as much as I can, dear sir, to be patient toward all that is unsolved in your heart and to try to love the *questions themselves* like locked rooms and like books that are written in a very foreign tongue. Do not now seek the answers, which cannot be given you because you would not be able to live them. And the point is, to live everything. *Live* the questions now.[16]

The classic formulation of the life-facing-death-and-life-taking-form-in-the-face-of-death philosophy in this century has come, as I suggested earlier, from the writings of the French existentialists, and especially those of Sartre and Camus. The constant motif in their writings has been

[13] *Ibid.*, p. 145.

[14] Siegfried Mandel, *Rainer Maria Rilke: The Poetic Instinct* (Carbondale: Southern Illinois University Press, 1965), p. 62.

[15] Rilke, *The Notebooks of Brigge*, p. 159.

[16] Rainer Maria Rilke, *Letters to a Young Poet*, trans. M. D. H. Norton (New York: W. W. Norton, 1963), pp. 34-35.

the cliff-hanging episode where the character is dramatically apprised of his utter finiteness, of the fact that he lives under the threat of annihilation at all times. The *personae* of their stories and plays have faced death by water, death by fire, death by battle, death by execution, death by illness, death by ostracism, death by almost every conceivable means of finalization. As Sartre put it in his massive philosophical treatise *L'Être et le néant,* nothingness lies coiled like a serpent at the heart of human existence.[17]

Unlike Kierkegaard, who has been called the father of modern existentialism, most of the literary existentialists in our century have been nontheists, insisting that the idea of God, and of what Kierkegaard called "the leap of faith," is basically dishonest and perjures the human imagination in the very act of seeking life. The most passionate, and in some ways cogent, argument of the modern viewpoint is to be found in Camus' *The Myth of Sisyphus,* where the author argues that the absurdity of human life without God is part of the very nature of our existence, which we cannot forswear without forswearing life itself. Camus began this book of essays with the statement that "there is but one truly serious philosophical problem, and that is suicide." [18] He discusses the apparent absurdity of our existence—the sense of imbalance and incongruity a man experiences when he first becomes aware of the difference between illusion and reality in the world of his relationships, so that he feels like an alien or a stranger there, in an irremediable exile. It is the sort of thing one finds dramatized so subtly and

[17] Jean-Paul Sartre, *Being and Nothingness,* trans. Hazel Barnes (New York: Philosophical Library, 1956), p. 21. It is interesting to note the difference of implication in this metaphor from that in Rilke's metaphor of the kernel growing in the fruit; one is negative and threatening, the other positive and assuring.

[18] Albert Camus, *The Myth of Sisyphus,* trans. Justin O'Brien (New York: Vintage Books, 1955), p. 3.

expertly in the novels of Kafka, or in Camus' own novel *The Stranger*: Man is divorced from his own life, and cannot get back to it again from where he is. When a man becomes aware of this absurdity, says Camus, he is tempted to end it all by taking his life. Such indeed was the decision of many when faced by the monstrousness of life during and following the war in Europe. But, says Camus, suppose the absurdity is grasped, and the problematic is seen as being of the essence of human life. Then the man who has seen through to the absurdity should realize that he is truly living, and that suicide is unthinkable. He should not want to escape from the absurd, for "living is keeping the absurd alive." [19] Kierkegaard was wrong, said Camus, for wanting to be cured. By throwing the whole burden of absurdity onto belief in God, he missed the very nature of human existence. One must not want to be cured—one must live with the ailment! [20]

It seems to me that this is an important strain of heroism in modern thought. It is not really atheistic, in the strictest sense. It merely insists that the business of man is to be human and not to want to be God, being immortal. As Camus expressed it is his journal: "Secret of my universe: imagining God without human immortality." [21] The notion declares unconditional war upon the kind of pie-in-the-sky eschatology with which much traditional Christianity may be justly charged; to use the language of traditional Christianity, it is a sin to transfer the weight of human existence from its locus in the created order into the locus of God in the uncreated.

To stay with Camus, there is a vivid example of this existentialist militance in *The Stranger* when, near the

[19] *Ibid.*, p. 40.

[20] *Ibid.*, p. 29.

[21] Camus, *Notebooks 1942-1951*, trans. Justin O'Brien (New York: Alfred A. Knopf, 1965), p. 12.

end of the story, a chaplain comes to see Meursault as he awaits execution. The chaplain is bent upon extracting a confession of belief from the prisoner. In the course of his "examination," he asks Meursault if he has never stared at the stone walls and seen the divine face appear there. Meursault replies that he has often stared at them, trying to make a face appear, but that the face he wanted to see "was a sun-gold face, lit up with desire"—his girl friend's face. The chaplain cannot accept that Meursault loves the earth so much.

> For quite a while he kept his eyes averted. His presence was getting more and more irksome, and I was on the point of telling him to go, and leave me in peace, when all of a sudden he swung round on me, and burst out passionately:
>
> "No! No! I refuse to believe it. I'm sure you've often wished there was an afterlife."
>
> Of course I had, I told him. Everybody has that wish at times. But that had no more importance than wishing to be rich, or to swim very fast, or to have a better-shaped mouth. It was in the same order of things. I was going on in the same vein, when he cut in with a question. How did I picture the life after the grave?
>
> I fairly bawled out at him: "A life in which I can remember this life on earth. That's all I want of it." And in the same breath I told him I'd had enough of his company.[22]

The gravest offense a man can commit against life is not in despairing of it, says *The Myth of Sisyphus,* but in hoping for another life and thus eluding "the implacable grandeur" of this one.[23]

One cannot help juxtaposing this passage from *The Stranger* with the one which was cited from Willa Cather's *Shadows on the Rock.* They are obviously a great distance apart in their understanding of the meaning of

[22] Camus, *The Stranger,* trans. Stuart Gilbert (New York: Vintage Books, 1946), pp. 149-150.

[23] Camus, *The Myth of Sisyphus,* p. 113.

life and death, even though they were written within a decade of each other. This might lead us to suppose that the real watershed in the interpretation of the significance of death was reached sometime in the years between the wars. Miss Cather represented an older generation, and earlier fashions in transcendence. Camus, on the other hand, spoke for the new generation, and for the coming "secular transcendence."

When speaking of Hemingway, I mentioned the close relationship of esthetics and spirituality in the sealed-off universe of the nontheist. It is probably true that there is an inverse relationship between the esthetics and the eschatological expectations of a person; that is, the stronger one's belief in life after death, the less concerned—I almost said the less frantic—he is to savor the fullest possible number and kinds of experiences in this life; and, conversely, the weaker one's faith in the afterlife, the more intent he is upon sensual experiences today.

We know that the early Christians had very little interest in the arts for their esthetic value. Such interest was apparently precluded by a feverish expectation of the end of all things. Aside from a few hymn snatches, there is little evidence of genuine literary composition in the New Testament writings—certainly nothing like the literary precedent found in the prophetic books of the Old Testament. And Wladimir Weidlé has observed that the earliest pictorial designs in the Christian community, from the walls of the catacombs and the toolings on the sarcophagi of the saints, were merely crude symbolic imitations of certain actions dramatizing the story of redemption.[24] There was no attempt, as Camus might put it, to make the world clearer through art;[25] things were clear enough in their minds.

[24] Wladimir Weidlé, *The Baptism of Art* (London: Camelot Press, n.d.), p. 9.

[25] Camus, *Notebooks 1942-1951*, p. 59.

Contemporary writings, on the other hand, soon betray the modern author's preference for the world that is concrete and attainable. As Hoffman says, our literature plainly emphasizes "the spatial qualities of life" (vis-à-vis the linear or eternal); it is "concerned with the density of objects, with their texture, with the specific values residing in experiences." [26] Writers are commonly in agreement with the testimony of Wallace Stevens when he says, in "Esthétique du Mal,"

> The greatest poverty is not to live
> In a physical world.[27]

It is the physical, the tangible, the sensible, that is most immediately dependable in human experience; anything else is tentative and illusory. Death, in such a schema, "turns us toward life (if it is a wall and not a door) and forces us to admire or cherish it (even though we despair of it as well), to begrudge the passing of time (which is signified by changes occurring in objects) and eventually to despair of conclusions." [28]

Post-Existentialism and Death

We did not suppose, twenty years ago, that it would be possible to go beyond existentialism in the achievement of a world view for the twentieth century. We had not reckoned with the fact of what Lewis Mumford in *The City in History* and Marshall McLuhan in *Understanding Media* have called "implosion"—the building up, once external limits have been reached, of internal pressures. We did not foresee the collapse of the old categories of time and space and meaning into the rubbish heap of

[26] Hoffman, "Grace, Violence, and Self," p. 440.
[27] From *Transport to Summer* (New York: Alfred A. Knopf, 1942).
[28] Hoffman, "Grace, Violence, and Self," p. 440.

total absurdity no longer organizable by human experience. Yet that is precisely the direction in which a significant corpus of recent writings has moved. In the novels and plays of the so-called post-existentialists, among whom are numbered such figures as Nathalie Sarraute, Alain Robbe-Grillet, and Samuel Beckett, the disorderliness of the universe is no longer something with which human beings cope, but something which they merely accept and experience. Time and death no longer stand over against life as its enemies, challenging it and giving it shape, but have become internalized in it to such a degree that they can no longer be regarded as catalytic.

What has happened in this avant-garde writing is that man is no longer regarded as a center of intelligence with a mandate for making sense of the impressions he receives from the world around him. Personality has been dissolved into environment. Beckett gives the clue to this in his famous essay on Proust when he says, "At the best, all that is realised in Time . . . , whether in Art or Life, can only be possessed successively, by a series of partial annexations—and never integrally and at once."[29] In other words, man is not the great unifier we thought he was; he exerts no force whatever on the disparate occurrences of life to bring them into meaningful relationship; he merely experiences things mechanically and serially, and possesses a degree of consciousness only slightly higher than that of other forms of life. Philosophy, in such a view, is folly.

This sentence from Beckett's *Proust* would serve as a fitting superscription for his one-act play *Krapp's Last Tape,* for the play graphically depicts the statement's meaning. Krapp, a myopic, unshaven old man, sits alone on stage with a tape recorder, listening to his own voice from years past recording his impressions and opinions

[29] Samuel Beckett, *Proust* (New York: Grove Press, n.d.), p. 7.

of life. It is obvious, from the fact that he is heard laughing on the tape at previously recorded material, that he has played the tape through the years, allowing his own reactions to be set down along with the original versions. Once he doesn't even recognize a word he used on an earlier occasion. It is the word "viduity." "Viduity," he murmurs; "viduity—viduity." He stumbles offstage and comes back with a large dictionary, in which he proceeds to look up the word. Most of the recording is now quite boring to him, some of it even embarrassingly so. Whenever he gets to a section of the tape where the voice is about to discourse upon some serious point of philosophy from his earlier thinking, he quickly speeds the tape ahead. The one thing he appears to be pleased with on the entire tape is something about an episode with a girl in a canoe—that alone has retained its meaning for him. Several times he switches the tape back to that account. It is the only real thing in his life. At the end of the play he has drunk too much again, and he sits staring into his hands as the end of the tape flaps idly around on the machine.

Is this what Hoffman meant when he said that concentration upon the spatial dimensions of life forces us to begin by admiring or cherishing life, then to begrudge the passing of time, and eventually to despair of conclusions? It seems, at least, to be the pattern in Krapp's life.

It is in Beckett and other post-existentialists that we see most clearly where the tenets of the French existentialists, pressed to their logical conclusions, must finally lead. The absurd, of which Camus wrote so descriptively in *The Myth of Sisyphus,* when seized relentlessly and maintained even when the dramatic atmosphere of wartime has been discharged, eventuates in a world where men are no longer capable of taking thought and acting in behalf of the world's redemption, much less their own. What is human becomes almost nonidentifiable. It is elided into the landscape, and ceases to be. As Prof. Wylie Sypher has put it, "Our *situation*—the field in which our experiences happen to us, if they be our experiences at all —seems to be more actual than the self on which these experiences are imposed." [30]

Sypher speaks of a kind of entropy among human beings analogous to entropy in the physical world, entropy being the tendency of an orderly universe to become increasingly random and at last completely disorderly, so that it cannot possibly continue to exist.[31] He sees the products of the anti-novelists and anti-playwrights and anti-painters of our time as evidences of an entropic neurosis in the human soul—a neurosis that is virtually incurable.

The characters in the plays which constitute the Theater of the Absurd are the most abject serfs in the history of the world. The biblical notion of the human being as one who exercises creative dominance over the other orders of life and existence is in these plays completely upended: man is at the mercy of virtually everything in the world. Beckett's characters are often clowns and buffoons who cannot even keep their hats from falling off or their trousers from festooning about their ankles. As Josephine Jacobsen and William Mueller have expressed it, they are like the poor circus comic who hangs from the tail of a galloping horse, unable to get up or to get down, but just forced to hang on.[32] Ionesco's people are crowded off the stage by proliferating objects—mushrooms, eggs, furniture, growing corpses—and easily merge into the animal world, becoming chickens or rhinoceroses.

[30] *Loss of the Self in Modern Literature and Art* (New York: Vintage Books, 1964), p. 67.

[31] *Ibid.*, p. 73.

[32] *The Testament of Samuel Beckett* (New York: Hill and Wang, 1964), p. 13.

The absurd has become absurd with a vengeance, and man is helpless to turn things right side up again.

Even death lies beyond his power in a new and frightening way. He is no longer able even to take life as he once was. Didi and Gogo, for example, the two tramps in Beckett's *Waiting for Godot,* cannot manage to get out of their dreary world by committing suicide. They try it, but the "rope" they have improvised from a belt breaks in the attempt. They are made to stick it out, even though all taste for doing so is gone. Time drags on and on with nothing to end it. The characters in *Endgame* are old and vile and decrepit, because they are overtaken by death but cannot die. Three of the four must have help not only to eat but to defecate. Apparently the landscape outside their house has been reduced to nothingness by something like an atomic holocaust; when Hamm asks Clov what he sees when he looks through the single aperture high above the stage, Clov replies that everything is "corpsed." They are the last pieces in the game—and they are not enough to end it. They are condemned to go on waiting and wanting to die. The play concludes as it began, with the invalid Hamm sitting in his wheelchair, his face covered with a bloody handkerchief. Perhaps it will begin all over again, the way Ionesco's *The Bald Soprano* is supposed to.[33] A parting word is aimed at the audience before Hamm goes under the handkerchief. He pauses, with the handkerchief spread out in front of him, and says, "You . . . remain." It is like the last word of Genet's *The Balcony,* where the audience, which has just been through an evening of tricks and illusions, is reminded that it goes home to its own illusions. "You . . . remain." Yes, and how remain? Like Hamm and Clov, and Nagg and Nell, the two

[33] The final stage instructions of *The Bald Soprano* call for the two couples in the play, the Smiths and the Martins, to exchange places, and for the play to begin again with the Martins saying exactly the same lines which the Smiths said at the beginning of the first playing.

old characters who reside in dustbins? Powerless to act in a world of utterly futile relationships? Is that the endgame the world has come to?

We see well enough what has happened. The transcendence that secularity had borrowed from earlier understandings of death and converted to its own minor key has now been dissipated entirely. There remains no sense of mystery at all, either for life or for the actual moment of death. Sensibility has played out, has become effete, and life itself is colorless as Sheol.

Is this man's future response to death? Are these authors far-seeing, prophetic figures, heralding a kind of zero age when even suicide is out of the question because man has become a mere scholarly vegetable? Is the blighting wind which has stricken these playwrights of the avant-garde only the forward edge of a chilling cloud about to settle on humanity as a whole? The debacle of faith among serious writers, and the movement of thought through naturalism and existentialist humanism to the present literature of nihilism, might indicate as much. The slightest glint of recognition, when one reads Robbe-Grillet or witnesses a production of Beckett, is sufficient to strike fear to the heart for what we may be already in the process of becoming.

What stance shall we take for facing this possibility? We cannot return to the age of the Count de Frontenac. It is not that simple a matter. We are where we are now, and we cannot forget what we have been through to get here. We cannot unlearn the responses born of a new kind of encounter with the secular, even if some would wish to. We can only act from where we are, as who we are. It is probably true, as Amos N. Wilder has said:

> If we are to have any transcendence today, even Christian, it must be in and through the secular. If we are to have any mystery it must be the lay mystery. If we are to find Grace

it is to be found in the world and not overhead. The sublime firmament of overhead reality that provided a spiritual home for the souls of men until the eighteenth century has collapsed.[34]

There is no turning back to the resolute structures of medieval theology. If the early Christians were right, if they were not grievously mistaken about the whole enterprise of death and transcendence, then we must have taken a wrong turn in the road somewhere. We must hear them again, and this time in language understandable to modern ears.

"Who shall deliver us from this body of death?" The words are St. Paul's in the book of Romans, but they are not unmodern at all. We can understand the question. It haunts us all. It lies, to appropriate Rilke's phrase, like a kernel in the fruit of contemporary writing, whatever the ostensible subject. We would like to be delivered from death. How shall we be saved?

But there, when we ask that question, we know that we have already taken a wrong turn. It is a misleading question. We have asked it often enough. The whole mission-structure of the church has been designed to coax it from the throats of men through the centuries. But we have always been misled by it because we put the emphasis in the wrong place. "Who shall deliver us?" We have ordinarily supposed that the speaker was interested in the delivery, when in fact he was really concerned with the *who*. "*Who* shall deliver us?" That is what the Christian gospel is about: It is about the Who who does the delivering, not about the actual business of deliverance; given who He is, the deliverance is bound to follow.

It seems rather clear from any careful examination of the New Testament today that there were two distinct

[34] "Art and Theological Meaning," *The Union Seminary Quarterly Review,* XVIII (November, 1962), 39.

strata of teaching about the Resurrection in earliest Christianity. At the first stratum, nearest the event itself, there was an apocalyptic excitement: As the firstfruits of the dead, Christ was a sign of the beginning of the end; God's sovereignty was being realized in creation. At the second stratum, the excitement had cooled somewhat, and various teachings about the resurrection of the dead began to be examined and argued about. The people of Corinth, for example, apparently thought that they had already passed into the resurrection state, so that it would not be necessary for them to die, and Paul tried to correct this understanding and help them to see that the mortal body must indeed die before putting on immortality.

The church of our time obviously occupies yet another level, a third stratum, characterized by a general confusion of belief heavily inclined toward agnosticism, or not knowing whether we believe anything at all. There are many in the church who do believe somewhat as the Count de Frontenac did, and who therefore should be placed somewhere in the second stratum, perhaps nearer the top of it, but there are numerous others who are either very close to or squarely within the secular positions we have been describing.

It should be rather obvious, I think, that the only viable answer for us is to return not to the second stratum, with its emphasis on how, when, and where the resurrection of the dead will occur, but to the first stratum, with its radiant concern for the Resurrection of Christ as the inauguration of a new age. Somehow we must get back into the state of incandescence where what matters is God and his Christ and the Kingdom, and not whether we shall sleep for an aeon or be raised in an instant or recognize the dead or anything else. We must reassign to mystery and to faith the things that belong to mystery and faith, and concentrate upon what it means to our lives here and now that we are in the age of the Christ.

Then we will realize, for one thing, that we are not so far from contemporary secular opinion about death as we had perhaps appeared to be, because we will not be so divided from secular opinion about the importance of life. We will see that being human, with a vengeance even, is not a particularly sub-Christian state to aim at. Genuine biblical faith is much earthier than some of us have ever imagined. At its very core is the notion of possessing the earth. The Hebrews were a worldly people, in the best sense, and Christ was no exception. The gospels are full of talk about a Kingdom of God, but always it is this world that is at the center of such talk. It was only later, when the Kingdom seemed impossible of realization in this world, that it began to be spiritualized, or, if you please, *spirited away* from the earthly setting. It is time we returned to the more basic meaning of faith, as a relationship between God and people who have daily business to transact. It is entirely possible that Camus, with his wonderful appreciation for life in the world, has something to teach us about our own lives as Christians.

Now suppose we are able to do what I have suggested, centering upon the reign of Christ and seeking the locus of our true existence as human beings in this world and not beyond it. What effect of this may we then expect to discern in the shape of our living and in our witness to the secular community? I phrase it this way because I think the two must be answered together.

When we become excited about God's inaugurating a new age and calling us to discipleship in it, so that our minds and hearts are upon God and his work in the world, not upon ourselves and some haven of rest in yet another world, then we will address the disjointed segments of time and human experience from such a vantage point as will unify them and cure their discreetness. We will find ourselves confronting life with the mystery which binds up our secular diversity and provides us with a context for meaningful freedom of action. We will not be able, in honesty, to claim absoluteness for such a view in the life of every man, for our experience has served as much as anything to remind us of the essential tentativeness of any structure the mind imposes upon the world. But we can again testify with enthusiasm to the peculiar vision of reality opened to us by the understanding that God was in Christ dealing with the things that matter.

This, as we have seen, is the problem with secularity, that it lacks a centralizing point of view, so that it must end at last in the most ridiculous kind of absurdity. The force in modern writing is usually centrifugal, spinning us away from any large and helpful images of humanity. Authors seem to have lost the ability of composing centripetally, so that we are brought back to some kind of inner unity as a basis for action. Nathan A. Scott has complained in a recent book entitled *The Broken Center* that artists have lost their contact with any significant body of belief that might facilitate the polarization of our diffused consciousness today. "Without something at least analogous to the sacramental vision of reality that is created for Christianity by its doctrine of Creation and of the Incarnation," he says,

> the likelihood is that, when faced by entangled and unpromising circumstances of life, the writer may be able to manage nothing better than a querulous retreat into the privacies of the isolate self: the kind of querulousness that is expressed by James Baldwin when he says that "there is no structure in American life today and there are no human beings," or that John Cheever, the author of *The Wapshot Chronicle,* expresses when he complains that "life in the United States . . . is hell." [35]

Secularity is really a kind of nonecclesiastical protestantism. It has no structure of its own. And when it has suc-

[35] (New Haven: Yale University Press, 1966), pp. 230-31.

ceeded in destroying the structures of other world views, it can only terminate in "the isolate self," which, from Melville to Hemingway to Camus and Beckett and Malamud, is surely the most distinctive myth of our time.

Death, in the secular view, can only be regarded as having a kind of vulgarity, for it is merely another indignity among many which the isolated self has suffered during its existence, and of a quality insufficient to distinguish it from all the others. There is of course more of a finality about it than about the other indignities, but the finality of all the others has been such as to cause the self to despair of life anyway. Death loses even its qualified, secular transcendence. Everything is, to employ the word used in Beckett's *Endgame* to describe the total landscape around us, "corpsed." We have arrived at the death of the self in the very midst of life, so that life itself is little more than death.

The Christian person should be capable of injecting into this chaos of particled existence a center of limited belief—not a timetable or cosmological chart, mind you, but a center of *limited* belief—which would enable men to rediscover their humanity. The faith originally had this character about it, which is essentially that of taking an oath or pledging undying commitment to the Christ of God, who, far from making everything plain, had only brought the mystery of God nearer and made it more manifest in human history. The word "sacrament," you may recall, which was the word the Latin Church used to designate the specific acts by which Christians identified themselves with the Christ-event, was the word for *oath,* in both the legal and the military sense. Baptism, as the initiatory oath of the Christian, was his official act of commitment to the new spirit in his life. Not everything was clear to the person committing himself. There was much that remained to be worked out. But the important thing was his acceptance of a stance, of a position from which a world view could be accomplished.

This, I suggest, is still the authentic stance of the Christian in an increasingly secularized world. Once this center of limited belief is chosen and occupied, it begins to polarize the free-floating bits of knowledge and belief which before had simply overwhelmed the person, and to enable him to engage in the formation of ethical decisions and the execution of those decisions in determinate action. Only then does humanity really fulfill itself in the person; until then it has lain dormant in creation, a mere potentiality waiting to be born.

William May, Professor and Chairman of the Department for the Study of Religion at Indiana University, argues that the loss of transcendence in death has led to an emphasis on life and a denial of death. Yet, excesses in the attempts to avoid and deny death actually affirm its mystery and sacral power. Christian faith, shorn of its other-worldly speculations, enables men to face death and its threat to human existence. Moreover, confidence in God frees man to live in this world and to serve his fellows.

V

The Sacral Power of Death in Contemporary Experience

William May

Theological reflection on the subject of death usually has an air of unreality because it has no contact with death as it is actually experienced by men in its sacral power. This is especially true of theology in an age that likes to think of itself as secular without remainder. Presumably there are no religious realities left to contend with. Men are relatively self-sufficient and autonomous, blessedly free of the incubus of religion in all its forms. The gospel has only to address itself to a world-come-of-age, commanded and populated by secular men.

Theologians of the secular persuasion may be right when they attempt to free the gospel from its earlier, uncritical ties with religion, but they are wrong when they assume that religion is dead. While religions, in the sense of official historical traditions, may indeed have entered a period of decline, the experience of the sacred is still very much with us. Nowhere is this more apparent than in the contemporary experience of death. This essay therefore will venture out against the stream of theology in the 1960's by exploring, at the very outset, the sacral power of death in contemporary life. Only then will it proceed to the theological interpretation of this religious reality and finally to the practical import of both analyses for the behavior of the church toward the dying.

Death in Its Religious Reality

Pastors rarely approach the gravely ill without noticing immediately the evasions and the brave lies that encircle the dying. Doctors often refuse to inform the patient of his true condition in the case of a terminal illness. Needless to say, most families cooperate readily with the doctor and his instructions.

A heavy silence surrounds death. I believe that this painful reticence has a source more profound than our childlike submission to the advice of a doctor. For the instructions of a doctor would not hold for a minute if men felt they had recourse in their words and actions against death. In fact, where else except from the dying has the doctor himself learned his reticence? He has seen too many men avoid asking the big question about their illness. Or he has heard them ask the question without being certain that they really wanted an answer.

Despite some charges to the contrary (which I will discuss later), I do not think of the doctor as the villain of the piece in this conspiracy of silence. Silence has its origin in the awesomeness of death itself. Just as the Jew, out of respect for the awesomeness of God, would not pronounce the name of Jahweh, so we find it difficult to bring the word *death* to our lips in the presence of its power. This is so because we are at a loss as to how to proceed on the far side of this word. Our philosophies and our moralities desert us. They retreat and leave us wordless. Their rhetoric, which seemed so suitable on other occasions, suddenly loses its power, and we may well wonder whether our words themselves are not caught up in a massive, verbose, uneasy flight from death, while we are left with nothing to say, except to "say it with flowers."

Without provision against death, our rituals and ceremonies are characterized by a powerful flight from its presence. This is a phenomenon that has already received savage treatment at the hands of satirists in the Anglo-Saxon world: Aldous Huxley, *After Many a Summer;* Muriel Spark, *Memento Mori;* Evelyn Waugh, *The Loved One;* and most recently, Jessica Mitford, *The American Way of Death.* Interestingly enough, all are English writers, and three of the four focus on the American attitude toward death. They are wrong, however, when they suggest that Americans believe in a triumph of technology over death by virtue of which they reduce death to the incidental or the unreal. Rites are evasive not because Americans react to death as trivial or incidental but because they feel an inner sense of bankruptcy before it. The attempts at evasion and concealment are pathetic rather than casual. The doctor's substitute diagnoses and vague replies and the undertaker's allusions to the "loved one" or to the "beautiful memory picture" reflect a culture in which men sense their own poverty before this event.

Men evade death because they recognize in the event an immensity that towers above their resources for handling it. In effect, death (or the reality that brings it) is recognized as some sort of sacred power that confounds the efforts of man to master it. James Joyce uses a particularly gloomy expression to convey this sense of death as sacred power in *Ulysses*—"*Dio Boia*"—the "Hangman God." Joyce happens to import the phrase into English literature from the Italian, but the reality of which he speaks crosses national boundaries—death recognized as the power before which all human efforts are ineffectual, longings to no avail; death admitted as the reality that may have inspired philosophers to meditate but brings these meditations to their conclusion, that may have crowned the hero or martyr with renown but eventually drags into oblivion even those whom it has lifted up; death honored as the power that unravels every human community, taking those fervent little intersections of human want—husband and wife, lovers, father and son—and eventually forcing all these intersecting lines to honor its presence with the rigid parallels of the graveyard.

So understood, death is not merely a biological incident that ends human life. It reaches into the course of life, gripping the human heart with love, fear, hope, worry, and flight, long before the end itself is reached. Whenever the concert is over, the meal is digested, or the career turns barren in one's hands, a man experiences the quiet, disturbing fall from life to death. Because death is more than the incident of biological demise, it is difficult to do justice to its scope without falling into parody of the psalmist's sense of the omnipresence of God. For the power that brings death besets men on every side. It drives men from behind as they flee into frenetic activities—the pursuit of career, virtuosity, or the display of some glory—hoping to escape their metaphysical solitude by outlining themselves against a dark background. It confronts men frontally as they mount their battles against their threatening enemies, whether that enemy happens to be soldier, competition, or sibling. It lies in wait and ambushes from the side—the young, the high-minded, and the frivolous—with the unexpectedness of a clipping at a football game. It stirs beneath human life in the profoundest of pleasures, as it touches with melancholy the marriage bed or as it ladens with guilt the relations between the generations. And at night, it settles down from above and breathes gently within men who are weary with all other forms of fleeing, fighting, and sidestepping death and who long now for sleep and the surcease of care.

If, in some such fashion, men experience death as a religious reality, then one might expect the language of religion to describe most appropriately man's primordial attitude toward the onslaught of the event. This is in fact the language that Joyce chooses in the opening passage of the *Dubliners.* A young boy—friend to a dying priest—muses on the word "paralysis," and offers therein a fine description of religious awe. " 'Paralysis' . . . it sounded to me like the name of some maleficent and sinful being. It filled me with fear and yet I longed to be near it and to look upon its deadly work." [1] Joyce's description captures beautifully that ambivalence of spirit that the phenomenologists of religion have recognized in all religious feeling and which they have variously termed: "awe," "dread," "astonishment," "wonder," or "amazement." A peculiar ambivalence, a strange vibration, a sort of motionless motion obtains in the religious man, an attentiveness somewhat akin to the attention that a hummingbird gives to a flower, when its wings beat furiously and yet it hovers at the spot. This is the way men relate to death in its dreadful reality.

The analysis has uncovered so far two basic responses to the event of death in contemporary culture: concealment and obsession. Only the category of the sacred explains their connection. Men are tempted to conceal death or to hold themselves enthralled before it only because they recognize death as an overmastering power before which all other responses are unavailing.

Geoffrey Gorer, the English sociologist, in his essay "The Pornography of Death," [2] brings together the phenomena of obsession and concealment by appeal to the religious category of *taboo*. On the one hand, death is a taboo sub-

[1] James Joyce, *The Dubliners* (New York: The Modern Library), p. 7.

[2] Reprinted as an appendix in his book, *Death, Grief, and Mourning* (Garden City, N. Y.: Doubleday & Co., 1965).

ject, the unmentionable event; on the other hand, death (and violence) is an obsession at every level of our culture. Gorer finds the solution to this oddity in a comparison with the Victorian attitude toward sex. A prudish culture in which personal sexual life is a taboo subject is also likely to develop simultaneously a pornographic obsession with sex. In contemporary culture, argues Gorer, the personal event of death has replaced sex as a taboo subject: Death has replaced copulation and birth as the unmentionable. At the same time, an obsession with violence has dominated our age. Concealment and obsession go together in the same culture.

The chief feature of pornography, of course, is an obsession with the sex-act abstracted from its normal human emotion which is love; the pornography of death therefore is an obsession with death abstracted from its natural human emotion which is grief. For the sake of his thesis Gorer might be altogether satisfied with the development of the James Bond movie. When the sexual act is abstracted from love it becomes somewhat repetitive and dull; therefore, pornographic literature rescues its readers from boredom by filling the fantasy with the sex-act performed in an endless variety of ways, each more elaborate or intense than the last. Interest is removed altogether from love to the technology of the act itself. Correspondingly, when death is abstracted from grief the same restless elaboration of technology occurs. It is difficult to maintain interest in the subject of death unless violence is done in a variety of ways. Thus technicians in violence have to equip James Bond with the ultimate in a death-dealing car that surpasses with exquisite ingenuity the death-dealing instruments that General Motors has already put on the road. And the makers of the movie *Thunderball* bring both lines of pornography to their absurd conclusion, inasmuch as lovemaking and murdering are somehow managed underwater.

The fascination with death in pornography and the concealment of death in the liturgies of polite society are both rooted in religious feeling. It is a religious enthrallment with death that eventuates in the strategies of helpless evasion in the homelike atmosphere of the funeral parlor and in the pornographic experimentations of the entertainment industry.

The traditional belief in the immortality of the soul does not seem to provide men with a sense of resource against the threat of death. In this respect the consciousness of the twentieth century has undergone a radical break with the recent Western past. Christian theologians from the Church Fathers through the Reformers of the sixteenth century held to a doctrine of the immortality of the soul. This doctrine was continued in an altered form by many theologians and philosophers (particularly those of idealist persuasion) in the eighteenth through the late nineteenth century. But today the situation has changed. Naturalists among the philosophers dismiss the doctrine of the immortality of the soul as just so much idealistic vaporing. Psychoanalysts interpret the longing for immortality as a perpetuation of infantile desires. Social critics have condemned the doctrine for its encouragement of an attitude of otherworldly indifference to social ills. Existentialists have opposed the doctrine because it distracts a man from his most essential task as an authentic human being: the appropriation of his own finitude and mortality. Even modern Biblical scholars have rejected the doctrine as they usually distinguish today between the primitive Christian hope of the resurrection of the body and the Hellenic-idealist doctrine of the immortality of the soul.

This is not to say that a belief in the immortality of the soul has had no hold upon modern men. The idealist tradition has had its defenders in Germany, England, America, and France. Dualists of the stripe of Unamuno have tried to reckon with the heart's longing for eternal life, along with the mind's crushing sense of death. Even existentialists, such as Marcel, have made appeal to the existence of a beloved community that transcends the empirical order of death. Finally, and somewhat less grandly, the ordinary man likes to think of himself as immortal, or at least, invulnerable. Tolstoy has observed [3] that the passion for finding out the "cause" of someone else's death is a way of satisfying oneself that the other fellow died accidentally or fortuitously by virtue of special circumstances affecting him (but not me). This shabby impulse, however, is hardly a serious expression of the traditional confidence in the immortality of the soul. Rather it is the hedonist's inveterate bargaining for a little more time in which to dawdle over just one more last cigarette.

Despite traces of contemporary belief in the immortality of the soul, the minister is ill advised to rely on it in the presence of death. Nowhere is the bankruptcy of the doctrine so evident as in a certain type of Protestant funeral service in which the minister strains to give the impression that the person "lives on" in the trappings of the service itself. The minister disastrously seeks to "personalize" the service, not by simple reference to the name and biography of the deceased, but by including his alleged favorite hymns, poems, prayers, and songs. We are supposed to have the impression that we are in the presence of a kind of *aurora borealis* of the dead man's personality, shimmering miraculously in the darkest hour of grief. Instead, however, the minister gives the sad impression that he has a repertory of three or four such "personalized" serv-

[3] Leo Tolstoy, *The Death of Ivan Ilyitch* (New York: Boni and Liveright), p. 8. See also Sigmund Freud, "Thoughts for the Times on War and Death," Collected Papers, Vol. IV, 1915, trans. Joan Riviere (London: The Hogarth Press, 1925), p. 305.

ices, designed like Sears Roebuck seat covers to fit any and all makes and models of cars. Its ill-fitting imposition upon the dead man only reminds us ever so forceably and comfortlessly that he is, indeed, dead.

Theological Reflection on Death

The attempt to cover up death in the funeral service is an unmitigated disaster for the church, preceded and prepared for by the church's failure to reckon with death in its own preaching and pastoral life. Many persons have said that they have never heard their minister take up frontally in a sermon the question of their own dying. This state of affairs, once again, is not entirely the fault of the professional. People tend to expect from the church service an hour's relief from the demons that plague them in the course of the week. In this atmosphere sermons on death would seem intrusive and unsettling. Better to avoid them and protect this hour from everything that jangles the nerves—even though the service comes to an end and the demons must be faced once again on Monday, fully intact, unexorcized, and screeching. The melancholic effect of this arrangement is that the church offers a temporary sanctuary, a momentary respite, from one's secret apprehensions about death, but inevitably they take over once again, without so much as a candid word of comfort intervening.

To preach about death is absolutely essential if Christians are to preach with joy. Otherwise they speak with the profound melancholy of men who have separated the church from the graveyard. They make the practical assumption that there are two Lords. First, there is the Lord of the Sabbath, the God who presides over the affairs of cheerful Philistines while they are still thriving and in good health. Then there is a second Lord, a Dark Power about whom one never speaks, the Lord of highway wrecks, hospitals, and graveyards who handles everything in the end. Under these circumstances, there can be no doubt as to which of the two Lords is the more commanding power. The death-bringer God already encroaches upon the sanctuary itself, inasmuch as people gathered there are so unsettled as to refuse to hear of his name.

The Christian faith, however, does not speak of two parallel Lords. The Lord of the church is not ruler of a surface kingdom. His dominion is nothing if it does not go at least six feet deep. The church affirms the one Lord who went down into the grave, fought a battle with the power of death, and by his own death brought death to an end. For this reason the church must be unafraid to speak of death. It is compelled to speak of death as the servant of Jesus Christ, the Crucified and Risen Savior, who has freed men from the power of the Unmentionable One.

But even when the church speaks about the subject, does the church evade it? Is theological reflection on the subject of death itself a method of circumlocution? Existentialism, after all, from Kierkegaard to Heidegger, has made men sensitive to the way in which objective discourse on the subject of death may be a way of escaping from one's own personal destiny as a creature who dies. Camus has condemned Christian thought on the subject of death for placing, in effect, theological screens before the eyes of the condemned.[4] Apparently the Christian hope of eternal life only serves to divert attention away from the stark conditions of life in the flesh. "The order of the world is shaped by death," says one of the heroes of *The Plague*.[5]

At the outset, then, by way of reply, it must be argued that Christian reflection, far from screening death from

[4] "In Italian museums are sometimes found little painted screens that the priest used to hold in front of the face of condemned men to hide the scaffold from them." Albert Camus, *The Myth of Sisyphus and Other Essays*.

[5] Albert Camus, *The Plague*, trans. Stewart Gilbert (London: Hamish Hamilton, 1948), p. 123.

view actually tears away the screens and forces men to look at death and to look toward their own dying. This is the unavoidable focus of a faith that has to reckon with the factual dying of its Savior. Even if men wanted to avoid death, they cannot if they look toward such a savior. In fact, he exposes the flimsiness of the partitions that men raise in order not to have to consider death. The purpose of this comment is not to outdo the existentialist in pessimism but to lay the only sure basis for Christian hope, a hope that is not based on screens, mirrors, or sentiment. It is based on the good news that men do not have to go beyond Jesus for a knowledge of death in its fullest scope; death is not an additional realm alongside of Jesus terrorizing men from the side.

Death in Jesus. In the light of Jesus Christ it is possible to explore the scope of death as it threatens a man in his three most fundamental identities as a human being. Death threatens a man's identity with his flesh, with his community, and with his God. (Insofar as the doctrine of the immortality of the soul abstracted the question of future life from these three fundamental identities, it tended to offer an impoverished if not ghostly sense of future existence.)

First, a man is identified with his flesh. He is not a ghost. The body is more important to his identity than words to a poet. He both controls his world and savors his world, and reveals himself to others, in and through the living flesh. Part of the terror of death is that it threatens a man with a loss of identity with his flesh, an identity which is essential to him in at least these three ways.

Too, man's flesh is the means to his control of his world. Except as he uses his flesh instrumentally (feet for walking, hands for working, tongue for talking), he could not relate to the world by way of mastery and control. When death therefore threatens to separate him from his flesh, it threatens him first with a comprehensive loss of possession and control of his universe. Death meets him as the dispossessor (Luke 12:15-21), even though he retaliates as best he can against his loss of control with an assortment of insurance policies. Quite shrewdly the medieval moralists saw a special connection between the capital sin of avarice and old age. Avarice is the special sin in which a man focuses his life on his possessions. The closer a man gets to the time of his dispossession, the more fiercely he clings to what he has and the more suspicion he feels toward all those who would dispossess him with indecorous haste.

Second, a man's flesh is more than instrumental, it is also the site for the disclosure of the world to him, the world which he will never be able to reduce to property but which is there for the savoring. Except as flesh is sensitive, susceptible, and vulnerable, a man could not be open to the world as it pours in upon him in a wild profusion of colors, sounds, and feelings. He could not fall under the spell of powers that both enchant and terrify him. When death therefore threatens to separate him from flesh it threatens also to separate him from the propertyless creation, the world which he may not control but which is his for the beholding in ritual, art, and daily routine.[6]

Third, flesh is more than instrumental and more than sensitive to the world; it is also revelatory. A man reveals himself to his neighbor in and through the living flesh. He is inseparable from his countenance, gestures, and the

[6] Karl Rahner has argued that the severance of a man from his flesh may mean not the loss of a world but rather a release of the soul from the more restricted world it knows in the flesh to an all-cosmic relationship that transcends the limitations of life within the province of a body. Even so Rahner must admit that this eventuality, if it be our destiny, is precisely the future which death, in its darkness, obscures. As we know it now, death threatens to separate us from the flesh and so banish us from that site through which the world is disclosed. See Karl Rahner, *On the Theology of Death*, pp. 29 ff.

physical details of his speech. Part of the terror of death, then, is that it threatens him with a loss of his revelatory power. The dreadfulness of the corpse lies in its claim to be the body of the person, while it is wholly unrevealing of the person. What was once so expressive of the human soul has suddenly become a mask.

We have referred to the *threat* of separation from the flesh in each case not only because a man can anticipate it before it occurs, but also because this separation does not occur all at once. It is shocking to encounter a young man who is dying and recognize a spirit that is still alive with its original power and promise while the flesh abandons it. Or again it is possible to look upon the aged whose spirits have long since absented themselves while their bodies persist so mindlessly alive.

Part of the melancholy of this loss of identity is that no frontal assault can be launched against it. The fear of death only intensifies insofar as a man plunges deeper into his possessions as a way of securing himself against the day of his dispossession, or gives himself over to the frenetic carnivals of a death-ridden age as a way of savoring his world, or takes daily inventory of his physical appearance in the quiet ceremonies before the morning mirror.

Death not only threatens a man with separation from the flesh; it also tears him away from his community. This threat has already been anticipated in the discussion of the revelatory power of the flesh. Death means the unraveling of human community. It divides husband and wife, father and son, and lovers from one another. Not even the child is exempt from this threat. In demanding the reassurance of a voice, the touch of a hand at bedtime, he shows that  he knows all the essential issues involved in a sleep that is early practice in dying. Death threatens all men with final separation, exclusion, and oblivion. And again, this threat is operative beforehand, as the fear of oblivion can prompt men to force their way into the society of others in ways which are ultimately self-isolating.

But death also threatens men with separation from God. This is the terror of death that men have never fully faced because they have never wholly honored the presence of God. But it is the terror of which all others are but prologue and sign. Men fear separation from their flesh because they know life in and through their flesh. They fear separation from community because they know life in and through their community. But what are these compared with separation from God, who is the source of life in the flesh and life in the community? This question remains partly rhetorical for all men inasmuch as they do not know fully what they ask. But it was the last question on the lips of the One whom Christians worship and adore in his cry of abandonment from the cross.

Jesus knew death in all its dimensions. The creed puts it: He "suffered under Pontius Pilate, was crucified, dead and buried; he descended into Hell." His death, like others, meant separation from the flesh. The narratives are utterly factual in detail about his ordeal in the flesh. He suffered dispossession: the king with no subjects, the teacher with no pupils, the healer who bleeds. He suffered severance from the world, reduced as it was to a sop of vinegar, the darkness of the sixth hour, and a spear in the side; and he, like all other men before and after him, suffered the final conclusion of his life in the unrevealing corpse.

His death meant also separation from community. One can see this separation at work beforehand in the persecution of the high priest, the ambiguities of the Roman governor, the fickleness of the crowds, the betrayal of Judas, the cowardice of Peter, and the sleepiness of followers in Gethsemane. It was consummated in his burial when he, like all other men, was removed from sight.

Finally Jesus experienced what men know only through

him: separation from God. The Son of God cries out, "My God, my God, why hast thou forsaken me?" The Son of God descends into the region that stands under the naked terror of the absence of God and stands fast there for every man.

Because the Son of God has done this, the Christian cannot be content simply to tell horror stories about the ravaging power of death. If in looking toward Jesus, he looks toward death in its full terror and power, so also he looks toward the Savior who exposes death in its ultimate powerlessness. No final power remains to death, if death itself has become the event in which Jesus exposes the powerfulness of God's love. Death can still menace, but it can no longer make good on its threats. In Jesus' death, God, flesh, and community are indissolubly met in self-expending love. For this reason, it is no longer necessary to stare in the mirror, worrying about the defeat of one's flesh, or to plunge into communities, worried about exclusion at their hands, or to lift up one's eyes to heaven, attempting in a blind fury of good works to force the presence of God. For the Savior who is identified, soul and body, with men in his descent is the one who remains their Lord in his ascent, to bring men new life—bodily, together, in the presence of God.

Life in Jesus. Usually when a man asks the question of eternal life, he wonders simply whether he will continue to live beyond the grave. Putting the question this way, he assumes that a human being can be separated from his ties with his flesh, community, and God. This is the assumption by virtue of which the doctrine of the immortality of the soul, in some of its versions, actually led to an impoverishment of the notion of eternal life. Eternal life, in effect, became an eternalization of death, as the soul projected itself endlessly into the future—deprived of everything that formerly made it jubilant with life. Cut off from its ties with its flesh, community, and God, the soul so imagined is spectral and wraith-like. Its daydreams about the future have turned into ghoul-ridden nightmares.

The Risen Christ, however, cuts through the nonsense of these daydreams about eternity with the sharp actuality of his life. He is not ghoulishly divested of a body; on the contrary, he shows himself to his disciples, his flesh still bearing the marks of his crucifixion. He is not banished from community like a spook (whose appearance always causes men to scatter and run); on the contrary, his appearance among men is such as to establish and nourish human community. Neither is he grievously separated from God; the account of his resurrection is followed by the acknowledgment of his ascension. This testimony to the ascension of Christ excludes the fantasy of a ghostly Savior drifting in the nether world between God and men. His proximity to God, in turn ("at the right hand of the Father"), is at the basis of his power to create a full-bodied life for his community among men.

Correspondingly, the eternal life that Jesus imparts to men is neither spectral nor rootless. Jesus extends to men the specific hope of future life in the body. "We wait for adoption as sons, the redemption of our bodies" (Rom. 8:23). Wholly consistent with this promise of a glorified body is the apostolic assurance of a new heaven and a new earth to which the body gives access. Man is not destined to live on perpetually in the tedium of a worldless "I." Neither however will he live on in isolation from his fellow. Jesus imparts eternal life to him through a community. As Ephesians puts it, "God . . . made us alive together in Christ." (2:4, 5) The word "together" in the passage does not convey the incidental bit of intelligence that others beside oneself are involved in the resurrection, as though men were like strangers, temporarily herded together to receive a fortune from a benefactor whom each knew in his private way. Rather God creates in the community of disciples a freedom for each other that would not be there except through participation in his life.

Finally eternal life means bodily life, together, in the *presence* of God. Resurrection means intimacy with God. Jesus says to the thief on the cross, "Today you will be with me in paradise." (Luke 23:43) The Christian hope is not simply for a deathless, endless life in which relations between a man, his body, and his neighbor have been set in order. To center hope on a perfected world alone is eschatological atheism. If God exists, eternal life cannot be defined apart from his presence. Without him the perfection of this world would be like the sterile order of a house that a woman kept immaculate for no other end than its own tidiness, as though she did not desire the presence of her husband. In the humblest of marriages the vital presence of the husband belongs to the joy of the house, so the presence of God fills out the joy of heaven.

Eternal life is the future destiny of man, but participation in this life is not reserved to the future alone. Just as death is not simply an event at the end of life but overtakes men by way of fear, worry, and disease in the present moment, so also the resurrection is not an event wholly reserved for the other side of the grave. Men can live now in the power of the resurrection. Surely the martyr faced death with hope in his heart for the future glory, yet he did so in the present enabling power of the resurrection. Otherwise the fullness of God fills only the future, fills only the far side, powerless finally to redeem the present and powerless to sustain men in the agony of dying itself. Men can look forward to the coming ages of his kindness toward them because he stands with them already on this side of the grave.

The fact of the resurrection of Christ, however, does not mean that the Christian is altogether removed from the experience of natural grief and sorrow. Were it otherwise, the Christian should be able to face his own death without a tremor, and he should be able to walk confidently into the sickroom, contending with its silence by "talking up" a victory that has not yet, apparently, reached the ears of those who await an imminent defeat. This is a professional Christian cheerfulness, a grisly boy-scoutism, for which there is no justification in Scripture. The apostle Paul expressed himself carefully: Only "when this corruptible *shall* have put on incorruption . . . *shall* there come to pass the saying that is written, Death is swallowed up in victory." (I Cor. 15:54, italics added.) The Christian knows grief in this life. He is not granted on this side of the grave a pure, steadfast, confident, and transparent sense of his limits—or the limits of his neighbor—before God. He tastes of eternal life in Christ, but not a life that removes him from death and the sting of death. The work of death is still very much evident in the inner and the outer man. Death remains the last enemy. Not until the gift of life beyond the limit has been granted to man is it possible for him to say wholeheartedly:

> O Death, where is thy victory?
> O Death, where is thy sting?

This does not mean, however, that nothing of importance has occurred. Although the Christian does not yet know an eternal life without death; he has reckoned in Christ with an eternal life under the conditions of death, that permits him to live hopefully in the crisis of his neighbor's death and his own. This is the basis for the witness of the church to the dying.

The Church's Behavior Toward the Dying

Let it be said at the outset that the church cannot act as though it possesses something that the dying lack. A demoralizing feature of illness for any patient is the condescending cheerfulness of nurses and friends, whose very display of good health reminds the mortally ill that they are about to be dispossessed of their world. The church cannot behave in such a way as to add yet another possession, i.e., Christian hope, that distinguishes the Christian from the unbeliever or the sorely tried believer who is mortally ill.

This consideration, however, produces an oddity. Does the Christian somehow have to assume the *unreality* of the resurrection in order to avoid removing himself from his fellowman? Must he ignore the resurrection so as not to appear like a self-assured Christ-dispenser in the sickroom? Does he find himself saying, in effect, that the resurrection has taken place but that its fruits are a long way off for all of us and therefore nothing has occurred that need disturb the humanity of my response to your illness and imminent death?

Actually, the reverse is the case. It is precisely in the absence of a sense of the resurrection that the Christian is tempted to think solely in terms of those possessions he has to offer the sick. He makes the painful assumption that he must be a God-producer, a Christ-dispenser, or a religious magician in the sickroom. Failing miserably, of course, at all these roles, he feels keenly his poverty. He makes a lame effort to produce the decisive and healing work, only to stutter and to fall silent. In the absence of a sense of resurrection he feels the terrifying lack of a gift between himself and the dying, a frightening gulf of silence between them. He is inclined therefore with every healthy fiber of his being to shy away from the dying to avoid his own poverty.

The resurrection of Christ frees a man for approach to the dying not because it arms him with a possession to give, but because it frees him from all this worry and confusion about possessions. Christ is already the decisive gift between the living and the dying, the mediator between them. There is no need to produce Christ in the sickroom when he is already there in advance of a man's approach. The Christian is mercifully free, therefore, to offer whatever secondary gifts he can—of anxiety, suffering, money, words, friendship, and hope—letting them be, wherever possible, signs of a divine love which they do not produce.

The Church's witness and separation from the flesh. It is angelism to assume that the sole witness of the church to the dying and the bereaved is the testimony of theology alone. A ministry to the flesh is a true and valid ministry. It need not be supposed that Christian witness is invariably something more than this. Admittedly the apparatus of medicine—doctors, nurses, and sanitary hospitals—can function as a shield behind which the larger community of health protects itself from contact with the dying. But this need not be the case. There is no reason why the machinery of modern medicine—awesome and impersonal though it is—may not yet serve human purposes and therefore function as a sign of a life that exceeds its own powers to heal. To do this, however, some sensitivity must be shown toward the several crises that a man experiences in his flesh.

It was noted earlier that sickness and death involve a traumatic loss of control over one's world. A man who has brutally exploited his body as an instrument of aggression against his world suddenly suffers a heart attack. The very flesh through which he exercised mastery suddenly explodes from within. He is helpless in the hands of others, unable even to control disturbing noises down the hall. Under these circumstances the apparatus of medicine can be frightening; it demonstrates to him his helplessness and therefore reminds him of the poverty of all his attempts to solve the problem of his existence through mastery alone. The machinery of medicine thus assumes the terrifying shape of a parable of judgment. It brings his past life to nought. At the same time, however, the apparatus of medicine can be a testimony to grace. It does after all serve the body; and in this it can be a mute sign of the Lord whose mastery took the form of life-giving and life-comforting service. Seen in this light, it is the special task of the church not to ignore the work of medicine as a sub-Christian activity but to accompany and to criticize it in such a way as to help it to serve this end of service.

The second crisis for the flesh is the loss of the world in its uncontrolled splendor and diversity. A toothache has a way of reducing the world to itself. Unfortunately, the apparatus of medicine, dedicated as it is to the medical recovery of the patient, presents the hospitalized patient with a functional but blank and abstract environment, devoid of the irrelevant details that make up a truly human existence. (Yeats once registered his complaint against the scientific formula, H_2O by observing, "I like a little seaweed in my definition of water.") Many European hospitals admirably manage to maintain gardens as part of their grounds. A functionally irrelevant expense, perhaps, in an institution dedicated to treating and discharging people as fast as it can, but some patients, after all, are discharged for burial, and it is well to maintain a sign for them of a world that has not shrunk to the final abstraction of their irremedial pain.

The third crisis for the flesh is the imminent loss of its revelatory power. The falterings of the body in old age increasingly prevent it from being expressive of the soul in its full dignity. There is warrant here for a sensitive ministry to the body in its infirmities which extends to the humblest of details in the daily routines of eating and cleansing. Upon death, moreover, there is warrant for a funeral service in which the body is not treated as a disposable cartridge to be thrown away like garbage. This argument for a fitting disposal of the remains, however, is hardly an apology for present-day funeral practice. Quite the contrary, it opens the way for an even more savage criticism of these practices. Precisely because the body has been (and will be) what it is only by the power of God to glorify it, it cannot become in Christian practice a lewd object of the mortician's craft. It is one thing for the mortician to minimize the violence done to the body by death, but it is quite another thing for him to impose upon the deceased the suggestion of a character other than its own. Only too often today Uncle John is not allowed to die. He must be prettied up with rouge on his cheeks and his casket opened so that his friends can see his face forced into a smile. Poor Uncle John never smiled in his life, but now he does—beatifically. It is not only the beautification of Uncle John, but his beatification that one attempts to achieve. The church won't canonize him but the mortician will. One is supposed to go to to the funeral parlor, look on the face of the corpse, and say about Uncle John, "Doesn't he look natural?" which, of course, is the one thing he does not look. Let death be death. There is no reason to add to its hideousness by mocking the inability of the dead to reveal themselves.

The witness of the church and separation from community. One of the most devastating features of terminal illness is the fear of abandonment.[7] Sickness has already isolated the patient from his normal identity in the community: Strong and authoritative, he is now relatively helpless; gregarious by nature, he suddenly finds friends exhausting. Ironically the very apparatus by which the community ministers to his physical need isolates him further. The modern hospital segregates the sick and the

[7] "The dying patient faces emotional problems of great magnitude, including fear of death itself, fear of the ordeal of dying and the devastating fear of abandonment." See Ruth D. Abrams, M.S., "The Patient with Cancer—His Changing Pattern of Communication," *New England Journal of Medicine,* Vol. 274, No. 6, p. 320.

dying from their normal human resources. One doctor has observed that in an Arabian village a grandmother dies in the midst of her children and grandchildren, cows and donkeys. But our high level of technological developments leads simply to dying a death appropriate to one's disease—in the heart ward or the cancer ward.[8]

Most desolating of all is the breakdown of communication between the dying patient, the doctor, and the nearest of kin. Substitute diagnoses are sometimes justified on the grounds that they establish an emotional equilibrium (homeostasis) essential to the health and comfort of the patient, but this justification ignores the fact that evasiveness can itself be emotionally disturbing. It is demoralizing for everybody concerned to get stuck with a lie, because, once told, life tends to organize itself around it. Even when the lie isn't working, even when it produces the anguish of suspicion, isolation, and uncertainty, the doctor may rely on it to keep his own relation to the patient in a state of equilibrium. Homeostasis, in other words, is a problem not only for the patient but also for the doctor and for the family. The family also grows accustomed to the explanation and enmeshes itself more deeply in the demands of make-believe. It seems too late for everybody concerned to recover an authentic relationship to the event. Isolated by evasion and lies, the patient is driven out of community before his time. He has forced upon him a premature burial. While trying to avoid the fact of death, the community actually reeks of death, for it has already excluded him.

It would be wrong, however, to make the doctor the scapegoat here and therefore to underestimate woefully the problems of sharing the truth. This was the mistake of

[8] Bryant M. Wedge, in discussion at the conclusion of a symposium on *Death and Dying: Attitudes of Patient and Doctor*, sponsored by the Group for the Advancement of Psychiatry, Symposium No. 11, Vol. V.

a group of psychiatrists in the previously referred to study of *Death and Dying: Attitudes of Patient and Doctor.*[9] The psychiatrists reported that 69 to 90 percent of physicians (depending on the specific study) were not in favor of informing the patient in cases of mortal illness. Meanwhile on the basis of their own interviews with patients, the psychiatrists reported that approximately 82 percent of patients in terminal cases actually wanted to be informed of their true condition. Several psychiatrists explained this discrepancy between the apparent desire of patients and the actual performance of doctors by appeal to the psychological defects of doctors or to faults in their training: (1) they are more afraid of death than other professional groups; (2) they shy away from dealing with chronic and terminal cases because such cases are a blow to the doctor's professional self-esteem; (3) they receive inadequate preparation in medical school for coping with the problem of handling terminal cases.

Doubtless, all these observations are valid in given instances, but I found the psychiatrists breathtakingly naïve in the evidence they accepted as proof that patients really want to know the truth. First, it is not clear that patients are so willing to talk about the possibility—or the inevitability—of their own death *with their own doctor,* as the percentages reported by the psychiatrists in their interviews with patients would indicate. Dr. Samuel Feder indirectly admitted this fact when he observed that "all . . . patients, when they were asked to see me as a 'new doctor,' reacted with great anxiety."[10] All but two of the patients, however, were delighted to discover that he was "only" a psychiatrist. He admits that this was

[9] See especially the essay by Herman Feifel, "The Function of Attitudes Toward Death," Ch. V. in *Death and Dying: Attitudes of Patient and Doctor,* pp. 633-37.

[10] Samuel L. Feder, "Attitudes of Patients with Advanced Malignancy," Chap. III in *Death and Dying: Attitudes of Patient and Doctor,* pp. 614-20.

a unique experience for him as a psychiatrist. Obviously patients were glad that "he was not one of those other doctors—those other doctors being the bearers of bad tidings."

Dr. Feder interpreted these anxiety reactions as proof that people knew that they were going to die. Therefore the doctors had no excuse for avoiding the subject. I interpret them, however, as proof that these people were frightened of hearing just this verdict from their own doctors. The doctor in charge is less approachable on this subject precisely because he is the keeper of desolate truths. By the same token, the psychiatrist is more accessible since he brings no final verdict. If this analysis is correct, then the doctor's reticence to discuss the subject cannot be written off solely as a question of his own fear of death or his oversensitive, professional self-esteem. The sacral dimensions of death are too awesome to admit of easy professional solution. The problem of isolation cannot be solved by handing out truth like pills since the truth itself can have a disturbing and an isolating effect.

Yet there are ways in which people can reach out to one another in word and actions and maintain some measure of solidarity before the overwhelming event of death. It would be pretentious to outline these ways since they are not fully given to men except in the concrete case. Nevertheless it is possible to clarify (and perhaps even to clear the way of) certain obstacles that men face in their behavior toward the dying. They divide very simply into those of word and deed.

The problem of words. Perhaps we are especially inhibited in our talk with the dying because the alternatives in language seem so poor. There are several types of discourse available to us: (1) direct, immediate, blunt talk; (2) circumlocution or double-talk; (3) silence (which can be, of course, a mode of sharing, but oftentimes, is a way of evading); and (4) discourse that proceeds by way of indirection.

Too often we assume (especially as Americans) that the only form of truth-telling is direct, immediate, blunt talk. Such talk seems to be the only alternative to evasive silence or circumlocution. On the subject of sex, for example, we assume that the only alternative to the repressions of a Victorian age is the tiresome, gabby explicit discussion of sex we impose upon the adolescent from junior high forward. So also on the subject of death we assume that truth-telling requires something approaching the seminar in loquacity. But obviously gabby bluntness in the presence of one dying is wholly inappropriate. It reckons in no way with the solemnity of the event. To plead for the explicit discussion of diagnosis or prognosis with every patient in clinical detail would be foolhardy. But the alternative to blunt talk need not be double-talk, a condescending cheerfulness, or a frightening silence. There is such a thing as *indirect* discourse in both love and death.

Perhaps examples of what I mean by indirection will suffice. One doctor reports that many patients instinctively brought up the question of their own death in an indirect form. Some asked him, for example, whether he thought they should buy a house, marry, or have plastic surgery done to their face. The doctor realized that the answer, "Yes, surely, go ahead—" in a big, cheerful voice was an evasion. Meanwhile the answer, "No," was a summary reply which would have made further discussion impossible. He found it important however to convey to them somehow that he recognized the importance of the question. From that point on, it was possible to discuss their uncertainties, anxieties, and fears. Some kind of sharing could take place. It was not necessary to dwell on the subject for long; after its acknowledgment it was possible to proceed to the details of daily life without the change of subject seeming an evasion.

Indirection may be achieved in another way. Although it may be too overbearing to approach the subject of death frontally under the immediate pressure of its presence, a kind of indirection can be achieved if death is discussed in advance of a crisis. The minister who suddenly feels like a tongue-tied irrelevancy in the sickroom gets what he deserves if he has not worked through the problem with his people in a series of sermons or in work sessions with lay groups. Words too blunt and inappropriate in the crisis itself may, if spoken earlier, provide an indirect basis for sharing burdens.

The language of indirection is appropriate behavior because, as it has been argued throughout, death is a sacred event. For the most part, toward the sacred the most fitting relation is indirect. The Jew did not attempt to look straight on Jahweh's face. A direct, immediate, casual confrontation was impossible. But avoidance of God's presence was not the only alternative. It was given to the Jew to hold his ground before his Lord in a relation that was genuine but indirect. So also, it is not necessary to dwell directly on the subject of death interminably or to avoid it by a condescending cheerfulness wholly inappropriate to the event. It is possible for two human beings to acknowledge death, be it ever so indirectly, and to hold their ground before it until they are parted.

The problem of action. Deeds are no easier to come by than words in extremity. Everyone grows uneasy. When nothing is left to be done toward the dying, a man is inclined to pay his respects, look at his watch, and fish out an excuse that fetches him home. Perhaps, however, our discomfort stems partly from a view of action somewhat inappropriate to overwhelming events. T. S. Eliot once said that there are two types of problems we face in life. In one case, the appropriate question is: what are we going to do about it? In the other case: how do we behave toward it? The deeper problems in life are of the latter kind.

But unfortunately as Americans, and especially as Americans in those professions that get tinged with a slight messianic pretension—medicine and the ministry—we are used to tackling problems in terms of the first question, and are left somewhat bereft, therefore, when that question is inappropriate to the crisis. If all we can say is, What are we going to do about it?, then the dying indeed (and our own death) is a fatal blow to professional self-esteem. But this is not the only question we can ask ourselves in crisis. In extremity it may not be possible to do something about a tragedy, but this inability need not altogether disable our behavior toward it.

The witness of the church and the threat of separation from God. Since this is the threat in which the name of God appears, it is assumed that the special witness of the church in this case is theology. It may indeed be theology—but neither invariably nor exclusively so and certainly not theology conceived as a series of truths that provide men with access to God while putting them at a comforting distance from the sting of death. Such a theology, while trying to screen death from view, would only succeed in shielding men from the presence of God. For who is God as the Christian knows him? He is the God and Father of Jesus Christ, crucified and risen from the dead. Possessed by Jesus Christ, the church is not removed from the sting of existence come to an end. Rather it lives by a concrete existence that cuts into death with all the power of God's love to make death itself the very instance of that love. Because this is the case, the church cannot shield death from view without seeking—foolishly—to place theological screens before the eyes of the redeemed.

The witness of the church to the presence of God is

not always direct and verbal. This fact has already been anticipated in our discussion of death. Just as an authentic acknowledgment of death can take place within the limits of indirect discourse, so also an authentic witness to Jesus Christ can occur without the inevitable footnote giving reference to his name. The Christian sense of the presence of God can express itself indirectly in the way in which the Christian responds to other levels of crisis. The calm with which he offers friendship in crisis may count for more than theological virtuosity in testifying to God's presence. The worry with which he offers advice will reveal more than the advice itself when he is really stricken with a sense of God's absence. But even in the case of failure he cannot, with Christian consistency, take his failure too seriously. God is the ultimate presence in death, whether men succeed in testifying to him or not. Neither life, nor death, nor the failure of Christians, will be able to separate men from the love of God. This is the message of Rom. 8 and the substance of Christian witness. When the church fails by its words and deeds to make this witness to the dying, let the dying among her members be brave enough to make this witness to the church.

Dr. Lloyd C. Elam was the Chairman of the Department of Psychiatry of Meharry Medical College, Nashville, Tennessee. He presently serves as president of that institution. Dr. Elam describes the place of death in man's psychological economy. He finds that interpretations of death usually reflect the meaning and maturity one has achieved in life. He finds also that a faith which will permit one to affirm death without making it the focal point of his life is the most beneficial stance. Finally, one ignores death and grief at his own psychic expense. He pays a toll for his avoidance both in inner conflict and in an inability to relate to the suffering in a helpful manner.

VI

A Psychiatric Perspective on Death

Lloyd C. Elam

A discussion of a psychiatric view of death might logically begin with a definition of the term. This may not be possible, for, as familiar as we are with death, until recently there has been little research on its psychological dimensions. One reason for this lack of research is our massive denial of death. We behave as though it did not exist for us. We believe that others will die, but we also believe that it will not happen to us.[1] Another factor which has hindered research in this area is our view of death as a biological phenomenon. Instead of seeing death as a regularly occurring and natural end to life, we see it as a result of disease, or of accidents, or of some other unusual event. The field of medicine has amassed a large amount of data about the things that hasten or postpone one's physical demise, but the investigation

[1] Sigmund Freud, "Thoughts for the Times on War and Death," *The Complete Psychological Works of Sigmund Freud,* trans. and ed. James Strachey (London: The Hogarth Press, 1916), XIV, 289, 296 f.

seems to stop at this point. Thus our attempts at definition are handicapped by our limited vision. One psychiatrist suggests the following as some of our unanswered questions:

> Does the moment of death coincide with some physical phenomenon such as cessation of heartbeat or of brain activity? How much are our lives enriched or made dull by our knowledge of the inevitability of death? Can death psychologically precede death physiologically? [2]

Yet when these limitations have been faced, we are still able to discuss psychological reactions to death. Leaving aside the physiological definition (which is usually thought to coincide with a certain amount of cellular structuralization from which there is no reversibility), we find that the interpretation of death varies greatly in different individuals. Further, it is apparent that persons respond differently to the knowledge of their own death than they do to the death of others. Finally, it is apparent that there are ways in which such knowledge enables us to be helpful to the dying and to the bereaved. These three concerns form the substance of this chapter.

Interpretations of Death

Sigmund Freud points out that our own death is unimaginable—our unconscious is inaccessible to the idea of our own death. Whereas we are able to think of death, it is largely thought of either as the death of others or as though a part of oneself will die. The psychoanalytic viewpoint then is that basically everyone is convinced of his immortality.[3]

The existential analysts on the other hand hold that

[2] K. R. Eissler, *The Psychiatrist and the Dying Patient* (New York: Hallmark-Hubner Press, 1955), p. 39.

[3] Freud, "Thoughts for the Times," p. 296.

the confrontation of death gives the most positive reality to life itself. Death is the one fact of life (say the existialists) which is not relative but absolute, and the awareness of this gives existence and what one does each hour an absolute quality.[4]

Rather than discuss the viewpoints of these schools of thought a discussion of the concerns of the individual when he contemplates his death should help in understanding his view of death. These concerns are reflected in traditions, religious practices, funerals, fears, and many other behaviors. There are few situations where the individual expresses his view of his death directly because rarely does he seriously contemplate his own death. (The contemplation of the death of another is an entirely different matter and will be discussed later.) The acts of the person about to commit suicide, suicide notes, the fears and the wishes of the dying patient, and occasionally the behavior of persons sentenced to be executed provide sources of public exposure of the private meaning of death.

For some, death represents the loss of consciousness (or awareness). Awareness of feeling, wanting, observing, thinking, knowing, and other phenomena is life, and its loss is death. Fear of the loss of consciousness is encountered in the presurgical patient and frequently must be dealt with before anesthesia can be given. The resistance of small children and certain mentally ill persons to sleep has been explained as a consequence of the fear of the loss of awareness. The desire to "die quickly" may be related to this view of death. Conversely, it is this loss of consciousness which is the attractive aspect of death to many suicidal persons. Their desire not to know, not to feel, etc., is expressed in suicide notes as being possible only in death. Many religions in which immortality is

[4] See Walter Kaufman, "Existentialism and Death," *The Meaning of Death,* ed. Herman Feifel (New York: McGraw-Hill, 1959), pp. 39-63.

a basic belief promise that awareness is the primary quality that will continue.

For some people, death may represent helplessness, or aloneness or separation from others. Concern about burial place, the dread of the terminally ill person when isolated, and the frequency with which suicidal persons choose public places for the act, are in part associated with the fear of separation from others. (This is not the only motivation for such behavior, for exhibitionism and hope for rescue are also involved.) This poses a particularly difficult problem in hospitals because of the tendency of people to avoid the dying person. Such a person is likely to have few visitors because would-be visitors are handling their own feelings about death by avoidance. The caretakers (physicians, nurses, etc.) also spend less and less time with the terminally ill patient, rationalizing that they must devote their limited time to those whom they can help. Actually, they too are handling their own feelings about death by having minimal contact with those whom they feel are dying. Other caretakers (ministers, social workers, etc.), have found ways to continue their availability to the dying by discovering means of being "helpful."

Mention should be made of a variation of this view of death—certain persons see death as a way of uniting or reuniting with someone else. This is frequently seen in the case of mentally ill persons who welcome death because of this belief. When it exists as a cultural or religious belief, it may serve as a neutralizer for the fear of loneliness in death.

Death may also represent immobility and loss of self-control. One may be concerned that he cannot alter his record after the moment of dying. The desire to get one's "affairs in order" reflects this view of death. Loss of identity, loss of bodily integrity, and nonexistence are additional expressions of fears about death.

There are other concerns and fears which reflect views which individuals have of death, but these should suffice to indicate similarities between one's view of death and the various conflicts which are seen at different levels of development. For example, at one stage of development the conflicts of a child indicate that his main task is the development of self-awareness. At this level all of the child's experiences—feeding, body movements, perceptions—serve to develop a greater self-awareness. At another level self-assertiveness becomes the central issue, and, at still another stage, identity and individual differentiation are central.[5] It seems to be a reasonable conclusion that one's interpretation of death, like his interpretation of all other life events, is dependent on his life experiences and on the developmental level at which he is operating.

Reactions to Death

Just as there is variety in the interpretation of death, so also there is diversity in the reaction to the fact of death. One's response to the knowledge that he is finite is not the same as his response to learning of the death of a stranger. And neither of these reactions corresponds exactly to a person's feelings upon the loss of a close friend or relative.

The main reaction to the idea of one's own death is denial. (Denial is a more or less conscious mental mechanism —as contrasted with unconscious mechanisms—which keeps experiences, feelings, and memories out of awareness.) Denial may take various forms:

1. One denies the absoluteness of physical death through belief in immortality of one's person and

[5] C. Knight Aldrich, *An Introduction to Dynamic Psychiatry* (New York: McGraw-Hill, 1966), pp. 83-187; and Erik H. Erikson, *Childhood and Society* (New York: W. W. Norton, 1963), pp. 247-69.

belief in the idea of another world where one's body or soul lives on forever.

2. One believes in the immortality of the world he leaves behind. (He may be mortal, but humanity or society is not.)
3. Fascination with danger is another form of denial. Many forms of entertainment are enjoyed because they are ways of flirting with death. It is quite likely that a part of our desire to take trips in automobiles on holidays despite the danger may be related to this form of denial.
4. Rejection of the dead and dying is still another method of avoiding the confrontation with death.
5. Even in our language we speak of people passing on, being deceased, expiring, or use other terms to avoid confronting the fact that they die.
6. The sacrifical death is a religious development of the denial of death as the individual believes that through this death, he achieves immortality.

Psychologically the mechanism of denial should not necessarily be understood negatively. For denial permits the knowledge of death to be close at hand so that a healthy respect for danger is fostered and, at the same time, far enough away so that dealing with it can be postponed. Denial of one's death is an appropriate defense, a mechanism of adjustment which, under ordinary circumstances, is adequate.

An alternative to the denial of death seems to be confrontation and dealing with death. Because of the unparalleled significance of this one event in his life, if the individual chooses to confront the question of his life ending in death, it may become a major issue and push other issues into the background. Everything is seen in relationship to death. Such a stance would emphasize Freud's death instinct—one of the least accepted of his concepts—to the virtual exclusion of his complementary life instinct. Though he insisted that the death instinct, which he related to aggression, was basic in determining behavior, Freud nevertheless felt a balance between these two instincts was necessary for healthy adjustment.

Thus, the acceptance of death as a part of life appears to be difficult, although not impossible. The usual reactions of either denial or focusing on death, while appropriate responses, may represent opposite ends of a continuum. Dealing with components of death, or dealing with it partially might be more appropriate.

Physicians who once believed that only by assisting the dying patient to deny could they be helpful are finding more and more that people are able to accept the inevitability of their death. More than that, some want to be told if the end is near. It would seem that, depending on one's maturity, the ability to accept death is dependent on the feeling of integrity concerning his life. For the individual whose life has been meaningful and full the acceptance of death is easier than for the individual who has felt dissatisfaction with his life.

It must be said that for a few the handling of the fear of one's own death is not accomplished. Instead of using denial, or integrating death into life, or making it the focus of life, they anticipate death, and some even commit suicide because it is more intolerable to wait for death than to hasten it when the fear of death is overwhelming. (To be passive in the face of danger creates more anxiety than any action taken, even if the action increases the danger.)

The reaction to the death of others—a much more acceptable notion—must be considered in two parts: (1) The reaction to the death of strangers, and (2) the reaction to the death of friends. Freud asserts that

> when it comes to someone else's death, the civilized man will carefully avoid speaking of such a possibility in the hearing

of the person under sentence. Children alone disregard this restriction; they unashamedly threaten one another with the possibility of dying, and even go so far as to do the same thing to someone that they love, as, for instance: "Dear Mummy, when you're dead I'll do this or that." The civilized adult can hardly even entertain the thought of another person's death without seeming to himself hardhearted or wicked; unless, of course, as a doctor or lawyer or something of the kind, he has to deal with death professionally. Least of all will he allow himself to think of the other person's death if some gain to himself in freedom, property, or position is bound up with it.[6]

He goes on to say that "towards the actual person who has died we adopt a special attitude—something almost like admiration for someone who has accomplished a very difficult task. We suspend criticism of him, overlook his possible misdeeds, declare that *de mortuis nil nisi bonum,* and think it justifiable to set out all that is most favorable to his memory in the funeral oration and upon the tombstone. Consideration for the dead, who, after all, no longer need it, is more important to us than the truth, and certainly, for most of us, more important than consideration for the living. The complement to this cultural and conditional attitude toward death is provided by our complete collapse when death has struck down someone whom we love—a parent or a partner in marriage, a brother or sister, a child or a close friend." [7]

Freud's comments about death are really related to the deaths of those whom we know. As far as the death of strangers is concerned, we react as though they were completely different—as though this were not an event of importance to ourselves. Our acceptance of man's death in war is as though the soldier were not quite a man. It seems that many of the tactics of war and the modern techniques

[6] Freud, "Thoughts for the Times," pp. 289 ff.
[7] *Ibid.*, p. 290.

of waging war are designed to increase our ability to deal with the death of soldiers as though they were not quite men. In our reports of the number of deaths, usually we call them casualties or something other than deaths. The weapons with which wars are now fought place the combatants at greater distances from each other so that they do not have to look at each other or come face to face with the realization that the other individual is a man very much like oneself. And as this is done for the combatants, so the distance is even greater for the people back home.

The reaction to the death of friends is quite different from what we have been describing. It is as though it were happening to us, as indeed it is. The physical death of a loved one requires a psychological reaction. This reaction is called grief or mourning. It appears that this mourning process has several steps which are related to one's management of death. The first step is the attempt at denial—the "it can't be" or the feeling of shock. This is the way death has been kept away from the individual before and at this moment he continues to try to keep it away from himself. After a period he recognizes that this cannot work because the reality is present; a death has occurred. This acknowledgment is followed by a time of increased interest in the positive aspects of the lost one. This is the stage described by Freud earlier in which we seem to admire the dead person and even to believe that he needs our admiration. Thus Freud was not talking about the handling of the death of strangers but of the death of friends. Since the dead person does not need the praise and good words which are directed in his behalf, what is the purpose of them? They are necessary for those who remain in order for them to handle their mixed feelings about the dead person. It is only after the living have gone through a period of feeling positively toward the dead person that they are able to enter into the third phase of mourning, which is being able to experience negative feelings about the dead person. If one goes through these steps then one is able to decrease the attachment to the loved one.

This orderly process of mourning is affected by any number of variables. The intensity and duration of grief is affected by marked ambivalence toward the dead loved one, the kind of involvement just before the death, the amount of time elapsed since the last contact with the dead, and the emotional state of the mourner just before the death. An interesting phenomenon is that if one is interrupted in the mourning process there is a greater likelihood of his developing a depression, a state in which the individual is convinced of his worthlessness. This has been interpreted as meaning that the depressed person feels that the loved one is dead because the depressed person is worthless or in other words, "If I had been better he would not have died and left me."

Being Helpful to the Dying and Bereaved

One final question should be asked: How does an understanding of death assist us in being helpful to other people? It has been pointed out that while denial of one's own death is an appropriate defense, this is not the only defense. The unfortunate result of dealing with death only by denial is that the dying person may be allowed to feel that he is abandoned or rejected. A less important result of handling death by denial is that this prevents us from using death as one of the organizing principles of life. Despite the propensity to deal with death as though it were absolutely unpredictible, how one dies and, to some degree, when he dies is determined by the individual and the culture in which he lives. It would certainly be possible for the fact of death to be used as an organizing principle without its becoming the central theme in the individual's life. Our ability to help the dying patient as well as the bereaved and the mourning is also greatly hampered by our approach to death.

Herman Feifel, who has done systematic studies of attitudes toward death, concludes that one's reaction to impending death is a function of interweaving factors. Some of the more significant ones appear to be:

1. The psychological maturity of the individual
2. The kind of coping techniques available to him
3. Variables of religious orientation, age, socioeconomic status, etc.
4. Severity of the organic process
5. The attitudes of the physician and other significant persons in the patient's world[8]

The approach to the dying patient should, therefore, differ for different people and should not be seen as a time to support his dealing only with matters other than death, but also as a time to support his dealing with the matter of death. Likewise, with the mourner, the work of mourning can be assisted by an understanding of what is going on and by making it possible for the mourning process to continue. Edgar Jackson in "Grief and Religion," indicates that the

> religious function within the community is to protect the bereft individual against destructive fantasy and illusion by surrounding the fact of physical death by a framework of reality that is accepted by both the grieving individual and the supporting community. This framework of reality is conceived to stimulate and make valid the expression of all the emotion that is a part of the process of mourning in a way that is acceptable to the community at the same time that it satisfies the deep inner needs of the personality. This expression of feeling is not designed to lead to despair and separation from the community but rather to make legitimate

[8] "Attitudes Toward Death in Some Normal and Mentally Ill Populations," *The Meaning of Death*, p. 126.

and more easily possible a reinvestment of emotional capital in the next chapters of life.[9]

Summary

Psychological economy is such that when an individual finds a solution for a particular problem he continues to use that solution as long as it works. Denial of one's own death is an appropriate defense and one which works. The individual, therefore, continues to use denial as a main form of dealing with the concepts of his own death and attempts to use it as a means of dealing with the death of others. It has been pointed out that this is not the only way of reacting to death in others or to the thought of one's own death. Because one's concept of death changes as he matures, he has a larger variety of possible methods of adjusting to the death of others and to the thought of his own death. It is necessary in studying death and in assisting persons who are either dying or reacting to the death of others to recognize this possible variety and the signs which indicate that a person is able to handle these facts of life in ways other than denial.

A brief discussion of grief and mourning indicated that (1) mourning is necessary in the adjustment to death of loved ones, and (2) that mourning follows an orderly progression. Interference with this orderly progression of mourning will very often lead to depression. The role of religion and indeed the role of the caretakers in society is to provide an environment which supports a reaction to death that fulfills the emotional needs of the individual in a culturally acceptable way. This in some way entails helping the individual see that death does not make life futile.

[9] *The Meaning of Death*, p. 231.

Ernest Q. Campbell is Professor and Chairman of the Department of Sociology and Anthropology at Vanderbilt University. He points out that the affirmation of death called for by Dr. Elam is difficult in our society. The rituals, ceremonies, and prescribed behaviors of any culture reflect its values and priorities. Death is a rite de passage *reflecting our attitude to life and avoidance of death. Thus, funeral directors serve as agents of the population. Despite protests, he insists that these agents provide what people want. Their role is symbolic of the secular take-over of death.*

VII

Death as a Social Practice

Ernest Q. Campbell

Death is a certainty of life and assumes a necessary importance in the affairs of men. The dead are social objects and as such they acquire social definition: how the body shall be treated, where the spirit is, what powers it has, how the living shall relate to it, what status and influence the dead shall have in the affairs of the living. Death poses immense tasks that strike closely to the basic organization of the community and the larger society. Associated with these tasks are normative definitions of bereavement behavior, an extensive industry for funerary arrangements, and fairly elaborate divisions of labor that bear on several major professional and quasi-professional groups; for example, physicians, ministers, and undertakers. Even the imperative death-work is substantial, not to mention the less central: the physical remains must be processed, the deceased placed in a new status, vacated roles filled and property disposed of, group and community solidarity reaffirmed, and the bereaved reestablished and supported.[1]

[1] See Robert Bauner, "Death and Social Structure," *Psychiatry,* XXIX (November, 1966), 378-94, and John W. Riley, Jr., "*Death and Bereavement*" (unpublished paper, 1966).

The organization of behavior around the event of death constitutes, in other words, a complex, interesting, and important social phenomenon.

Yet death practices have received rather little systematic attention. This is because death is a taboo subject. Many people regard discussion of death as morbid and depressing, and even wonder whether anyone who investigates it may perhaps have perverse motives. Physicians are often observed to be immensely uncomfortable concerning discussion of death, whether with patients, the relatives of patients, or even representatives of the lay and scientific communities.[2] A rather interesting and full language exposed to parody in Evelyn Waugh's *The Loved One* creates an unusual imagery of dying and the dead that seems to deny the facts to which it relates.[3] Extensive funeral customs, as exposed in widely circulated publications during the early 1960's, seem to reflect and encourage illusory notions regarding the reality of death.[4] These very practices may themselves be a worthy subject for our attention as social analysts; they constitute a set of cultural definitions of social objects and events, and they help define expected behavior for those affected by the event of death.

[2] For a strong, even fierce, attack on medical views and social norms, see Herman Feifel, "Scientific Research in Taboo Areas—Death," *The American Behavioral Scientist,* V, No. 7 (March, 1962), 28-30.

[3] James Agee catches this circumlocution and ambivalence poignantly in his novel *A Death in the Family.* A mother tells her school-age children of their father's accidental death in a lengthy, discursive statement during which at various points she says: "Daddy didn't come home. . . . He isn't going to come home any more. He's gone away to heaven. . . . God wanted him. . . . God let him go to sleep and took him straight away with Him to heaven." Finally, Rufus, her son, asks directly: "Is Daddy dead?", and "Her glance at him was as startled as if he had slapped her." Pp. 190-91.

[4] See for example: Ruth Mulvey Harmer, *The High Cost of Dying* (New York: Collier Books, 1963); Jessica Mitford, *The American Way of Death* (New York: Simon and Schuster, 1963); Roul Tunley, "Can You Afford To Die?," *The Saturday Evening Post* (June 17, 1961), pp. 24-25, 80-82.

Every society is confronted with the reality of death. It is an important confrontation, philosophically because it challenges the assumption of continuity and permanence that societies make about themselves; organizationally because it requires the replacement of personnel in all the various statuses that make up the social order; interpersonally because it dislocates role networks and has immense emotional tone; psychologically because it requires each and every actor on the human scene to acknowledge the transitory nature of his own existence.[5] This paper deals with the set of social behaviors, adjustments, and definitions that cluster around the nature and fact of death. We will discuss, more or less in turn, the nature of death as a social role; the social functions of the funeral; the social meanings of grief and how the circle of grievers is defined; the subterranean work of the medical profession in giving performance cues; and, finally, the cemetery as a social symbol.

Death as a Social Role

Even as we begin, it is important to acknowledge that "death" itself is subject to cultural definition and has no obvious meaning. The Melanesians make their most meaningful distinction, for example, not between life and death but between health and illness, and in consequence the socially important transition for the individual in his relations with his associates occurs at the time of his loss of health rather than at death.[6] Likewise, our common use of the words *dead* and *death* to refer simply to the termination of given relationships suggests the possibility of alternative meanings, as in the observation, "Their mar-

[5] Erik Erikson uses the term "ego-chill" with reference to the sudden awareness that one's non-existence is entirely possible. *Young Man Luther* (New York: W. W. Norton, 1958), p. 111.

[6] W. H. R. Rivers, "The Primitive Conception of Death," *Psychology and Ethnology* (New York: Harcourt, Brace & Co., 1926), pp. 36-50.

riage is dead." Sudnow has shown that even in the physical sense, nurses and doctors may treat the critically ill as dead while life still remains. For example, he observed a nurse to spend several minutes trying to close the eyelids of a woman she explained was dying: "After several unsuccessful moments she managed to get them to stay shut and said, with a sigh of accomplishment, 'Now they're right.' When questioned about what she had been doing, she reported that a patient's eyelids are always closed after death so that the body will resemble a sleeping person. After death, however, she reported, it was more difficult to accomplish a complete lid closure, especially after the body muscles have begun to tighten; the eyelids become less pliable, more resistant, and have a tendency to move apart; she always tried, she reported, to close them before death; while the eyes are still elastic they are more easily manipulated." [7]

Death is a role, and like many other roles it is marked by ceremonial passage rites and by adjustments in the behavior of the role incumbent and of those with whom he relates. Each person prepares himself for performance in this role, as do others with whom he interacts prepare for the changed role relationships that will result from his death. Certainly death is not a typical kind of role: It obviously is not like entering into the role of college student or into marital, occupational, or parenthood roles, though with each of these it shares some common characteristics in an analytical sense, particularly the advance preparation commonly called anticipatory socialization. One as the object of death does not literally perform in different role relationships because of his death. All who are in any given circle of acquaintances must to some extent readjust the set of relationships that characterizes them as human beings because of the death of anyone within the circle.

[7] David Sudnow, *Passing On: The Social Organization of Dying* (Englewood Cliffs, N. .J: Prentice-Hall, 1967), p. 74.

Death, the exit from life, is thus the exit from a relational system, and this departure requires the restructuring of that relational system in much the same way that divorce, change of residence, an argument among friends, or any other transition requires the reorganization of relevant interpersonal networks. We must think of the totally unattached—the unclaimed bodies of potter's field—to find an exception.

In two lengthy works the British anthropologist Frazer, after reviewing a suggestive body of cross-cultural data, concludes that it is typically the case that man is thought to be more hostile to his descendants after his death than during his lifetime.[8] His concern is with the fear of the dead, which results ofttimes in elaborate precautions to prevent the return of the dead to this world, and with actions that are adopted to protect survivors from the departed just in case their efforts to thwart his return are not successful. One interpretation of these elaborate precautions is that they acknowledge the final, ultimate exit of the departed from a set of role relationships, and a desire on the part of those who remain to restructure relationships so that order and meaningfulness in relationships can be continued. If survivors can be made comfortably certain that the deceased will not reenter the role system, directly or under guise, it follows that they cannot be held accountable to the deceased for role realignments that they make (e.g., remarriage, change of residence, new friendships, changed organizational affiliation) nor is there any danger that reentry will mess up an evolving system of new interpersonal connections.

Frazer also observes that those thought to be in greater danger are those who were closest to the dead; indeed he suggests that intimates' fear of the dead is a substantial

[8] Sir James George Frazer, *The Belief in Immortality and the Worship of the Dead* (London: Macmillan & Co., 1913); *The Fear of the Dead in Primitive Religion* (New York: Biblo and Tannen, 1966).

source of the religious thought that has characterized humanity "ever since people began to meditate on the great mysteries by which our little life on earth is encompassed." This concern to assure the permanent exit of the dead, this care in making sure that they don't come back, suggest the fear that post-death relationships might be restructured as it were for nought. "The King is dead. Long live the [next] King." And may the deceased King be truly departed, for were he to return and lay claim to the throne our personal lives and our social order would be in for terrible chaos! Malinowski dwells on a similar theme, stating that love of the dead and fear of the corpse work to create very contradictory emotions in us.[9]

Except in the case of unexpected death, all those who will be affected by it engage in advance preparation, which is to say that their behaviors are to some extent affected by the anticipation of death. Indeed, the greater the social connectedness, the fuller the preparation, so that the degree of advance preparation (and of bereavement, as we shall see later) may be revealing clues to the nature of the social network. The plaintive plea, "How can I live without him?", and the greedy anticipation of an inheritance from an unloved uncle merely set the opposite extremes (and probably detract from our full comprehension) of a full range and large body of role work that is carried on because of anticipated death. Though we do not openly discuss even this because of the taboo nature of death, it is at least normatively appropriate to commend and admire anyone who, preparing for his own death, draws up his will, arranges his affairs, sets his house in order, and makes a neat departure, i.e., reduces to a minimum the potential confusion and disruption occasioned by his exit. But it does not seem normatively appropriate, though it may be of equal if not larger significance, to acknowledge

[9]Bronislaw Malinowski, *Magic, Science, and Religion* (Anchor Book; Garden City, N. Y.: Doubleday & Co., 1954).

that those who will survive him also plan beyond his departure and substantially engage in role work anticipatory to his event. The two conditions—the joint though silent adjustments that A makes in his affairs and relationships, and those which A's associates make in their relationships with him and to each other—have the common, conjoining effect of easing the readjustments required by the transition from life to death.

Our common tendency is to perceive grief and funeral practices as oriented toward the past. Someone has departed, and the rites and ceremonials serve the purpose of mourning the dead, reliving the past, reviving treasured memories, honoring the departed who will not return. Certainly this is a part of the picture. But a more useful view is to see funeral rites and death attitudes as serving the purpose of assisting the survivors to restructure their relational system. The vital functions of these ceremonies relate really to the future, and not to the past: the restructuring of relationships occasioned by the absence of someone from an established set of relationships.

It must not escape our attention that in the social no less than the physical sense funeral ceremonies are commonly simply the terminal point of a gradual process begun long before. Physiologically the long-term process is one of degeneration; socially it is one of disengagement.[10] In an important sense, the human being learns to be dead, and practices being dead, and those around him also practice his death, his departure. In the life-cycle one begins life in a tiny social set consisting of his immediate family; and in infancy and early childhood one is in contact with relatively few people. But we expect an expansion outward from these early primary groups as the child grows into adolescence and adulthood: in school and col-

[10] A full statement of disengagement theory appears in Elaine Cumming and William E. Henry, *Growing Old: The Process of Disengagement* (New York: Basic Books, 1961), pp. 162-79.

lege, dating and work, and in varied organizations, the number of acquaintances he has is supposed to increase, particularly in an urban society; indeed, the popular meaning of "personality" suggests poise and skill in extending one's range of contacts. But this expansion does not continue throughout the life-cycle; rather, as one moves toward old age, the person begins cutting away—not merely ceasing to form new intimacies—but cutting away, reducing his circle of contacts, reducing the frequency of his interactions.[11] From the human actor's standpoint, we can say that he is preparing for death, the absence of relationships.

So the death process, in a social sense, begins typically a long time before the burial ceremony. And it begins not only with the person himself but with those who relate to him as well. His friends, his business associates, his family come to the point where they no longer encourage him to enter into new business ventures or to take up new hobbies or to develop new activities or to meet new people. That is, they begin to plan for his departure. Just as the actor takes on what we might call death behaviors—by which we mean dissociation and disengagement behaviors of various kinds—so do those around him begin to reciprocate in kind. They do not treat him as they treat the young family with children that has moved in next door, or the college freshman, or the new vice president in the company.

At the societal level these and related practices are best seen as reducing the harm to the general community oc-

[11] It is interesting to note that an everyday expression concerning the very old—"He's getting childish"—refers really to a changed orientation toward interpersonal relationships and a changed structure of demands on one's associates. Mary Lou Parlagreco, "The Very Old," in Cumming and Henry, *Growing Old,* pp. 201-9, noting that persons in their eighties are inwardly directed, absorbed with self-concern, and freed from social norms, and that friends are those who "do things for you," draws a specific analogy to childhood, suggesting that the aged have indeed come full cycle.

casioned by death. This mutually endorsed disengagement helps alert the potentially bereaved to the impending change in their role systems. It also benefits the general society: forced retirement is one of the best cases in point; made totally routine and orderly, it permits the social system to schedule its withdrawal of dependency on any given member. The societal shock waves from death are lessened in proportion to how few are those whose work or emotional routines are linked into the departed.[12] So the physical event of death, except in the case of sudden death, is preceded by interpersonal preparation by a whole set of people, specifically those whose role networks will be influenced by the change in status of the person.

All rites of passage, all major role transformations, involve an exclusion, as in death, followed by a new integration, that is, a new birth. So in death, is it not likely that the sudden—the unexpected—death grasps our attention so much the more precisely because we have not been ready for it, because it demands of us a sort of crash program of adjusting to a role network that will either have a void in it or for which a substitute must be found? Transitions from group to group and from one social situation to another cannot be effected with a snap of the fingers or a wave of the wand. Some formalized public statement and also a period of transition are necessary during which everyone becomes accustomed to the new circumstances.[13]

[12] Blauner, in "Death and Social Structure," suggests that the equilibrium of social life is disrupted by death to the extent that death creates a "social vacuum," which depends in turn upon the degree of the deceased's engagement in the life of the society. Anything a society can do to reduce the importance of those who die will contain the impact of mortality.

[13] Arnold van Gennep, *The Rites of Passage,* trans. Monika B. Vizedom and Gabrielle L. Caffee (Chicago: University of Chicago Press, 1960). Van Gennep observes that *rites de passage* divide logically into stages. They begin with rites of separation, during which the central party removes himself from his old ties; he goes off (or is sent) into the wilderness, or into the garden to pray, or away from his former friends in the nonfraternity world. Following a period of waiting, there are

As we have been emphasizing, it is essential that we not overlook the anticipatory and preparatory phases that begin long before actual death. There is, nonetheless, the culminating event, the event of death itself. There remains the fact that whatever the extent of prior, gradual dissolution of social bonds, the final, permanent, and complete separation of man from his fellows occurs, and ceremonials inform the public of this change in circumstances. It is to consider the nature of these rituals surrounding the acute event of death that we turn now.

Social Functions of the Funeral and Grief

Death, we have suggested, is a *rite de passage*. As widespread belief systems define the matter, the passage occurs for the deceased as well as for the living: the person who dies passes into another, perhaps eternal, system of role relationships just as those who are left behind pass into another system of role relationships. We never directly observe the former instance; this is a matter of belief and faith, though various rites and ceremonies exist to facilitate this passage. These may be quite literal, as in the form of providing the Happy Warrior with hunting equipment to use when he gets to the Happy Hunting Ground, or they may be totally symbolic, but clearly this belief in passage from the visible to the invisible world affects the nature of the funeral ceremonies, the social definitions of bereavement, and the condition of human hope. It will carry us too far afield to consider the effects of belief in existence after death on the behavior of individuals and the affairs of society. Surely, in the face of adversity and failure, or when the morally unclean are observed to prosper, the devout and the scrupulous find sustenance in the ideas of changed status, eventual justice, final payoffs,

---

rites of aggregation which induct or aggregate the person into his new status, thereby concluding the sequence.

and ultimate reward-and-punishment systems. Surely, too, the multiple decisions of daily life, mundane or momentous, are affected, sometimes directed, in the case of believers and even of the uncertain, by the assumption of continuing existence and eventual reckoning. But we are not really interested at this point in the human actor's passage into postlife status, but rather in the rituals and ceremonies pertaining to this passage that are conducted by and in the name of those who survive him. It is with this interest in mind that we inquire into the social meanings of funerals and other bereavement behaviors. What do funerals accomplish, beyond the obvious physical disposition of the dead; that is, what do they say to the living? In considering these questions we may inquire at two separate levels: the immediate circle of the deceased, the changes occurring in their behaviors and role networks; and, the meaning of death at the level of the society.

From the standpoint of those directly affected, funerals announce to the community that the bereaved are now in a new and unaccustomed status, and that normal role performance is not to be expected from them for awhile. From the societal standpoint death is an occasion for summing up an individual's social personality; no better proof exists than the content of the obituary pages themselves. The treatment of the event of death varies with the social position of the dead; to treat the death of person A as immensely important and the death of person B as less important is to affirm the values of those things that person A was and person B was not and to remind everyone that it is worthwhile (because it is rewarding) to try to be like person A. Hence people should be motivated to wish to be those things that produce a lengthy obituary column.[14] Funerals represent a public reformula-

[14] We are reminded that Don Birnam in Charles Jackson's novel *The Lost Weekend* is detained from suicide precisely because he cannot bear to be absent when his associates react to his death.

tion of social norms by the way they sum up an individual's social personality, restate the roles he has played, the positions he has occupied, and, at least by inference, suggest an evaluation of the way in which he has conducted himself during his lifetime.

But not only must the normative order be affirmed, communities must be kept intact, and burial ceremonies, by their special honor to the dead and their special consideration of the bereaved, make their contribution here as well. Perhaps the point can be made most forcefully by asking the innocent question, Why do we insist on being nice to the dead? Why can't the unloved wife say, "I'm glad he's gone," and why does not the fundamentalist minister say decisively, "Here's a man who's going to burn in hell. If ever we've had a beautiful case, this is it" ? Probably the reason is that this would not contribute to the solidarity of the living; it would pit group against group, family against family, and would, of course, injure and hurt the bereaved. Since funeral ceremonies function to reintegrate the group and attend to the needs of the living, it would seem dysfunctional to pronounce judgment on the dead, even within those religious traditions that give heavy emphasis to everlasting reward and punishment systems and are explicit as to the determining conditions. "Speak ye not evil of the dead," not in the interest of the dead but of the living.

Let us turn at this point to look at an additional side of the picture. What is grief for? What use does it serve? We most commonly view grief as a spontaneous manifestation of personal loss and a relatively uncontrollable expression of personal emotions. There is a useful perspective from which we see that grief serves to unite the living, to reaffirm dominant social values and dominant group relationships, just as it is that the ceremonies of death not only manage, control, and direct the grief of individuals who are bereaved, but also, and more importantly, assert the sanctity of the group that now grows closer together because of the absence of the departed. The point is that society loses some part of itself in any man's death, and it must have means of recuperation, means, as it were, for reweaving its webs.

We should expect the volume of grief occasioned by a death to be, indeed, proportional to the number of persons whose role systems are dislocated or threatened, and to the sum of the severity of the dislocation.[15] Again, the extreme negative case is the unmourned, those unclaimed bodies carried to potter's field, buried by the public sector because the deceased participated in no meaningful private networks. The more diffuse and nonspecific the obligations, the more intensive and enduring the interaction within a network, the more severe are the dislocations that occur when any member is removed.

To understand the nature of a social network, let us take the case of the family unit. Like any other social network, it may be said to have an agenda, a business that consists of things that must get done if its essence is to be preserved. We are saying that there are certain tasks that must be accomplished if the family unit is to preserve itself in any interactional form that we will recognize as a family. Some of these are economic, of course, and some involve sheer maintenance, but many are emotional, affect-laden tasks. Importantly for our argument, they involve countless customs and assumptions about, to take examples, how each member is to address every other member, who can give orders and who can not, how affection is

[15] This is somewhat similar to the "social loss theory" as stated by Barney G. Glaser and Anselm L. Strauss in "The Social Loss of Dying Patients," *American Journal of Nursing*, LXIV (June, 1965), 119-21. They argue that nurses bestow more loving and extensive care on dying patients who are perceived to have high social value. An example of very high social value (hence high social loss) would be a middle-aged man with dependent children who in his occupation makes an obviously important contribution. An example of low social loss would be the aged.

expressed, what acts are to be private, which public, which semi-private. In their nearly infinite subleties, these behaviors give definition to what a father is to a child, what a wife to a husband, what an older brother to a younger brother, etc. Any lost member of such a network will be severely mourned, partly of course for other and more sentimental reasons, but partly also because the task of finding and adjusting to his replacement is such a severe one.

To point the contrast, all members of a social network consisting of a city bus driver and his (even regular) passengers are easily replaceable; its essential agenda is accomplished in much the same way if given passengers or drivers are removed. It is unlikely that any member of such a network will give more than passing thought to the death of any other member. Thus, those persons will mourn the dead who must realign their role relationships the most, and the larger the number of persons whose role relationships must somehow be realigned, the greater the total grief that a death will occasion.

But personal grief, even when severe network dislocation is involved, is not purely either a private or a spontaneous matter. The larger community has a legitimate interest in influencing and directing the nature of bereavement behavior. Social networks are not closed systems; each person normally links into a number of networks, and thus the number of networks ultimately affected by mourning a single death is quite large. Some impairment of the normal routines and efficiency of all such networks continues for as long as survivors are in bereavement status. To take a single example, one's coworkers on the job are affected as long as he is away, or preoccupied, due to a loved one's death. Therefore, we should expect to observe a reasonably explicit consensus regarding the rules for bereavement behavior, varying by the nature of the relationship to the deceased and perhaps by certain attributes of the person himself such as sex and age. The immense public admiration for Mrs. John Kennedy's conduct following the President's assassination occurred precisely because she bore the loss more bravely than we had any right to expect.

Bereavement behavior, it is interesting to note, is controlled by both normative and structural elements in the society. Mourning, says Emile Durkheim, is not spontaneously expressed private emotion: "[It] is not a natural movement of private feelings wounded by a cruel loss; it is a duty imposed by the group. One weeps, not simply because he is sad, but because he is forced to weep. It is a ritual attitude which he is forced to adopt out of respect for custom, but which is, in a large measure, independent of his affective state." [16] Speaking specifically of contemporary American society, Riley observes that the normal orientation requires the bereaved to do their grieving both quickly and within the confines of family and close associates, which is to say privately.[17] It is probable also that a rational, secular, efficiency-oriented society produces norms that encourage early termination of a mourning attitude. The set is toward the future rather than the past; there is an impatient "let's-get-on-with-it" concern that requires the survivor to pass quickly through bereavement to the resumption of his normal social tasks.

Structurally, and continuing to limit our attention to the present-day United States, it seems likely that physical mobility of the population and the decline of the extended family have significant effect on how bereavement is expressed and experienced. As to the former, the ecology simply is not right for protracted expressions of grief. Survivors must often come great distances for interment ceremonies, and they return quickly to settings which provide neither the social support nor the physical induce-

[16] Quoted in Jack Goody, *Death, Property, and the Ancestors* (Stanford: Stanford University Press, 1962).

[17] John W. Riley, Jr., "Death and Bereavement."

ments to grief. If we follow Eliot in regarding bereavement as in its nature a family (or primary group) affair,[18] then the number of persons experiencing sorrow surely is less than when the nuclear family is the prevailing pattern and the number of offspring is typically small.[19] But probably the most fundamental structural effect on the nature of bereavement in American society is the lengthening life-span of the population. As Parsons has pointed out in an important paper,[20] death through adventitious circumstance has become less frequent, so that we confront death more frequently as the termination of a normal life-cycle. An increasingly large proportion encounter death only after completing the significant life-tasks associated with work careers and family roles.[21] The most acceptable death is that which comes at the end of a full life in which opportunities have been reasonably maximized and worthwhile goals reasonably well achieved; when these have happened, the sense of fulfillment and of completeness dilute the sense of grief. Thus, a major social force tending to de-emphasize prolonged and expressive grief behavior is the increasing longevity of the population.

[18] Thomas D. Eliot, "The Bereaved Family," *Annals of the American Academy of Political and Social Sciences,* CLX (March, 1932), 184-90.

[19] Of course, the matter is much more complicated than this: very strong ties develop between members of small systems such as the American family, and personnel are not interchangeable. To complicate matters further, it is probably that the same smallness and intimacy and the intensive interaction in the small nuclear family intensifies not only love but also elements of guilt and hostility, and that these latter feelings must be managed in the bereavement process. See Edmund H. Volkart and Stanley T. Michael, "Bereavement and Mental Health," *Death and Identity,* pp. 272-93.

[20] Talcott Parsons, "Death in American Society" (unpublished paper, 1967), see especially pp. 6, 18.

[21] One striking evidence of this is the extension of the joint survival years. Now more than one third of the marriage period of the average American couple is spent in the "empty nest" stage, after all children have grown up and left home. Paul Glick, *American Families* (New York: John Wiley and Sons, 1957).

The Subterranean Work of the Medical Profession

Death is an uncertain, a problematic, state, in that though it surely comes for all of us its precise coming for any one of us normally cannot be known. Because of this, death has been conceptualized as a nonscheduled status passage, in that the human actor passes from living to dead status according to no man-made or imposed schedule.[22] Death derives some of its power, fright, and mystery precisely from such a feature. Now scheduling is much to be desired where possible in human affairs, and this fact should alert us to the possibility that various procedures and communications exist among humans for the purpose of establishing the most probable time of death, of making the time more definite than it otherwise will be. But having observed that death is a taboo subject, we should expect there to be substantial slippage, that is, ambiguity and imprecision, in these elements of the death complex.[23] Nonetheless, knowing when a person is going to die is useful information to have: it is useful to the immediate subject, to his survivors, and to the community at large; so it should not surprise us if a fair amount of human energy is devoted to calculating such matters. The person himself wants to arrange to set his affairs in order, and those who will be left behind wish to have as much advance knowledge as possible as to how their affairs, including their emotional and relational life, will be affected.

Now the problem of establishing the probable time of death rests in our society largely with the medical profession. Whether it be annual health checkups, medical

[22] Glaser and Strauss, "Temporal Aspects of Dying as a Non-Scheduled Status Passage," *American Journal of Sociology*, LXXXI (July, 1965), 48-59.

[23] For an insightful discussion of how hospitals are arranged and physicians conduct themselves so as to hide the truth of impending death, see Glaser and Strauss, "Awareness Contexts and Social Interaction," *American Sociological Review*, XXIX (October, 1964), 669-78.

record maintenance, communications with the afflicted, or assistance to the survivors in establishing proper bereavement behavior, the responsibility of the medical profession is substantial and central. The tasks involved in this complex are not as simple as they may at first appear. The doctor, in the midst of his professional tasks of relieving pain and sustaining life, is called upon to help the patient and others involved decide whether death will occur, its probable time of occurrence, and the conditions that will affect its coming. He also has to decide how much information should be given, when, and to whom. He must of course announce the occurrence of death itself, and select the proper time and manner for this announcement. Even this latter is no simple matter since, as Sudnow perceptively observes, those closest to the deceased have the right to hear first, and an elaborate precaution and ritual system must operate to insure that people do not hear out of turn.[24]

These tasks of the physician are essentially nonmedical in nature.[25] Nonetheless, he is aided in his task by various medical appurtenances, not the least of which is the physical setting of the hospital itself. Thus, moving the patient to an intensive care unit clearly places him in a new status, as may placing the patient on the critical list, or wheeling him into surgery, or inducing flurries of activity that break the routinized processes of patient care. The physician is in clear control of the setting in which the definition of death takes place, and if he elects to tell even nurses nothing until death is certain, it is his perogative to do so.[26]

[24] David Sudnow, *Passing On,* p. 160. It appears that it was felt improper to have a relative of one kin-class, say children, brothers-sisters, aunts-uncles, cousins, etc. be told of the death of a relative by a member of a kin-class more "distant," formally speaking, from the deceased.

[25] Glaser and Strauss, "Awareness Contexts." An appropriate term to describe him in this role is that of "transition technician."

[26] John Gunther, in *Death Be Not Proud* (New York: Harper & Row, 1949), pp. 29-30, writing of his own son's prolonged death, gives

One of the dominant features of modern death is that it occurs in the hospital, a physical setting devoted to the practice of medicine and clearly controlled by medical personnel: a major consequence of this is that many aspects of death are removed from the public's domain. It is in fact removed from the public's eye, occurring in bureaucratized settings under highly routinized processes.[27] The processes of medical care, handling of the terminal patient, and post-death arrangements are in large part separate from, and not the responsibility of, the general public—in contrast to days in which folk remedies were administered by neighbors and lay physicians and the body was prepared for burial by a citizen whose avocation it was to do so.[28]

The Cemetery as a Social Symbol

If the dead by virtue of death became irrelevant to the living community, it would be necessary merely to provide a sanitary disposal system. Instead, cemeteries exist, often occupying immensely valuable land and involving substantial financial investments by individual citizens; the cemetery is, in other words, a substantial, significant element in social organization. It is remarkable how little attention we have paid to the cemetery as a form of land-

---

the following description of how he first learned: "Five minutes after I got there I knew Johnny was going to die. I cannot explain this except by saying that I saw it on the faces of the three doctors, particularly Hahn's. I never met this good doctor again, but I will never forget the way he kept his face averted while he talked, then another glimpse of his blank averted face as he said goodbye, dark with all that he was sparing us, all that he knew would happen to Johnny, and that I didn't know and Frances didn't know and that neither of us should know for as long as possible."

[27] See Robert Blauner, "Death and Social Structure."

[28] Fulton comments on our tendency to segregate the dying so that relatively few citizens have had direct contact with the harsh facts of death. Robert Fulton, "The Sacred and the Secular," pp. 89-104, *Death and Identity*.

use and a representation of public sentiments.[29] The only major work has been done by W. Lloyd Warner, to whom the cemetery is meaningful both because it partakes of the sacred and because it reflects so much of the secular: "The cemetery reflects many of the community's basic beliefs about what kind of society it is, what the persons of men are, where each fits or is fitted into the secular world of the living and the spiritual society of the dead." [30] A place dedicated to the dead of God, it symbolizes to him the certainty of man's own death made safe by tradition and by religious sanction. It is sacred earth. Whereas the funeral is a time-bound event that moves the human being from the time-bound existence of humanity to an enduring spiritual status, the cemetery is a timeless place; it bridges time, connecting eternity to human time. That is, the cemetery locates the dead in time and space, thus maintaining their reality to those who wish to continue relations with them. It unites the living and the dead and forces the living to rethink their own situations. To be able to believe that the dead still live is to be able to believe that one will also live after he dies. The cemetery, then, is a collective representation expressing the social structure of the living; it is a spiritual symbol, as well. Tied to the cemetery is the undertaker.

The undertaker takes charge after death. He prepares the dead for viewing, and he stages and arranges the

[29] For limited exceptions, see W. L. Warner, "The City of the Dead," *Death and Identity*, pp. 360-81; William M. Kephart, "Status After Death," *American Sociological Review*, XV (1950), 635-43; Walter Firey, *Land Use in Central Boston* (Cambridge: Harvard University Press, 1947).

[30] *The Living and The Dead* (New Haven: Yale University Press, 1959), p. 280. I didn't know how common this is, but Warner happened to study a community in which the position of the graves neatly reflected the community position of the family owning the gravesite. That is, the area of the wooden headstones was down at the lower levels where the dirt washed out, and the large plots were up on top of the hillside. So that as you went up, you went up. This is but one instance of the relevance of cemeteries to the social organization.

funeral ceremony. There is a production, a final public presentation of the deceased.[31] The living are the consumers of the services offered by the undertaker; he performs this ritually unclean and physically distasteful work in a manner that is demanded by the living and at a cost that they are willing to bear. Thus, as in the typical case, when there is a cosmetological triumph by which the dead is made to look as though he were only asleep, and the pillowed, mattressed arrangement of the body supports the illusion, it must be said that this production, as set in motion by the undertaker, is presented on commission of the bereaved. Importantly, it is presented also in the name of the larger community. That is, if perchance the undertaker treated the dead in ways that were thought to be unfitting or inappropriate, he surely would hear about it; there would be a hue and outcry. The fact that this does not happen on any large scale should suggest to us that the undertaker acts as a representative of the community, and the things that he does with the deceased, and the differences between the things that he does with deceased A as against deceased B, somehow fit with the beliefs in the community at large about how things are and about how things ought to be. Here we are reminded again that the ceremonies of the dead affirm the values of the living. Though several recent efforts spoof and ridicule those whose business it is to process the dead, nonetheless, we must view the undertaker as an agent of the community. He does things that are generally approved; another way of confirming the point is to observe that a less secular age, an age in which the church were more dominant in the affairs of men, I think, would simply not permit the

[31] And it may be viewed as a highly complex effort by the bereaved to present a final public definition of the deceased, as well as to make a contribution to the public's image of the family name and of those who provide him. For provocative analysis, see Erving Goffman, *The Presentation of Self in Everyday Life* (New York: Doubleday & Co., 1959).

take-over of the affairs of death as completely by the undertaker and the funeral home as has happened in at least the urban segment of contemporary society.[32]

Summary

Karl Mannheim once raised the innocent, disarming question, what would society be like if there were no death? [33] His answers seem relevant to the basic perspective of this paper. Because members die, he suggested, roles must be filled by new participants. This permits some slippage in transmitting the culture, which in itself facilitates social change. Further, the arrival of new role performers almost automatically assures a fresh perspective, also abetting change and adaptation. Societies, he implies, are in their essence affected by the fact of death, and would be immensely different and vastly more rigid if death did not occur.

This essay tries to suggest the central relevance of death and death-related behaviors to social organization. It tries to suggest, indeed, that the ultimate determinants of the response to death rest in the needs and nature of the social system.

[32] See Robert L. Fulton, "The Clergyman and the Funeral Director: A Study in Role Conflict," *Social Forces*, XXXIX (May, 1961), 317-23.

[33] *Essays on the Sociology of Knowledge* (London: Routledge and Kegan Paul, 1952).

James T. Laney, Associate Professor of Christian Ethics at Vanderbilt Divinity School, suggests the "axiological presence" of death and a transcending faith as a basis for ethical reflection. Without acknowledging this presence, individual life loses its uniqueness, and daily decisions forfeit their moral seriousness. Without a transcending faith, the affirmed presence does not necessarily lead to constructive attitudes and practices. Thus Christian Ethics requires an affirmation of both death and grace. On this basis, Mr. Laney considers truthtelling, euthanasia, organ transplants, and suicide.

VIII

Ethics and Death

James T. Laney

This essay on ethics and death is divided into two parts. The first part consists of an examination of some implications of the fact of death for the ethical enterprise, i.e., what it means to undertake ethical reflection under the sign of mortality. The second part is a consideration of several specific ethical issues which arise in acute form at the time of death, such as truthtelling, euthanasia, and suicide.

Some Implications of the Fact of Death for Ethical Reflection

Even a casual reader in contemporary Christian ethics will be struck by the fact that many of the most popular and influential writers conspicuously avoid treating death as an ethical problem. For example, Charles West in an early review of *The Secular City* noted the lack of any mention of the problem of death or suffering in Harvey Cox's best seller. While many of the specific issues surrounding death could well be relegated to more comprehensive ethical studies, such as Helmut Thielicke's *Theological Ethics* or the ethical portions of Barth's *Church Dogmatics,* one must still inquire whether the way he sees life and hence "does" ethics is not fundamentally altered by his interpretation of the meaning and significance of the fact of death. Karl Rahner has observed that much of the excitement surrounding the discovery of secular man's prowess in a technological age is tenable only by ignoring the inescapable fact of each man's death. This, he notes, issues in a perspective upon the world which is more technological than historical.[1] To be sure, headlined advances in surgery and genetics underscore man's increasing mastery over what had once been considered unalterable determinants of life. These spectacular successes foster visions of man's control over life—and hence, by implication, even death—making any reminder of man's continuing creaturehood seem both incongruous and unappreciative. Yet obviously the question of death is not raised simply for negative reasons. Rather it is to point out that while *man* doesn't die (insofar as we mean mankind) short of the extinction of the species, nevertheless, each man must fashion a responsible life within the limits of a given life-span.[2] Serious ethical reflection, then, should take into account the particularity and finality personal death imposes as well as the questions which scientific control has raised for policy and decision making.

For example, when ethical reflection relies too exclusively upon a generalized perspective on life, all values tend to find a common denominator and thus become

[1] This point is discussed at length in his essay "Christianity and the 'New Man,'" *Theological Investigations* (Baltimore: Helicon Press, 1966), V, 135-53.

[2] Kierkegaard develops this idea more carefully than any contemporary. See especially his *Concluding Unscientific Postscript,* trans. David F. Swenson and Walter Lowrie (Princeton: Princeton University Press, 1944), pp. 147 ff.

commensurable, that is, exchangeable for one another. This is because an overview on life as a whole diminishes the uniqueness it invariably has for a person. On such a broad view, the problem of death can be met by the substitution of life for life. An extreme case is found in statistical abstraction. Modern society abounds in such statements as, "The incidence of highway death is 48,000 per year," or, "The kill ratio in Vietnam is six to one." Obviously these kinds of concepts are essential to control over the environment. They represent the quintessence of rationalized modern society, where even life and death are reduced to manageable integers. On the basis of such statistical margins, rational judgments as to relative courses of action are reached. But while acknowledging the place for and necessity of this kind of ethical evaluation, questions must still be raised as to the adequacy and sufficiency of this kind of rational value as a basis for Christian ethics. One does not have to resurrect the nightmare of Nazi terror nor invoke the specter of Orwell's controlled state to suggest the dangers inherent in an ethical calculus which cannot distinguish intrinsic and thus irrevocable values from a putative good, abstractly conceived. To take the most obvious case, the question of justice has always served to remind us that there are certain values (life, liberty, etc.) which cannot with moral justification be sacrificed to the larger good, no matter how great that good purports to be. Such protection of individual life is based upon the root conviction that each man's life is unique and unrepeatable; that the finality of death sets an inescapable limit to any generalized calculus of good or rational assessment of value.

Much of the current protest movement can be understood in morally intelligible terms as a refusal to reduce life—its uniqueness and unrepeatability—to rational control. It is not merely protest against the galling impersonality of major decisions affecting the lives of so many, as though any effort to locate the responsible person behind policy decision were doomed to frustration in a Kafkian sense. More importantly, this moral protest is directed against the kind of impersonality which would deal with life interchangeably—one life for another, one job for another—all the while denying what life seen under the sign of mortality inescapably is, viz., utterly singular. Similarly, the moral activism of many of today's protestors grows out of concrete imperatives in which an awakened moral consciousness is bound to specific situations and particular people—imperatives which constrain the moral consciousness despite its evident conflict with rational policy. At stake here is not whether parallels drawn between Hitler's policies and the American government's today are valid (as many protestors claim), but whether a too-ready reliance upon abstract ethical calculus does not serve to blunt moral sensibility for real—that is, incarnate—value. An appreciation of the uniqueness of life deriving from the fact of death offers an indispensable component for ethical reflection, one that should be held in tension with the more abstract, general, and rationalized approaches to modern ethical decisions.

What are some of the implications for ethics growing out of a consideration of life now seen as that interval bounded by birth and death? Hannah Arendt suggests that one of its primary characteristics is to be found in the distinction between life seen as *bios* rather than *zoe*.[3] One characteristic of the former is that it provides the basis of a story, or history, and is not the subject of mere duration. Another lies in the movement from the strictly natural to the personal as the primary mode of life. Death sets the unavoidable limitation upon life's "time" in such

[3] *The Human Condition: A Study of the Central Dilemmas Facing Modern Man* (Anchor Books; Garden City, N. Y.: Doubleday & Co., 1959), p. 85. Indeed, the whole book reflects the kind of sensitivity toward death to which this chapter is indebted.

a way as to invest it with utter singularity. The very nature of temporality as a fundamental constituent of life drives us to wrest meaning and significance from it, which, if possible, can transcend self and self's final end.

Death then not only sets the limits within which ethical reflection must take place, the awareness of death colors all decisions in life and freights them with moral seriousness. This has been referred to as the "axiological presence" of death throughout the whole of life.[4] Death in this view is no longer only value-negating. Rather, the anticipation of that final negation as far as historic life is concerned serves to provide the basis for value-affirmation, for a deepened sense of time's unique preciousness and the singular opportunity. Because time is thus limited, possibilities are also, and every choice means not only to entertain a certain possibility but to forego others. In this sense every decision entails a sacrifice of value, a denial of options, a foreclosure of yet other opportunities, but always for the sake of a concrete possibility. Time's movement toward death not only requires a concentration upon the one choice among the many, it also bespeaks the irrevocable nature of that choice and thus of life itself. Responsible moral life will seek to be sensitive to both these dimensions of death impinging upon life.

A second implication death holds for ethics concerns the manner in which one responds to this axiological presence of death in life. Our response to death and its pervasive presence in life reflects a value context expressed in all ethical decisions. Evasion of the fact of death is flight from moral seriousness into triviality or preoccupation. Karl Jaspers has put it this way, "If to philosophize is to learn how to die, then this learning how to die is actually the condition for the good life. To learn to live

[4] Karl Rahner, *On the Theology of Death* (New York: Herder & Herder, 1961), p. 77.

and to learn how to die are one and the same thing."[5] This bears close affinity with Kierkegaard's observation that the development of a person consists precisely in his active interpenetration of himself by reflection upon his life in light of his end, i.e., death.[6] The import of such responses to death are not to be construed as morbidity or a fatal pessimism. They emerge out of an appreciation of the once-for-allness of the given character of life, in all its singularity, and the intrinsic possibilities which inhere in such particularity. It must be readily admitted that such considerations find little resonance among many contemporaries. Yet it would be a mistake to misconstrue a consideration of death as the antithesis of action and participation in life. The thoughtful person would want to insist that such awareness and response are the *conditio sine qua non* of responsible action, the urgent prerequisite for any ethical stance. What this means in a "world come of age" is that the new responsibility afforded to man by greater and greater extensions of power over life (and over the boundaries, but not the fact, of death), is to be exercised in light of a *mortal* perspective and not from a vantage point above history as a timeless master. While such remarks may seem obvious to the point of banality, a review of some of the less restrained discussions bearing on ethical decisions in a new age indicate that consideration of man's essential condition as creature is salutary.

It needs to be acknowledged frankly, however, that this "axiological" presence of death throughout life does not necessarily insure a constructive attitude and response. In the absence of hope and without constructive faith transcending our temporal end, the presence of death in life can lead to a clutching at value, to an "ethics of death." Whether issuing in a morbid preoccupation with death

[5] Quoted in Jacques Choron, *Death and Western Thought* (New York: Collier Books, 1963), p. 228.

[6] Kierkegaard, *Concluding Unscientific Postscript*, p. 151.

itself or an evasion of the consciousness of death, life's transiency serves to erect defenses or drive one into nihilistic abandonment. A consideration of the future—under such circumstances taking the "long view"—can only be disconcerting and unnerving, for its only promise is loss and descent, if not into the grave, then *ad inferos*.[7] The ever-narrowing space-time alloted to us leads to ever more frantic grasping after something. It is important here to reject the notion that an anxiety born of awareness of death is a disease peculiar to a certain class of existentialists. Those who would reject consideration of death do so by immersion in a kind of adolescent enthusiasm for life which would deny any necessity of transcending the temporal. Real maturity, according to such views, can accept finitude without flinching and make the most of what is possible during life. One cannot help admiring such matter-of-factness before the problem of death. Yet the accuracy of such observations is open to dispute. In a careful study of a group of adolescents, Robert Kastenbaum suggests that even during the most robust period of life when there is little or no manifest anxiety over death, lurking beneath confident visages is widespread uneasiness occasioning just the questions we have been discussing.[8] Death as enemy, mocker, and caster-into-oblivion is not so easily defeated, and certainly not by evasion or repression. To minimize the problem of death as the universal *terminus ad quem* for each person allows for a trivializing of life and tends toward a total rationalization which ends only with the denial of individuality and uniqueness.

But on the more personal level, awareness and acceptance of mortality are not enough. Only a faith which

[7] This term is found in H. Richard Niebuhr's *The Responsible Self* (New York: Harper & Row, 1963), pp. 99-100.

[8] "Time and Death in Adolescence," *The Meaning of Death*, ed. Herman Feifel (New York: McGraw-Hill, 1965).

enables one to transcend death can offer the freedom to deal in responsible love with those who are dying. Ethically speaking, there are two consequences an affirmation of the axiological presence of death might have for the Christian. The first is what we shall call, in Erik Erikson's phrase, "responsible renunication."[9] It is not only the recognition and acceptance of one's own death—with a consequent anticipation of its implications—but it is as it were a preparation for the final renunciation by way of a reordering of life about a center beyond the self. The release of the self's commitment from self-protection and concern to one who alone is eminently worthy of such loyalty and support is the prerequisite. This mode of life bears resemblance to Heidegger's idea of authentic existence made possible in light of one's death. But it also contains the notion of cause or purpose beyond the self—a felicity to that life which transcends death. Such fidelity makes possible what Karl Rahner terms "free self-possession" and is the condition for a "good" death.[10] Rahner's point is sustained by experiences we all have had in the presence of the death of others. The bitterness and resentment which some exhibit in the face of their own impending death contrasts sharply with the attitude of those in whom a prior self-renunciation has already enabled them to overcome the terror of death. This quality, Rahner suggests, is verifiable by observation. Such an achievement—or better, grace—is a lifetime's work, made possible in Christian terms by "dying with Christ" in faith, thereby relinquishing a clutching after life. Such responsible renunciation is not to be confused with a kind of supine acquiescence. On the contrary, it becomes the basis for a new kind of self-possession, one no longer shaken by the thought of death either of self or neighbor.

[9] *Insight and Responsibility* (New York: W. W. Norton, 1964).
[10] *On the Theology of Death,* p. 39.

Death transmuted by the cross now becomes the condition for, rather than the limit to, life.

This recognition of a cruciform pattern to all of life illumines how each life stands for another, how sacrifice is the door to life. Only through such an affirmation can the inescapable law of entropy be overcome. Whether it is understood in psychiatric terms as "individualization" or in existentialist terms as "authentic existence," for the Christian it is summed up in the confession of Paul that one has "died with Christ."

A second consequence flowing from an affirmation of the axiological significance of death may be described in terms of availability, or as Marcel has described it, *disponibilité*.[11] Quite obviously the openness implied in such a concept is only possible after a measure of responsible renunciation has occurred, wherein death is not the inevitable foreclosure upon life but enables one to be with another. It is through a posture of availability that one becomes alive to others and is enabled to "stand with" them in time of their death. Marcel has described this as the transition from an egoistic response which "cadaverizes" life to an availability which "consecrates" life. This has implication far greater than just for the moment of death itself, although it is most stringently tested at such a time. There is a natural revulsion to death common to us all. When death occurs under particularly brutal and dehumanizing circumstances this revulsion is heightened. Still it may be asked whether greater depths of inhumanity are not reached when we allow people to die in isolation, walled off from effective community with others under the cover of medical necessity. To the extent this occurs we "cadaverize" life. On the other hand to assist persons under conditions of suffering to achieve a measure of re-

[11] Gabriel Marcel, in his essay "Value and Immortality," explores at length this suggestive term, *Homo Viator* (Harper Torchbook; New York: Harper & Row, 1962).

linquishment because they are being affirmed by their companions may constitute one of the genuine expressions of grace. To have come to terms with one's own death and in faith to have achieved a degree of "responsible renunciation," may make possible our overcoming this revulsion and allow us to be "available" to another at his death.

Death, then, provides an inescapable reminder of the historicity, particularity, and concreteness of each life in its personal and social reality. Its axiological significance in light of the incarnation lies in the unrepeatable—and thus utterly morally serious—character of life. God becoming man is not so much a transcendent alchemy allowing a kind of escape from the givenness of this life, as the supreme ratification of the very earthly coordinates of this life. It is out of these materials and under the severe limitation they impose that moral maturity is to emerge.

But the incarnation under the sign of the cross also points to the vicarious mutuality of life and the possibility of a this-worldly transcendence through an availability to and identification with others. The sanctity of life remains, but no longer as an automatic ethical touchstone. Rather, its employment in ethical reflection moves beyond the boundary of protection to render death an opportunity for achieving through grace a kind of self-transcendence. What some of the implications are for specific instances, especially heightened by the imminence of death, will be briefly explored in this next section.

Some Specific Ethical Issues at Time of Death

By all odds the most recurrect ethical dilemma arising in connection with impending death is that of truthtelling. The question "Am I going to die?"—whether asked in a silently imploring look or framed directly—surely is one of the most unsettling of all experiences. How is it to be dealt with, and what considerations qualify one's response? Patently, the issue is not resolvable into the simple alternative of shielding the patient from or exposing him to the "facts." It is settled neither by an appeal to the patient's right to the truth in some general sense, nor derived from one's universal obligation to veracity in a Kantian sense.

On the surface, at least, there appear two kinds of considerations which might qualify whether, when and how truth is communicated. The first relates to the context of the patient himself—his maturity, strength, and capacity to comprehend and incorporate such existential knowledge. The second concerns the relationship between the patient and the one to whom the question is addressed directly or indirectly. Whether this person is doctor, friend, or pastor, the question consists of the degree to which the relationship is marked by sufficient trust and confidence to support and affirm the dying regardless of what the truth might be. These considerations distinguish "truth" as communicated within a relationship from the utterance of cold objective "facts." Truth under such conditions cannot be dissociated from the "sphere of intentionality" where the relation between the persons in question and the import of the remarks brings new and volatile forces into play.

It is a widespread experience, for example, that information about the patient's condition which confirms his worst suspicions often appears to precipitate a decline and hasten death. This may occur even when objective prognosis would not have pointed to such a rapid deterioration. The psychological dimensions of assurance are too well known to require recounting here, and every doctor knows the value of a placebo under certain circumstances. Similar devices, medical and verbal, should not be rejected out of hand, although their use quite obviously calls for sensitivity and circumspection. More important, however, is the attitude of others to the patient, that nonverbal realm of communication which often expresses their true expectations to him. Here a distinction should be made between accepting the "facts" regarding one's condition while still acknowledging their tentativeness or penultimacy. Marcel makes the point that a too ready consent to the impending death of another may constitute a betrayal, since it is in effect giving him up to death.[12] One may accept a provisional prognosis without consenting to it as inevitable. Thus the manner in which those close to the patient respond to the prognosis may be of greater moral importance than how and to what extent they communicate the specific terms of that prognosis.

Two points need clarification here. On the one hand we are not being responsible to the patient if every conceivable means is taken to deceive him and thereby evade confrontation with the actual situation. Often such avoidance results in a whole tissue of fabrications and subterfuge. This can have the effect of tainting otherwise beneficial supporting relationships. At the same time consideration of the sensibilities and feelings of others may become as important as the truth. Avoidance of direct confrontation with a near-certain verdict may be initiated by the patient himself to spare others as much pain as possible. Sometimes the truth is known on both or all sides, but is simply not bandied about. Each knows the other knows, but refrains from imposing what might be an intolerable strain. Silence in such cases is not tantamount to evasion. It is more akin to responsible restraint. Under such circumstances the formalities of life—those much maligned structures of indispensable protection—may serve to hold back a descent into disintegration.

[12] *Ibid.*, p. 147.

Similarly one is not being responsible to the patient merely by bludgeoning him with the truth. This applies especially to physicians whose time seldom allows for them to prepare the patient to receive such truth. Here "speaking the truth" is framed by an appreciation of the necessity of a free acceptance of death, made possible by sustaining mutual relationships. The importance of coming to terms with a death which does not have to be seen as being left forsaken and abandoned cannot be overemphasized. Truth is responsibly uttered when it assists one to come to terms with death and yet at the same time "win" his life.

This points to some of the dangers of withholding the truth under a false consideration for the patient. Such "protection" can engender false hope and thereby constitute a grave disservice to the dying. One must be alert to the possibility that the reason often springs as much from the desire to avoid the awkwardness of a painful confrontation as out of a genuine concern for the patient's total self-possession. Bonhoeffer's insistence upon the "limits of responsibility" enters in here. One has no right, he avers, in interposing one's own feelings of propriety and consideration to the exclusion of allowing another to come to terms with his own destiny.[13] We must be careful not to deprive another of the "patrimony of his own soul," to use a phrase of Erikson. At the same time there are real dangers in romanticizing the attitude of Karl Holl, the German theologian of the early part of this century, who replied upon his deathbed when asked if he wanted morphine, "Nobody shall deprive me of my death." Such determined acceptance of death in its most self-conscious sense smacks of posturing as much as integrity. Nevertheless, it does serve to remind us of the extent to which we have come to view death as a reality

[13] See Dietrich Bonhoeffer's *Ethics,* ed. Eberhard Bethge (Paperback ed.; New York: The Macmillan Co., 1955), pp. 166 ff.

to be evaded at all costs, and minimized when it cannot finally be avoided, by withholding the truth from terminal patients. Part of the insistence upon the moral significance of death in the first part of this paper arises from the conviction that a discussion of the specifics of death must take place within a total context of its meaning for life as a whole. Thus the determined evasion of any confrontation with impending death is more a reflection of a contemporary ethos which seeks to deny the axiological importance of death at all costs than an expression of genuine human concern.

For this reason the discussion of the place of truth at the time of death involves more than the question of psychological tactics or religious imperialism. Thielicke rightly notes that our concern is with a truth to which we must be led, a truth which is not a presupposition, but a goal.[14] But such truth is never merely individual, even in death. No matter how intensely personal death inescapably is, it entails communion if it is to be met and transcended. This suggests that the modern penchant for isolating terminal patients, psychically if not physically, may constitute the great untruth of society. Minimizing physical pain takes the place of "being with" the patient. The terror and loneliness which are often so much a part of dying today can only be transcended by one who is affirmed and supported to the end. That kind of identification is the presupposition of truth, and it establishes the context in which the patient can be led to hear and also comprehend the truth. Only a responsible renunciation on the part of those with the patient can translate the irresponsibility of delivering the truth as a verdict into the sharing of truth through a bond which sustains even in death.

[14] Helmut Thielicke, *Theological Ethics* (Philadelphia: Fortress Press, 1966), I, 551 ff.

If the question of truthtelling is the most universal moral dilemma encountered at the time of death, that of euthanasia raises the most far-reaching implications. As Barth defines it, euthanasia is the sonorous Greek term indicating a gentle, painless, almost beautiful death by means of which those whose lives are intolerable to themselves or others are ended.[15] For our purposes here it has to do with taking the lives of those condemned to advanced, incurable illness, done as a favor to the sick and his relatives. It consists of an intentional shortening of a tortured and intolerable life by means now at our disposal through modern science.

It must be admitted that for most people the very thought of euthanasia is so repugnant that it is difficult to discuss with composure. The question arises in acute form at that point where the doctor can no longer help the patient to recover but can put an end to his suffering. In such a case, proponents of euthanasia inquire, may not the patient have the right to ask the doctor to end his own life, and does he (the patient) not have the right to have it granted? Further, they ask, in cases of extreme disability, cannot relatives request the same right?

There is no denying the element of mercy or humanitarianism involved in these requests. One of the strongest aspects of the argument in favor of euthanasia consists in citing the growing incidence of cancer-caused deaths, many of which entail extreme and prolonged suffering, a prolongation made possible today through the use of various medicines and surgical techniques. The all too frequent case of a person kept alive biologically in a comatose state by means of intervenous feeding provides the extreme case in point. Sometimes unusual methods adopted with the hope of provisional recovery only result in the

[15] Karl Barth, *Church Dogmatics,* III, 4 (Edinburgh: T & T Clark, 1961), 424 ff.

perpetuation of a vegetable-like existence. Yet deliberate withdrawal of such measures would constitute indirect killing. When life continues under artificial means for months and even years, the demoralizing effect upon all concerned is obvious. At the same time the refusal to employ every means possible to save life becomes an implicit consent to death. Advocates of euthanasia point to the dilemma posed by the ability to extend life almost indefinitely while not having the accompanying right to decide when such measures are unwise or even immoral.

The first general category of euthanasia has to do with death requested by the patient himself. The strongest case emerges when the request of the patient finds concurrence among the family and with the doctor or group of doctors. Obviously the controlling circumstances would be very compelling indeed: terminal illness coupled with acute suffering and rapid deterioration of the personality. When the patient pleads for such a death—or "release"—in reality it would take place by his own hand were it possible. The moral implications of this from the standpoint of the patient can be referred to a subsequent discussion of suicide. Parenthetically, however, it should be noted that requests from a patient under such circumstances are almost always accompanied by severe depression. One must ask whether the patient is in fact his own master in that case. Here the concurrence of relatives and family becomes pivotal. What are some of the moral implications for them of such acquiescence? Inevitably the question of true motivation arises. Is consent really for the sake of the patient, or for the convenience of those who live after? The impossibility of ever knowing one's true motives for sure, coupled with the high likelihood of acting from mixed motives, raises the more long-range question of what such consent might do to a sensitive person who would be prey to ineradicable guilt feelings. Under what circumstances, if any, can a close relative "consent" to a patient's death without betraying, as Marcel suggests, the one whose life we relinquish? This does not constitute an *a priori* denial of any possibility under which euthanasia could be necessitated, but it does raise the question whether the stipulation of certain conditions of moral responsibility in advance can provide unquestionable moral justification.

What about the physician under such circumstances? When family and patient request death, and diagnosis indicates no hope, is he morally free to perform the necessary task? Again the problem of the limit of responsibility must be raised. To what extent does a doctor have the right to assume a position of conscious arbiter over life and death? It is one thing to acknowledge that a doctor deals on the boundary of life and death every day, and quite another to conclude that the fundamental orientation of his work, namely protection and enhancement of life, can be discarded in favor of an act which takes life.

The second major category of euthanasia has to do with instances where it is not requested by the patient (either because of mental illness, deficiency, or unconsciousness). Here the importance of a categorical refusal to allow ethical reflection to be dominated by utility is underscored. Once the question is allowed to stand unchallenged, "Of what use is such a life?" (i.e., extreme disability, age, sickness, etc.), we have entered a realm of rational calculus which is fraught with peril. The venerable concept of the sanctity of life not only has served to protect the weak and "useless" from destruction, but quite as importantly, has served to keep men from becoming inhuman in their treatment of each other. Possibly a more pertinent question protecting the sacredness of life should be, "Is there a will to live?" When no such will is evident and life has presumably run its course, one may inquire whether we have the right to force the continuation of life by extreme means. Not to consider the question would constitute a denial of the right to die. Countless persons who are of no use to society or to others nevertheless cling tenaciously to life. Such life must be protected. Sperry sagely observes that questions of involuntary euthanasia have a way of losing their pertinence when one confronts the actual persons whose lives are to be taken.[16] Any diffusion of the responsibility for decision in this area which would enable one to evade direct decision and accountability constitute for Sperry the most insidious undermining of moral responsibility.

Having said all this, it should be admitted that one of the complicating factors today is the relentless determination to push the frontiers of medicine back. There is often an operative, but unstated, assumption that any death is a medical defeat. Consequently responsible medicine dictates the use of every conceivable device and strategem for the prolongation of life. There is no question that the artificial extension of life has exacerbated the question of euthanasia. But it may be that a more sensible solution would lie in the frank recognition that death invariably comes to all, and that while medicine is dedicated to life and health, it is not to be abused by forcing upon another the mere continuation of life in a biological sense. The more difficult judgment arises before the question of euthanasia itself is an issue, namely, at the time when a physician must exercise wisdom as to the total well-being of his patient. This kind of judgment has always been a part of the doctor's portfolio, and only with the advent of spectacular advances in technical medicine has an insistence upon a kind of physical-literal guarantee of the validity of his judgments become a prime issue.

[16] Willard L. Sperry, *The Ethical Basis of Medical Practice* (New York: Paul B. Hoeber Books, 1952), pp. 157-58.

In any case of euthanasia, however, the possibility of mistaken medical judgment remains. While it must be acknowledged that instances of such error might be rare, the fact remains that they do occur. In light of what values is euthanasia so necessary that it can afford to run this risk? At this point a contrast with the progressive elimination of capital punishment is in order. The very arguments forwarded by opponents of capital punishment seem to contradict those which support euthanasia. Is it a gain in moral responsibility to eliminate retributive death and instate utilitarian death? While this question takes us far beyond specific cases to the area of social morality, its urgency is a matter for general ethical concern.

I would suggest that the moral question here is not really addressed by raising the question of euthanasis. In light of our larger theological perspective, such a question is already an evasion of moral responsibility. Instead, moral sensibility is to be seen as an inescapable dimension of medical prognosis simply because we are dealing with human beings and not mere organisms. This being the case, the prior question becomes, what makes for wholeness in the patient and among those to whom he is related, and how can death be accepted as constitutive to life as a whole and not merely its termination?

One last problem demands a hearing today. What are the moral implications of organ transplants? The sudden rash of experimental attempts on heart patients has made this an urgent issue. The intent of the practice certainly cannot but be affirmed. Yet certain precautions must be insisted upon. In an eagerness to obtain an organ questions concerning the termination of life arise all over again. Here we must reassert the earlier point that life cannot be deliberately taken. Sacrificial euthanasia courts the same dangers and perils as suggested above. Yet the opportunity to have one's death be the occasion for possible new life for another does offer a means of transcending the negative aspects of death. Here only certain cautions can be entered. One, there should be no hint of pressure in bringing about a decision to donate an organ. The decision must be a free one reached by the patient himself, or if impossible, in his behalf by his family. Second, care must be taken to avoid any direct inducement of the hastening of death itself. Even a feeble life may not be terminated for another. Third, while the initial cases of transplant must always be fraught with great risk, putative advances in medical science should not be used to justify unnecessary haste and inadequate preparation. Life must always be treated with respect. One can only observe reluctantly that the spate of heart transplants within a short span of time smacks more of medical and institutional competition than humanitarian concern. To raise false hopes and expectations through unseemly notoriety neither enhances overall confidence in the medical profession nor supports an image of moral integrity.

The third and final dilemma arising before impending death is suicide. In this essay we are only considering suicide as it relates to terminal illness, whether administered by one's own or another's hand. In face of the ignominy of becoming a complete invalid and of being a total burden upon others, can a moral case be made for suicide? Bonhoeffer's counsel is wise: "If this action [suicide] is performed in freedom it is raised high above any petty moralizing accusation of cowardice and weakness."[17] Suicide, under certain circumstances, may be viewed as a supreme effort at self-justification, a heroic attempt to wrest a fragment of dignity from a life which has become impossible. The fact that suicide has an honorable place in certain cultures would indicate that it is an acceptable way of dealing not only with shame, but more importantly, with the impotence which may accompany age and illness.

[17] Bonhoeffer, *Ethics,* p. 167.

Yet for our purposes and in light of our theological affirmations, suicide remains the final act of despair, a judgment not only upon the uselessness of the life taken, but upon the supporting fabric of those about him. Suicide, at least in our culture, remains an enigma. Even when explanatory notes are left behind, true motivation and intent remain shrouded in mystery, inviting interpretation. Suicide is inescapably unethical not only because it is a taking of life, but because it is invariably social. Suicide cannot but be a negative condemnation of the whole of life, and thus of the relations of those who live on after.

Joseph Fletcher, in his book *Situation Ethics,* cites an instance of a young father afflicted with an incurable illness.[18] He knows that if he lingers on his insurance will not be renewed and the financial burden upon his family will become severe if not intolerable. Fletcher seems to suggest that when one considers all the circumstances—financial, emotional, etc.—the man would be justified in taking his own life for the sake of his family. The apparent force of this reasoning must be acknowledged. Maybe in certain homes there would be relief. But the basic presupposition underlying the presentation of this case is a kind of social hedonism whereby the maximization of "good" (here equated with the minimization of pain and hardship) is the basis for moral justification. But would a wife and family necessarily see it that way? If they felt some measure of sincere affection for the husband and father, would not his taking his own life become an indictment upon their loyalty and love? Are there no bonds of human trust which can withstand hardship, or which may not be subjected to it? Such questions are not raised by Fletcher. But surely a careful consideration of suicide can hardly avoid them.

[18] (Philadelphia: Westminster Press, 1966), pp. 165-66.

While suicide may solve certain immediate problems and thus presumably have some kinds of "good" consequences, are its "abiding consequences" those which survivors can live with? These considerations, rather than a recital of legalistic prohibitions, appear germane to the problem of suicide.

Conclusion

I have been suggesting in this paper that the finality of death must be included as a basic datum for moral theology, and further, that only in light of a Christian response which frees one from bondage either to evasion or mere pragmatism with regard to life can the specific issues death invariably raises for us today be responsibly addressed.

The theological premise underlying these considerations consists of an unalterable respect for life which is denied if its end is dealt with abstractly or calculatingly. Possibly more than with any other ethical problem, reflecting upon the moral aspects of death demands a personal faith stance —acknowledged and explicated—out of which one achieves the freedom to be for life even at death, and in so doing to respect life's dimensions which transcend death. Such faith alone can provide the sensitivity and capacity to examine the concrete issues involved at the time of death in such a way that even in death, life is affirmed.

Liston O. Mills is Associate Professor of Pastoral Theology and Counseling at Vanderbilt Divinity School. He writes this essay on the assumption that the pastor's ministry to the dying and to the bereaved continues as an important aspect of his work. The needs of both the dying and the bereaved are neglected in society's tendency to deny and to evade death. Such neglect enhances the temptation they already feel to despair of love and meaning. By his willingness to be present with *the dying, the pastor may participate in their quest to complete their lives and to die with integrity and with hope. By his public and private ministry to the bereaved the pastor is able to assist them as they accept the reality of their loss and reaffirm life in the face of death.*

IX

Pastoral Care of the Dying and the Bereaved

Liston O. Mills

Traditionally the ministry of the Christian pastor to the dying and the bereaved has been anticipated and accepted with gratitude. As a representative of the community of faith and hope, he was a reminder of a love transcending death. When one confronts American society's tendency to deny death and to isolate the dying and the bereaved, it becomes apparent that the pastor's presence is needed still. Yet strangely enough, many contemporary pastors are defensive about their work in this area. They feel that the medical profession cares for the dying and the funeral director cares for the bereaved.

This essay is written on the assumption that such defensiveness is unwarranted. It maintains that the pastoral care of the dying and the bereaved continues as an important aspect of the pastor's work. By understanding the needs of the patient and the bereaved, and by a grasp of his own heritage in Christian faith, the pastor may serve to help break down the barriers that anxiety about death continues to raise.

The Pastoral Care of the Dying

The Christian pastor who takes seriously his ministry to dying persons finds little written by his colleagues to assist him in his work. One token of the secularism of our time is that psychologists, psychiatrists, and sociologists are the current sources of our information on the dying person. Despite this fact the impression gained from a reading of this sensitive and humane material is that the presence of the pastor with the dying was never more important than it is now. For they describe a central tendency of our time to be the denial of death and the isolation of the dying person. They also insist that many dying persons wish to complete their lives, i.e., to come to some sense of integrity about the meaning of their relationships and commitments. By bearing witness to a love which does not deny either life or death and which transcends both, the pastor may be able to stand with the dying and to participate in their quest.

Perhaps the most important lesson the pastor can learn about the dying is of their fear of isolation and of the tendency of American society to segregate them. Dying persons are not so much afraid of death as they are of the process of dying. They fear progressive isolation, and they fear being forced to go it alone. Herman Feifel, after commenting on the relief some of his patients expressed when given an opportunity to share their feelings, says, "There is almost nothing as crushing to a dying patient as to feel that he has been abandoned or rejected." [1] In a study of patients with a predilection to death, Drs. Weisman and

[1] Herman Feifel, "Attitudes Toward Death in Some Normal and Mentally Ill Populations," *The Meaning of Death,* ed. Feifel, p. 125.

Hackett found them to be characterized by an absence of living human relationships in their final illness. They conclude that "isolation in itself did not evoke the image of appropriate death, but it undoubtedly encouraged the conviction that death was desirable. All showed little interest in the world of living people." [2]

Despite our knowledge of the negative effects of isolation on the dying, the trend seems to be for persons to die in hospitals. Studies reveal that most persons prefer to die at home. They are less apprehensive and less withdrawn with the people they know. Yet in 1964, 53 percent of the deaths in this country occurred in hospitals.[3] It is no indictment of the medical profession to say a personal death is difficult among strangers. Dr. Elizabeth Ross suggests that it is "understandable that physicians, whose vocation is to heal and to help, find it hard to 'give up,' to accept their failure. It is also understandable that they find it hard, if not impossible, to *help their patients die.*" [4] Since doctors and nurses have had no training in the special needs of the dying, their temptation is to neglect or to isolate the patient when there is "nothing more to do."

Another factor which serves as a handicap to relationship with the dying is the reluctance of many doctors to tell the patient the seriousness of his illness. Herman Feifel has done perhaps the most thorough study of this evasiveness. He records the resistence he encountered from doctors when conducting his study and concludes that "death [to medical doctors] is a dark symbol not to be stirred or touched, . . . it is an obscenity to be avoided." He points to

[2] Avery D. Weisman and Thomas P. Hackett, "Predilection to Death," *Death and Identity,* ed. Robert Fulton (New York: John Wiley & Sons, 1965), p. 325.

[3] Feifel, "Attitudes Toward Death," p. 119.

[4] Elizabeth Ross, "The Dying Patient," *Chicago Theological Seminary Register,* LVII (December, 1966), 3.

the "interesting contrast" between physicians and patients on whether or not the truth should be told. Depending on the study, 69 to 90 percent of physicians favor not telling. In contrast, 77 to 89 percent of patients want to know the truth. Feifel points out that "our embarrassment at looking at the individual face of death forces the seriously ill person to live alone on the brink of an abyss, with no one around to understand him". [5]

Although those involved in research on this subject seem to agree with Feifel that the truth is best, they also join him in a word of caution. The way in which the truth is told is all important. Sensitivity to the individual and a sense of timing should temper the truth. "Truth can be cold and cruel, or it can be gentle, merciful, and hopeful." [6] Gerald Aronson devised four guidelines designed to give the patient the truth and at the same time allow the person a "sense of individuality and identity to the end." First, "Do not tell the patient anything which might induce psychopathology." Second, "Hope must never die too far ahead of the patient; either hope of getting better, or hope of enjoyment of conversations tomorrow, etc." Third, "The gravity of the situation should not be minimized." Fourth, know "the duration of [his] psychological present [so you can manage] telling [him] . . . in such a way as to avoid [having him just] idly sitting around, awaiting death." [7]

The pastor walks a narrow ridge in this matter of truth-telling. He knows that not to tell compounds the patient's already weighty loneliness, and the pastor knows that the "falsity around him and within him [may do] more than

[5] Feifel, "The Function of Attitudes Toward Death," *Death and Dying: Attitudes of Patient and Doctor* (Group for the Advancement of Psychiatry Symposium No. 11 [New York: Mental Health Materials Center, 1965]), pp. 635 ff.

[6] *Ibid.*, p. 635.

[7] "Treatment of the Dying Person," *The Meaning of Death*, ed. Feifel, pp. 253-54.

anything else to poison [the patient's] last days."[8] Yet despite this conviction the pastor sometimes finds himself caught by the directions of the doctor, the requests of the family, and the questions of the patient. In such situations he may consult with those directly responsible about the advisability of being more open. And he may be careful not to miss any hint from the patient of his desire to talk about death. But the pastor may not usurp medical authority and tell the patient what he may know of the prognosis. Beyond these measures the pastor should be aware of the effect truth sometimes has on a patient. Pluegge mentions three phases through which he observed a patient to move after he had become aware of his prognosis: (1) "A first reaction of 'spurious hope,' based on denial, illusion, and self-deceit"; (2) "A period in which anxiety, rebellion, and despair were accentuated." (3) "But at long last, sometimes even in the very last stages of the illness, . . . [there was] a third period with new hope, quite different from the first one." In this transition he observed marked changes of personality in the form of increased patience, tolerance, and humility.[9]

A final aspect of the tendency to isolate the dying patient concerns his family. We cannot imagine that their concern is always for the patient's welfare. On occasion this is less a problem because the patient is comatose or there is general agreement as to how the matter will be faced. But during prolonged terminal illness, one must expect the family to bring to the experience of death the whole history of their lives together. Ambivalent feelings, old antagonisms, old guilts and griefs, and malignancies are sure to appear either overtly or covertly. Moreover,

[8] Leo Tolstoy, *The Death of Ivan Ilyitch*, in *Six Russian Short Novels*, selected by Randall Jarrell (Anchor Books; Garden City, N. Y.: Doubleday & Co., 1963), p. 282.

[9] Cited by Paul W. Pruyser, "Phenomenology and Dynamics of Hoping," *Journal for the Scientific Study of Religion*, III (Fall, 1963), 90 f.

cultural attitudes toward death affect family members. They must often experience a period of adjustment and grief before they can *be with* their relative.

The family's ambivalent feelings and rejection of the dying are often apparent in their behavior around the patient. Anger may be cloaked as solicitousness. Rejection of feelings may appear in a desire to be practical, which usually means checking the will. And a request that the doctor employ more medication to "ease the pain" may be a way of avoiding the dying patient. The "rituals of preparation" such as drawing the shades and speaking in hushed tones reflect totally unnatural attitudes. Weisman and Hackett say such activity indicates "complete capitulation, abandonment, and, in fact, premortem burial." These family attitudes often lead to "premortem loneliness, *bereavement of the dying.*" [10]

A way in which families sometimes reject the dying is in refusing to give up hope. They deal with their own fears of death and reject the patient by refusing to accept the medical diagnosis. An example of this attitude is the family of a thirty-one-year-old housewife who was dying of cancer and who knew she was dying. When told by the husband of the physician's report, the mother's response was, "Well, it sounds to me like you have given up on her. Well, we are not like that. . . . We've got lots of hope." Communication between the family and patient was superficial. Whenever the patient would mention death, her mother would reply, "If you don't stop trying to talk about dying, I'm going home because I don't want to hear about it." The patient's brothers and sisters insisted, "We know you will be all right, just keep fighting this thing. It's not like the —— family to give up so easily." The father refused ever to be alone with his daughter.

[10] Weisman and Hackett, "Predilection to Death," *Death and Identity*, p. 325.

Many, perhaps most, family members experience this same anguish and ambivalence in death. But given pastoral attention, some of them deal with their grief and enter new and deeper relationships with their dying relative. A hospital chaplain, while attempting to assist a dying woman, had her husband confess the difficulty he was experiencing in visiting his wife. "I have to force myself to come," he said. He was having many of the same feelings as his wife. He felt cheated by life. He loved his wife and did not want her to die and leave him and their two small children. Subsequently, the chaplain met with this man to discuss his feelings of anger and frustration. For a brief time during these talks the husband found it impossible to visit his wife, but the chaplain explained this to her. As he became more comfortable, the husband requested the chaplain to go with him to visit his wife. For a long time they simply looked at each other. Then they began to admit what they had been going through—their fear, their anger, the grief they both felt. Their reconciliation to the fact of her death and to each other led them away from despair and toward hope.[11]

The purpose which guides the pastor's striving for community and relationship with the dying patient is an awareness of the patient's "built-in need for completeness." [12] One doctor has said that a fact of major psychological significance is "how many people enter their terminal illness with a sense of defeat, failure, and unfulfillment." [13] To seal off the patient precludes coming to terms with either commonplace concerns or past failures. It can also lead to a despair of love and a sense of hope-

[11] W. E. Wygant, Jr., "Dying, But Not Alone," *American Journal of Nursing*, 67 (March, 1967), 574-77.

[12] Margaretta Bowers, *et al., Counseling the Dying* (New York: Thomas Nelson & Sons, 1964), p. 22.

[13] Arnold A. Hutschnecker, "Personality Factors in Dying Patients," *The Meaning of Death*, p. 237.

lessness. Thus the pastor works on the assumption that even if a life has been uncreative, there remains a thrust to meaning and fulfillment. And this quest for meaning, for personal integrity and dignity in death, affords the pastor his best opportunity to serve the dying.

The course which this quest for completeness takes is determined not by the pastor but by the patient. People die as they have lived; one cannot look to overturn the history of a life in its final moments. Insofar as a man gains personal integrity and meaning at death, it must stem from a coming to grips with the truths of his own blood. It is important for a pastor to affirm this. It is important that his anxiety about death not lead him to seek a hollow assent to this or that doctrine. His presence is a reminder that one's own truth may be set within the context of a love which is not destroyed by death. But it is not a presence which seeks to rob an individual of his responsibility to decide about love and relationship.

The grant of such freedom on the part of the pastor insures that a person will have the chance to find his meaning. Some, like Pope John XXIII, have their bags packed. Death for them is not so much a crisis as the completion of a fulfilled life. For others death is a welcome relief. A life of turmoil and conflict or of pain can be let go. But for some, death may call in question all the values of their lives. They bring to mind the words of Ivan Ilyitch, Tolstoy's respectable and proper government official, as he lay dying of an unexpected malady: "In them [his wife, his daughter and his doctor] he saw himself—all that for which he had lived—and saw clearly that it was not real at all, but a terrible and huge deception which had hidden both life and death. . . . [He] then restrained himself no longer but wept like a child. He wept on account of his helplessness, his terrible loneliness, the cruelty of man, the cruelty of God, and the absence of God." [14]

That ingredient of life which most often hinders the search for meaning and completeness is guilt. Ivan Illyitch was no exception. Every man has memories of wasted opportunities, indifference to others, withered talents, and unworthy goals. In the words of Joseph Haroutunian, when the guilt of breaking our bonds with each other is not admitted, then the emptiness of our lives is confirmed, "and the hope of human life is reduced to a sigh, if not replaced by despair altogether." [15] Lives cut off from love by guilt are also cut off from faith and hope. The question of such lives is whether any righting of these wrongs is possible, and, if not, whether any forgiveness for them is credible. For some, informal conversation assuages their guilt; for others, the rituals and the sacraments of their faith give sufficient answer. A general absolution grants them community with those they love and reaffirms their faith in God.

But there are dying patients for whom ritual practices and sacramental acts are not enough. They wish to speak of specific sins, and sometimes the talk is difficult. One such person was a middle-aged woman dying of cancer. The chaplain noticed that she became somewhat agitated when he visited. She always seemed glad to see him and requested that he return, but the air was tense during his visits. After several such calls he asked if there was anything he could do for her. Her response was, "Yes, there is, chaplain. I wonder if I could take Holy Communion." He assured her that this request was perfectly in order and made arrangements to comply with it. The next day after the General Confession and the Communion she seemed relaxed. She appeared at ease with him for the

[14] Tolstoy, *The Death of Ivan Ilyitch*, pp. 296, 290.

[15] "Life and Death Among Fellowmen," *The Modern Vision of Death*, ed. Nathan Scott (Richmond: John Knox Press, 1967), p. 91.

first time. However, a few days later he noted the reappearance of the tension and that she continued to avoid accepting any of the openings to talk he sought to give her. Finally, after a brief chat, and as the chaplain was preparing to leave, she asked if he could stay a moment longer. She told him then that she had hoped the sacrament would ease her mind, but that she was still bothered and needed to talk. As a teen-age girl she had a child out of wedlock. She had placed the child through an adoption agency, had finished school, married and lived a full life. But the early experience continued to bother her; she wanted assurance that God could forgive her act.

The dying patient's quest for meaning and completeness may also be hindered by a sense of failure. The knowledge that unfulfilled tasks are left often leads a young or middle-aged person into bitterness. Dr. Elizabeth Ross describes her relationship to a man with "piles of rage and anger." He was angry with doctors who neglect patients whom they can no longer help. His death, he said, was untimely. It was like "a man who was in the midst of building a big house; he felt that his creation was only half complete." But as they talked, he came to a different conclusion about his life's meaning. A man must face the fact that he will never "finish" anything, he said. Tasks must be left to those who follow; each man is responsible only to contribute his part.[16]

The rage expressed by this patient over a life cut short raises the last hindrance to the dying's quest for completeness we shall consider. Implicit in his cry is the question "why"—why death, why suffering, why me? At times the question "why me?" comes as persons seek a reason for their suffering. Guilt convinces them they are being punished by a vengeful deity for past wrong deeds. But the pastor who deals faithfully with this misunderstanding,

[16] Ross, "The Dying Patient," pp. 7-8.

who helps undo the strain of guilt, still finds himself pushed to the other two—why death, why suffering? For these we have no answer. We may intellectualize on the "problem of evil," but those who have stood dumb before death's mystery in a pediatrics ward know how little solace and assurance it brings to parents. Before this onslaught the pastor does not speak with glib conviction of the theological "solutions" he has read. Instead he simply stands, and points. His standing with the person confesses him as mortal too, caught in the same suffering, facing the same death, and in need of the same comfort with which he seeks to comfort others. His pointing is to the source of his faith, the God of Jesus Christ who took death upon himself and beckons us to trust that his resurrection is an earnest of our own. The pastor can only hope that this willingness to stand with the dying and to bear witness to a faith will lead the patient back into an affirmation of his oneness with humanity and a trusting hope that death can be overcome.

The discussion above indicates some of the reasons the pastor's place with the dying person continues to be important. The question remains, however, as to whether the pastor is willing to be with death. The answer lies with the pastor; it depends on his attitude toward death in general and his own death in particular. He is bound to absorb some of his culture's alienation and its fear. He is as tempted as anyone to "conquer" death by avoiding it, by turning it over to doctors and morticians, to hospitals and retirement villages. And his alienation and avoidance may appear in his work with the terminally ill. He may be, in Marcel's term, "unavailable." Thus one minister reported feeling as though he would faint each time he called upon a dying person. Another, a seminary student, was unable to recall anything that occurred in a visit with a friend who was dying of leukemia. As Dr. Bowers points out, some deep emotion in these men had undoubtedly been touched and identified with the condition of the patient.[17] It caused them to be preoccupied, encumbered with themselves.

The pastors who have dealt with their own alienation and fear of death are "available" to others. The dying patient and his family sense this; they know the pastor is at their disposal. And with this knowledge they will talk with him or be silent with him. They know he is not hiding. Perry LeFevre suggests that what Martin Buber says of the role of the mother to a child might also be said of those who are willing to be with another in death. "Because this human being exists, meaninglessness, however hard pressed you are by it, cannot be the real truth. Because this human being exists, in the darkness the light lies hidden, in fear salvation, and in the callousness of one's fellow-men the great Love." [18]

Yet even in speaking of the pastor's availability and of his willingness to be with the dying, care must be taken that we not delude ourselves. We must remember that some dying persons turn away from a relationship to the pastor. Whatever need for community and completeness they have, they keep to themselves. In Karl Rahner's phrase, they appear to choose an "autonomous death." Whether they do in fact, or whether they simply seem to die alone, we do not know. Other dying persons choose not to discuss the matter of their death with a clergyman. They choose another person and do not seem to suffer on this account. The pastor should recall, and do so rather frequently, that it is not his responsibility to have everyone respond to his presence. It is his responsibility only to make that presence available.

[17] Bowers, *Counseling the Dying*, pp. 63 ff.

[18] Quoted in "On Being 'with' Another," *Chicago Theological Seminary Register*, LVII (December, 1966), 25.

The Pastoral Care of the Bereaved

The pastor's ministry to the bereaved bears much resemblance to his work with the dying. His attitude toward death influences his willingness to be with those who mourn just as it did with the dying. He still must depend on the work of behavioral scientists for insights into the bereaved's special needs. With the notable exceptions of Jackson, Irion, and Rogers, he will find little material directed specifically to him.[19] And he encounters the same tendency to separate life and death and to shunt the bereaved and his grief off the stage of life as before. In some respects his task is similar also. Both the dying and the bereaved face separation, the sting of death. But whereas the dying look at life to prepare for death and the loss of all relationships, the bereaved must look at death and the loss of one relationship in order to be free to live and love again. To assist the bereaved in his sometimes painful passage through grief and back to life, the pastor must have some knowledge of his psychological needs and of our culture's practices in dealing with death. He must also be aware of his own heritage as a pastor and of the strength Christian faith and community bring to those who mourn.

Research on Grief and the Funeral

Psychological Research. Erich Lindemann's paper, "Symptomatology and Management of Acute Grief," is the classic psychiatric study of acute grief.[20] Although research by

[19] See Edgar Jackson, *Understanding Grief* (Nashville: Abingdon Press, 1957), and *The Christian Funeral* (New York: Channel Press, 1966); Paul Irion, *The Funeral and the Mourners* (Nashville: Abingdon Press, 1954), and *The Funeral: Vestige or Value* (Nashville: Abingdon Press, 1966); William F. Rogers, *Ye Shall Be Comforted* (Philadelphia: Westminster Press, 1950).

[20] *American Journal of Psychiatry,* 101 (September, 1944), 141-48.

Freud, Abraham, Klein, and others preceded his, Lindemann's investigation of the reactions of bereaved persons, many of whom had lost friends or relatives in Boston's Coconut Grove fire, has come to be the starting point for any consideration of grief. It contains several conclusions which are essential to the pastor's understanding of the psychological needs of the bereaved.

One of the most helpful observations Lindemann makes is that acute grief presents a definite clinical picture. Wise pastors have always been aware of the sorrow surrounding grief and have learned over the years to recognize grief's face. However, Lindemann removes the understanding of the bereaved from the realm of intuition and trial and error. He found a patterned reaction among his subjects; both their physical and emotional symptoms exhibited a remarkable degree of uniformity. Five characteristics form the basis for his description of persons experiencing acute grief: (1) somatic distress such as sighing, shortness of breath, fatigue, and digestive complaints; (2) a preoccupation with the image of the deceased; (3) guilt; (4) hostile reactions, irritability, and a wish to be left alone, and; (5) the loss of patterns of conduct as manifested in talkativeness, restlessness, and an inability to initiate and maintain organized activity. Lindemann says these feelings tend to come in waves and cause extreme discomfort. Indeed the bereaved person may refuse to see visitors because expressions of sympathy and conversations about the deceased bring on these distressing reactions.

Another helpful conclusion drawn by Lindemann concerns the complex nature and intensity of grief. It is no simple emotion. It involves the whole network of feelings which characterized the relation to the deceased, and its intensity is determined by the quality and closeness of that relationship. Paul Irion notes that "often in the past only the positive feeling of sorrow because of loss has been recognized and associated with grief." [21] What Lindemann and others show is that negative feelings such as bewilderment, fear, guilt, and anger are usually quite involved in the grief reaction.

A third conclusion reached by Lindemann has to do with the duration and resolution of grief. One grieves he says, until he completes his "grief work" or mourning. Grief work signifies the process by which the bereaved frees himself from bondage to the deceased, readjusts to a world in which the dead person is absent, and establishes new patterns of life and love. To do this work requires the honest acceptance of the pain of loss and a frank facing of one's memories of the deceased. This is no easy task; memories bring suffering. But Lindemann offers no way to freedom and new adjustments and relationships except through this pain of mourning. No amount of simple comfort or reassurance can substitute for thinking of the deceased and striving to come to the freedom which the powerful emotions of grief can prevent.

Lindemann then describes those persons who are unwilling or unable to accept this pain and distress. The binding power of their emotional attachment to the deceased and the suffering of bereavement is more than they can accept. He describes these persons as manifesting a "delayed" or a "distorted" grief reaction. By seeking to deny the pain of grief, or out of preoccupation with other things, one may have a delayed reaction. Other persons, seeking to flee the experience altogether, may have their grief appear in distorted form. One cause for distorted responses lies in the basic personality structure of the bereaved. The loss causes too much conflict within the self to be confronted and moved through. Among the symptoms Lindemann describes as characterizing this reaction he includes: changes of behavior, the development

[21] *The Funeral and the Mourners,* p. 31.

of symptoms belonging to the last illness of the deceased, medical diseases such as ulcerative colitus and asthma, and furious hostility against specific persons. Proper attention can transform these distorted pictures into normal reactions.

What Lindemann gives the pastor is a clue to understanding the psychological dimensions of grief. With this understanding, the pastor is able to support the bereaved as he accepts reality and moves through the painful process of mourning. Moreover, this picture of grief provides the pastor with a guide to evaluate the bereaved person's behavior. He has an excellent set of criteria by which to estimate his progress.

Cultural Research. Awareness of the psychological dimensions of grief is indispensable to the pastor. However, questions about the provisions made to deal with this crisis lead him to see that success in mourning is not solely determined by psychological factors. Cultural values and attitudes towards death also help to shape the bereaved's response. Society's influence on the mourner becomes obvious in the public and private rituals provided to support his grief work and to aid him in reaffirming life. Professor David Mandelbaum says a society must do three things at the time of death: it must dispose of the corpse; it must help to orient the bereaved; and it must assist the group to readjust itself after the loss of a member.[22] Therefore, in his work with the bereaved the pastor must be aware of the rituals provided by society at the time of death, what values they reflect, and whether they approximate the needs of the bereaved.

Sociologists and anthropologists who study the public and private rituals of death in America describe them as undergoing profound change. They indicate a growing

[22] "Social Uses of Funeral Rites," *The Meaning of Death,* p. 189.

dissatisfaction with the traditional funeral and a trend towards the "deritualization of death." [23] Critics are unhappy with the funeral, first, for its denial of the psychological needs of the bereaved. The patterns of the funeral, they say, are designed either to avoid reality or to control grief.[24] The attempt to create an "illusion of life" (Your "loved one" is "resting" in the "slumber room.") denies the reality of death. A contrived atmosphere stifles the expression of genuine emotion. The emphasis on privacy and the isolation of the service in a funeral "home" minimizes personal involvement and corporate support. Other critics are not so concerned with this denial of reality as they are with the religious overtones of much funeral practice. Robert Fulton says, "There is an increasing tendency for modern man to believe that sacred ceremony is out of date. It is, he believes, empty, artificial, and wasteful of time and money." [25] His study of the attitudes of the American public toward death revealed that a small percentage of people see the funeral as primarily religious in nature.[26] One other criticism often made of current funeral practice is largely economic. Jessica Mitford's *The American Way of Death* complains of the manipulative and exploitive practices of the funeral director.[27] She accuses him of monopolistic control, price-fixing, and profiting from the grief of the bereaved. Though her study leaves much to be desired, the recent increase in the number of memorial societies attests to the prevalence of the sentiment.

This dissatisfaction with the traditional funeral reflects

[23] *Ibid.*, p. 214.

[24] Irion, *The Funeral: Vestige or Value*, pp. 44-59.

[25] "The Sacred and the Secular: Attitudes of the American Public Toward Death, Funerals, and Funeral Directors," *Death and Identity*, p. 101.

[26] *Ibid.*, p. 92.

[27] (New York: Simon and Schuster, 1963).

both the drastic social change and the shift in values of American society. The move to urban centers cuts contemporary man off from the context in which values were certain, meanings were clear, and rituals accorded with his understanding of life. Science and the higher criticism call into question many of the religious convictions once devoutly held.

The more basic reason for disenchantment with the funeral, however, arises from the shift in the understanding of life and death which science, technology, and social change helped bring about. Modern man places a premium on the rational and pragmatic control of life. "His dependence upon technology and his faith in science and its ability to solve all problems move him away from the contemplation of himself as a mortal being." [28] He chooses to contemplate youth, vitality, a new home, a long vacation, and "lovely children." Death for him is not the wages of sin but the results of an accident or of negligence. It is a disease for which we will soon have a cure. In the meantime he chooses "to disguise [death] and pretend . . . it is not the basic condition of all life." [29] Fulton finds this wish to evade mortality behind the denial of death in funeral rites, the wish of memorial societies to remove the body from funerals, and in the rise of "retirement cities" which by removing those most likely to die from our midst "enables us to avoid almost entirely the grief and anguish of death." [30]

This trend and the values it represents fail to grasp the importance of public ritual at time of death. Pastors would join Fulton as he laments the pragmatic approach which neglects the positive benefits of ceremony. "Ceremony traditionally not only related man to his god or

[28] Edgar Jackson, *The Christian Funeral,* p. 7.
[29] Fulton, "The Sacred and the Secular," pp. 100-103 *passim.*
[30] *Ibid.,* p. 102.

to the sacred in the way of a sacrifice but also to his fellowman in the form of a gift—to be given and received." [31] It gave opportunity for man to reestablish his relationship to God and to his fellows. Moreover, it afforded an occasion for the controlled expression of anger and the lessening of guilt. New forms may be needed; not everyone wants a religious funeral.[32] But the values of sacrifice and gift-giving and the depth of meaning which an honest confrontation with death may bring to life are lost when rituals are abandoned at death.

The cultural attitude of the denial of death and grief manifest in the controversy over the funeral is even more obvious with regard to private expressions of grief. The customs which formerly guided the bereaved such as wakes and special occasions for meetings with friends have all but disappeared. Only a few religious and ethnic groups supply guidance and support in the expression of grief. Geoffrey Gorer did a study of British grief and mourning and later compared it with practices in the United States.[33] He concluded that during the period of intense mourning (following the funeral), the bereaved are "more in need of social support and assistance than at any time since infancy and early childhood." [34]

Despite this need Gorer found a complete breakdown of traditions of private mourning among his sample. There was a decline in the number of persons who wore mourning dress at funerals. Moreover, those who wore widow's weeds resumed normal dress in less than a month after bereavement. Men no longer wore black armbands. Few of the sample refrained from any social or leisure activity after the death. Of his sample Gorer says, "The

[31] *Ibid.*, p. 101.

[32] Paul Irion discusses the pros and cons of a "humanistic funeral service" in *The Funeral: Vestige or Value*, pp. 136-43, 189-99.

[33] *Death, Grief, and Mourning* (Garden City, N. Y.: Doubleday & Co., 1965).

[34] *Ibid.*, p. 134.

vast majority hid their grief and . . . acted 'as if nothing had happened' in any situation where they could be observed." [35]

Friends of the bereaved also betrayed a lack of knowledge as to how they should behave. Usually after the funeral the mourners would gather for a family meeting. In the days immediately following the death special visits by friends and relatives were fairly common. But many of the bereaved thought they saw less of friends after the death. They felt they made their friends uncomfortable since conversations were usually brief. They noted also that friends seemed at a loss for words; they tried to distract the bereaved and to divert attention from his grief.

Gorer concludes that both British and American society seek to ignore death and mourning. The bereaved should take out three days, at most a week, and then return to life's routine as though nothing had happened. Moreover, he found that the expression of grief is often interpreted as weakness; giving way to grief is stigmatized as demoralizing, morbid, and unhealthy. It is certainly not understood to be psychologically necessary. Gorer concludes that the lack of accepted rituals means the bereaved lack the alternating companionship and privacy they need. And for this lack they pay a price in "misery, loneliness, despair, and maladaptive behavior." [36]

This survey of cultural attitudes to death should convince the pastor of the importance of his task. It should also cause him to seek to deal realistically with the needs of the bereaved for whom he is responsible. Otherwise they will be left alone. The want of meaningful ritual will force each one to find his own way through mourning. Few men are successful at this task. They usually push their pain away, and it goes underground. Lindemann

[35] *Ibid.*, p. 135.
[36] *Ibid.*, p. 135.

suggests that it may appear later as asthma or as ulcerative colitis.[37] And Shoor and Speed confirm Rollo May's judgment that among children and young people it may appear as delinquent behavior.[38] It is because of these things, the needs of the bereaved and the denial all about them, that the pastor must seek ways to care for those who mourn.

The Pastor and Grief

The pastoral care of the bereaved requires the pastor to set the psychological and cultural understandings of death beside that of Christian faith. When this is done at least four guidelines emerge which shape this ministry.

The first guideline to emerge from these perspectives is the necessity to affirm the finality of death and the reality of separation. All persons confronted with death are tempted to deny its presence. The early remarks of the bereaved often reflect his struggle between fantasy and reality. Statements such as, "I can't believe it happened," or, "It all seems like a bad dream," manifest a natural tendency to avoid the pain and distress of separation. The pastor does no kindness by yielding to the temptation to soften this blow. The token of grace here is the willingness to affirm the loss and the pain and to stand with the sufferer.

There is theological justification for this affirmation of the finality of death. It stems from the biblical view of man and death. Biblical teaching on man presents him as a unity. He is body, soul, and spirit; he is a *whole* creation whose life is from God. Even so, death is the death of the whole creation. No *part* of man is by nature immortal; no *part* of man escapes death. "To die is to come to an

[37] Lindemann, "Symptomatology and Management of Acute Grief," p. 145.

[38] Mervyn Shoor and Mary H. Speed, "Death, Delinquency, and the Mourning Process," *Death and Identity*, pp. 201-6.

end, not so much the end of *this* life as the end of *life*. . . . Normally, throughout the Bible it is supposed that when a man dies, the whole man dies, both body and soul. To die is 'to be no more.' "[39] It is over against this radical view of death that the New Testament sets the hope of resurrection. It is the death which defeats the whole man that God overcomes with a resurrection of the *whole* man, a resurrection of the body. Thus, rather than denying death, the hope of the resurrection rests on the final nature of death. By relating life, death, and resurrection to God, the Christian pastor can affirm both the finality of death and the reality of hope.

There is a strain in Christian thought which runs counter to this description of the radical nature of death. The incursions of Greek philosophy represent a dualistic view of man and influence many pastors.[40] According to this view, man consists of a mortal and finite body and an immortal and eternal soul. Death represents victory; the soul is freed from its unnatural home to return to its source in God. The division of man into a body and soul enables pastors who reflect this view to emphasize the spirit and life and to play down the body and death. One such pastor wrote a paper on the funeral for his congregation which said: "Too many funerals show a direct and obvious contradiction between what the clergyman says and what the congregation does. The minister's words indicate that what counts is the soul and only the soul, because it is still alive, and that the now dead body is no longer of any importance. But if the casket is left open and people pay respects to the body, this indicates that . . . what counts is still the body and only the body."[41]

[39] Fred D. Gealy, "The Biblical Understanding of Death," *Pastoral Psychology*, 14 (June, 1963), 33-34.

[40] See Chapter II in this volume, "The New Testament and Death" by Leander Keck.

[41] Louis Cassels, "Minister Writes Instructions for a Simple Christian Burial," United Press International News Release. A student handed

Such a division of man contradicts biblical teaching on man and death and tends to obscure the reality of death for the bereaved.

The attitude toward the body represented by the Greek dualistic view of man raises the question of its place in the funeral. Many persons are convinced that it should be ignored. The mortician's skill in creating an "illusion of life" and his promise to preserve the corpse in perpetuity cause some to argue that an emphasis on the body denies the finality of death. Other persons speak from the vantage point of Greek dualism and insist that attention to the body misleads the mourners on the real meaning of death. And still others maintain that "viewing the remains" is grotesque. It merely stirs the emotions and fails to recognize the body for the lifeless shell it is.

Some of these objections merit attention. If the intention of the body's presence is to create an "illusion of life," then it certainly is not helpful to the bereaved. Moreover, good taste dictates that the coffin be closed during the funeral. Yet, if one acknowledges that the fundamental issue is the reality of death, then viewing the body prior to the funeral and having it present at the service may have a positive effect. For one thing, time spent with the body of the deceased can aid the bereaved to accept the reality of death. This may become quite important now that families relinquish all preparations for the funeral to professional morticians and have no personal contact or involvement in these activities. Moreover, viewings of the body often aid in confronting one's memories of the deceased. The desire to "remember him as he was" may be a desire to evade the reality and pain of separation. Again, having the body present at funerals is sometimes helpful to mourners other than the family. It reminds them that the service is not just to comfort the bereaved

me a reproduction of this item, and I have been unable to locate the exact source.

but it is also to commemorate a unique life. To one who holds a unitary view of man, respecting the body's presence may be an act of gratitude for the person. However, the initial observation must be repeated: the fundamental issue is whether attention to the body faces or evades the reality of death. This remains the essential point regardless of the disposition of the body.

One of the ways the pastor may support the bereaved in their acceptance of reality is by his attitude toward the presence of the body in the funeral. He may also work toward this goal through what he says and reads and quotes in the service itself. Moreover, his personal contacts with the bereaved need to have this acceptance of reality and pain as a primary aim. Reality in its full impact comes slowly. The bereaved need to speak often of their loss as its implications and the emotional pain it brings come increasingly into view. They may need to tell "how he died" and of their last days and hours together and of the plans they had made. When one appreciates the significance of the story, his patience permits him to listen quietly while it is repeated.

The pastor encourages the bereaved to accept death's finality so that they will begin to mourn. Once reality is affirmed, feelings may emerge. Thus a second guideline of the pastor's work with the bereaved is to encourage mourning. If the mourning person is to deal with his memory of the deceased and move toward freedom, then the pastor must encourage the expression of genuine emotion in both public ceremonies and private conferences. This is not easy in our country. We tend to deny deep feelings of any kind, whether of anger or affection. Yet Edgar Jackson is right when he describes grief as "an honorable emotion." [42] It is composed of all the love and joy, all the anger and frustration people know in their

[42] Jackson, *The Christian Funeral*, p. 35.

lives together. It is compounded by the fear and bewilderment, the loneliness and frustration that characterize separation and the call to new adjustment.

There is a taboo on the public expression of grief in the funeral. Emotion cannot be avoided, but it can be kept superficial if the bereaved respond to the synthetic stimuli of soft lights, tremulous music and sentimental words rather than to the harsh reality of death.[43] Careful family placement also reflects this taboo on public grief. They are segregated, placed behind screens or in private rooms, so they will not "embarrass themselves" with public displays of grief—as though there was something wrong with honest emotion. The pastor sometimes plays a part in this suppression of mourning. He "keeps it brief" and often selects his scripture and prepares his sermon with the goal of not arousing feelings. Moreover, some pastors leave the impression they are unaware of the deep and dynamic nature of grief. In their actions or speech they indicate that a stoic and unfeeling acceptance of death is somehow more Christian. James Carlin reports that his sample of Baptist pastors in the South did not think it wise to raise "emotional subjects" in funeral meditations. The majority of them also thought it best "never" or "rarely" to call to mind painful memories of the dead.[44]

The pastor should encourage the development of an atmosphere in the funeral in which mourning is acceptable. Paul Irion maintains that one criterion of a Christian funeral should be: "Will the funeral permit and even encourage the mourners to accept their feelings toward their situation, toward the deceased, and toward themselves? "[45] Edgar Jackson insists that the pastor be "aware

[43] Irion, *The Funeral: Vestige or Value,* pp. 45-46.

[44] "Grief Work and the Pastoral Care Practices of Baptist Ministers," (Unpublished doctoral thesis, Southern Baptist Theological Seminary, Louisville, Ky., 1962), pp. 81 ff.

[45] *The Funeral: Vestige or Value,* p. 181.

of the powerful emotions that are at work and [try] to fulfill the feelings rather than deny them."[46] Thus one goal of the funeral should be the fostering of a climate in which the bereaved is able to recall the deceased. Surrounded by friends who hold up his hands and commend him to God, the mourner may begin to face his pain and let go the past. Furthermore, the ritualized acts of the funeral give many the opportunity to work through feelings and convictions that are not easily spoken. The pastor's sensitivity in the selection of scripture and in his meditation can also acknowledge the reality of loss and pain.

For a few persons this ritual of public ceremony and the support of friends suffices to deal with their feelings. However, most bereaved people need the pastor's private as well as his public ministrations. William Rogers suggests that the conversation of the mourner follows a pattern.[47] As they seek to make real their loss and express their sorrow they talk first of the present and the immediate past. They may want to talk of the last illness or the fatal accident. They may seek to reassure themselves that they did all they could for the deceased. Gradually, the bereaved begins to speak of the past and of his total relationship to the deceased. He will move from the recent to the remote past, eventually telling, for example, how they met and where they were married and how his folks felt about it.

It is essential for the pastor to stay with the bereaved throughout this experience. Lay persons are often helpful, but they sometimes become frightened at the depth of the feelings expressed. Indeed, it is not unusual for the bereaved person to fear for his sanity. He is surprised at his sudden changes of feeling and at his ambivalence to the deceased. Freud and Abraham recognized that the

[46] *The Christian Funeral,* p. 35.

[47] "The Pastor's Work with Grief," *Pastoral Psychology,* 14 (September, 1963), 24.

grieving person was an angry person.[48] But the bereaved is often disturbed at the depth of his frustration and hostility. Guilt is also a frequent emotional response. Conflicts are recalled which were not reconciled. Regrets are expressed that something was not done differently or that he had not been more sensitive throughout the years. And the thread of sorrow and deep sense of loss weaves its way into all this design. The bereaved has periods when he wants to be alone; he has days when he's "not sure it's worth the effort anymore."

Finally, it would seem wise for the pastor to recall that it is individuals who mourn. This caution will save him from preconceived notions on how people "ought to react." He should remember that memories differ, feelings vary in intensity, and the cords binding the bereaved to the deceased are not all equally strong. Both circumstances and cultural expectations influence mourning. The man who has not seen his sister for twenty-five years may feel guilty that he has no sense of loss at her death. The man who cries at a funeral may feel less a man for having done so. The woman who feels relief when her invalid father dies may avoid admitting it. Yet all of these are legitimate responses when the circumstances are known. The point at which concern is appropriate is when all known circumstances do not account for a response. Sudden changes of conduct, extreme hostility against specific persons, withdrawal from all social intercourse—all these may be signs that the bereaved need medical assistance. Yet even when these symptoms appear, it is important to ask whether it is an isolated instance or an emerging pattern. Pastors who give attention to such individual dimensions of mourning are strong supports. They make it easier to move through feelings and to look for meanings.

[48] Cited by Paul Irion, *The Funeral and the Mourners*, p. 52.

As the bereaved person works through his grief, he gradually begins to seek a sense of direction. Death has caused him to suspend life for a time. But as his feelings about the past become more clear, he starts to emerge from his indecision. Thus the third guideline in the pastoral care of the bereaved should be their crisis of meaning. This is the pastor's attempt to participate in the bereaved's movement towards a reaffirmation of life.

The crisis of meaning for the bereaved has at least three dimensions. The first dimension concerns the past relation to the deceased. The meaning of life is tied to persons. Our sense of place and identity, our values and decisions, our directions and commitments—all these are bound up with the people to whom we are close. When these persons die, our meanings are jeopardized; there is a tendency to feel that everything important is gone. However, as feeling subsides it becomes apparent that many of the commitments once shared may be continued alone. Some of the ideals which fashioned joint enterprises may continue to motivate activity. Many of the tasks begun may be continued. It is important for the bereaved to rescue these values from the past. It gives continuity to their lives and serves to identify them with the deceased.

The demand for a new self-definition is the second dimension of the bereaved's crisis in meaning. He becomes aware that he is no longer who he was. The bereaved goes through life understanding and defining himself in terms of close relations. When the relation is removed, he must discover again who he is. A wife must become a widow. Parents become a "childless couple." Of course, the intensity of this crisis varies with one's past and with the closeness of the relation. But even a son who has long been on his own feels subtle changes of self-understanding when his father dies. He feels he must somehow be more sensitive to commitment and responsibility.

The third dimension of the bereaved's crisis of meaning

emerges from his confrontation with death. The experience of bereavement produces many different effects. Some persons walk away from grief and despair of love. Meaning in any deep sense left the life of a young father embittered over the death of his infant son. The death of a close relation can also stir the bereaved's fears of his own death so that he tries to avoid any suggestion of his mortality. He is never free of the commands of his fear; it controls his life. However, some persons permit their encounter with death to make an authentic statement on their own existence. Their confidence in love enables them to accept the limitation of their life. By this act of faith they realize in a more profound sense the uniqueness of their own lives. Their freedom to love and work attests to their assimilation of death.

The pastor's task is to work with the bereaved as they engage in this quest for meaning. He seeks to participate as a fellow sufferer in the bereaved's affirmation of life. His loyalty to the bereaved assures him that the values of the past were not counterfeit goods. The groping for new self-understanding can be encouraged by the pastor. And he can support the bereaved as they seek to come to terms with the mystery of death. Moreover, the pastor can be aware of the constant temptation to shrink back. He can encourage faith and not despair as the bereaved wrestle with old habits and dependencies.

The importance of community in this reaffirmation of meaning is obvious. Indeed one of the continuing themes of this discussion of the bereaved person has been the devastating effects isolation may have on him. At every point of the grief process the support of friends encourages him to accept his loss and not to despair of love. A final guideline for the pastor's ministry to the bereaved, then, is a reiteration of the positive effects of a supporting community.

Community is important to the bereaved because grief

and loss are more readily admitted in a group than when one is alone.[49] They are more likely to confess how deeply they hurt when they know that others face that hurt also. Sorrow is more easily expressed when one sees that others share his loss. Group participation in the bereaved's sense of loss causes him to lose his self-consciousness. Suddenly it becomes all right to feel as he does. He is understood. It is this feeling of being understood in grief, of not feeling bereft of all relationship, that makes it important for funeral services to encourage honest emotion.

Community support is beneficial also in the affirmation of meaning. Grief and sorrow left to themselves lead to despair. But the congregation who stands with the bereaved short-circuits despair with affirmations of faith. The group does not permit his sorrow over separation to lead to despair of love, but rather they point him to the hope of resurrection which is the victory of love. This is the reason a funeral should be primarily a service of worship. For comfort comes to the bereaved person in the affirmation of his loss and in affirmation of the God whose love transcends that loss.

Finally, the life of the congregation is important as the bereaved seeks to establish new relationships and to reaffirm life. It gives him room to make "false starts." It offers him opportunity to test his new identity. The confidence of the congregation in him and their affection for him enable him to work out the meanings of his new life. They are, in short, the patient friends who stand with him while he learns to live and love again. Joseph Haroutunian says, "The living God who saved us through a man still saves us through our fellowmen."[50] And so it is with the bereaved.

[49] Edgar Jackson, *For the Living* (New York: Channel Press, 1963), p. 94.

[50] *God with Us: A Theology of Transpersonal Life* (Philadelphia: Westminster Press, 1965), p. 53.

Conclusion

Despite contemporary man's attempts to disguise death, its sting can still be felt. Its force is seen in modern man's frantic effort to have a good time and in his regard of all talk of death as morbid. Its pain is seen in his consignment of those who face death to loneliness. The Christian pastor who takes his ministry to the dying and to the bereaved seriously finds himself moving against this cultural stream. For he moves on the assumption that the deepest meanings of life are met at the point at which the deepest issues are joined. He assumes that it is only by confronting the end of life and the destructive power of death that a man is able to rise and to do his daily work in love. These convictions about life did not originate with the pastor. Jesus of Nazareth has taught him that flinching in the face of death and the temptation to despair of love are no new thing. But Jesus who is the Christ has taught him "that neither death, nor life, nor angels, nor principalities, nor things present, nor things to come, nor powers, nor height, nor depth, nor anything else in all creation, will be able to separate us from the love of God" (Rom. 8:37-39). Because he has heard these words, and because he represents the speaker, the pastor's ministry at the time of death is important.

index